Compadrinazgo
Ritual Kinship in the Philippines

COMpaDRINaZGO

Ritual Kinship
in the Philippines

by
Donn V. Hart

Northern Illinois University Press

Library of Congress Cataloging in Publication Data

Hart, Donn Vorhis, 1918–
  Compadrinazgo: ritual kinship in the Philippines.

  Bibliography: p.
  Includes index.
  1. Sponsors—Philippine Islands. 2. Kinship—
Philippine Islands. 3. Philippine Islands—Social
life and customs. I. Title.
GN671.P5H37   301.42'1'09599   75-15015
ISBN 0-87580-062-9

To
Harriett and Susan
For Aid and Comfort in the Field
and
Morton J. Netzorg
Generous Critic, Valued Colleague

Contents

Illustrations

xi

Maps

Graphs

Photos

Preface

For the Philippines, this book combines personally gathered field data with some manuscript research material of other American and Filipino anthropologists, published sources, student reports, and theses. I first studied Caticugan in 1950; I made shorter visits to the village in 1955 and 1957; and I reestablished residence in Caticugan in 1964–1965. The summers of 1968 and 1972 were spent in Caticugan checking earlier drafts of this study. Lalawigan was studied in 1956 and has not been revisited.

My Philippine research was sponsored by the Fulbright Program. The Philippine-American Educational Foundation, the agency now administering the Philippine Fulbright Program, was responsive and cooperative to all my research needs. Silliman University, Dumaguete, and its capable faculty were helpful in many ways when I resided in Negros.

Cooperation and assistance have been received from many persons, Filipinos and Americans. I wish to express my sincere appreciation for the privilege of living in Caticugan and Lalawigan. Nearly every resident in these villages has contributed to this book; their traditional gracious hospitality and almost unlimited patience never wavered in explaining the obvious. It is hoped that this publication will be accepted as a token for an unrepayable debt of gratitude owed them.

No acknowledgement of this nature can be made without recognizing the contributions made by my perceptive research associates: in Caticugan, Mr. Dioscoro Ragay (1950, 1955, and 1957) and Mr. Isidro Somoza, Jr. (1964–65, 1968, and 1972); and, in Lalawigan, Mr. Felipe Dala. During the several years it took to write this study, they generously responded to frequent questions that required them to obtain information from key informants in Caticugan and Lalawigan.

To these colleagues must be added Professor Mary Hollnsteiner, Ateneo de Manila; Dr. Agaton Pal, then at Silliman University, Philippines; Dr. Daniel Scheans, Department of Anthropology, Portland State University; and Dr. Willis Sibley, Cleveland State University, who shared materials from their unpublished field notes. Information in this publication therefore includes some material beyond what appears in these authors' publications on Hulo, Esperanza, Suba, Camangahan, and Manalad.

This book has profited from critical reading, in several preliminary drafts, by the following colleagues: Dr. Fred Eggan, Department of Anthropology, University of Chicago; Dr. Stephen Gudeman, Department of Anthropology, University of Minnesota; and Dr. Arthur Rubel, Department of Sociology and Anthropology, University of Notre Dame, Indiana. "Jock" Netzorg not only offered skilled assistance in editing various manuscript versions of this study, but he also suggested sources that had been overlooked. His frequent challenges to clarify concepts are acknowledged with keen appreciation.

Some data for Siaton poblacion were collected by a group of Filipino students who were members of a seminar on field research techniques taught in Dumaguete (and Siaton) during the summer 1972.

The valuable assistance received from my wife, Harriett Colegrove Hart, and daughter, Susan Elizabeth, will be understood by those fortunate field workers who have had a spouse and daughter as members of their research team.

Donn V. Hart

Department of Anthropology and Center for Southeast Asian Studies
Northern Illinois University
DeKalb, Illinois

Compadrinazgo
Ritual Kinship in the Philippines

Chapter One

Introduction

The basic purpose of this investigation is to describe the history, structure, and functions of compadrinazgo in the Philippines. This ubiquitous feature of Christian Filipino social organization rarely has been a major research interest of scholars specializing in the Philippines; detailed data are limited to a handful of the major cultural-linguistic groups in the nation. Yet these deficiencies do not justify postponement of a comparative review of what is known about Philippine compadrinazgo.

Compadrinazgo, often called the *kumpari* or compadre system in the Philippines, is the godparenthood complex (Jocano 1968b: 27). *Godparenthood* is used synonymously with *compadrinazgo;* it is not limited to its occasional association with Protestantism (Gudeman 1972: 69, footnote 6). The concept of compadrinazgo subsumes those of padrinazgo and compadrazgo. Padrinazgo (or spiritual godparenthood), more in accord with Canon law, emphasizes vertical relationships, the ritual linkage between godparents and godchildren. Compadrazgo (or ritual co-parenthood) stresses horizontal relationships, or ritual ties binding adults—godparents and natural parents. Compadrazgo has assumed an additional meaning among the urban middle class in Santiago, Chile, where it refers to "a system of reciprocity which involves a continuing exchange of complimentary services (*favores*) performed and motivated within an ideology of friendship. . . . and should not be confused with the ritualistic Catholic institution of Godparenthood" (Lomnitz 1971: 94). Since *compadrazgo* has several meanings and refers technically to only one of the two sets of relationships associated with the godparenthood complex, *compadrinazgo* has been proposed, and accepted in this book, as a term to describe the complete sets of ritual relationships (Ravicz 1967: 238).

A second purpose of this book is to compare Latin American, and to a lesser extent European, compadrinazgo with the Philippine variety. Such a comparison was urged as early as 1942 by Benjamin Paul. The

Spaniards brought the godparenthood complex to both Latin America and the Philippines. This form of ritual kinship was modified by the indigenous cultures of the New World and Asia. Consequently, there are numerous differences between Latin American and Filipino godparenthood complexes, although they have more features in common than either does with the Spanish system from which both derive.

Comparative data from Hispanic America and Europe are summarized in several later chapters, indicating the similarities with and differences from Philippine compadrinazgo. In these later chapters various theoretical issues related to the godparenthood complex are analyzed, e.g., social classes, urbanization, influence of spatial factors on the selection of sponsors, etc. In addition to furnishing a comparative context for Filipino ritual kinship, these chapters challenge and modify previous generalizations concerned with compadrinazgo in general.

As a setting for later chapters, Chapter One briefly summarizes the cultural contours of Christian Filipino society; greater detail is given to the research areas in eastern Samar and southern Negros. A short concluding survey outlines the historical development of compadrinazgo, including Church-prescribed and folk occasions for sponsorship and recent efforts to classify them.

Although compadrinazgo was mentioned more than 100 years ago by Tylor (1861: 250–51) as an aspect of Mexican life, Gillin commented only a few decades ago that "it is strange that this type of linkage [compadrinazgo] between persons and families [in Latin America] has not received more extensive treatment in the sociological and ethnological literature" (1947: 104). Since 1947 godparenthood in general and compadrazgo in particular have attracted considerable attention from anthropologists working in Latin America, and, to a lesser extent, in Spain, Italy, the Balkans, and Greece.

> The compadrazgo was the first distinctive aspect of Latin American social structure to be discovered by anthropologists, and it quickly became the prototype for the broader category of fictive kinship. In a series of studies beginning with Spicer's pioneering *Pascua* (1940), and including among many others Paul (1942), Gillin (1947), Mintz and Wolf (1950), Foster (1953), Sayres (1956), and Deshon (1963), the dimensions of the compadrazgo have been determined, and its near-infinite variety has been documented (Foster 1969: 263).

Although scholars have studied the Latin American godparenthood complex for several decades, our knowledge remains inadequate in two ways:

> First, most accounts represent ideal culture, the answers given by informants when asked to describe how the system works. Very little analysis of the institution has been based on real behavior in real situations.... Second, there has been almost no quantitative analysis of large samples aimed at revealing the inner dynamic of compadrazgo, especially with respect to the exercise of choice, as it is manipulated in the building of social networks (Foster 1969: 263).

The godparenthood complex in Latin America is "characteristically found in mestizo communities featuring bilateral kinship systems" (Middleton 1975: 461). Middleton adds: "It is therefore interesting that while bilateral systems have been analyzed increasingly within a framework of strategy and choice, and of adaptive viability, *compadrazgo* has remained largely outside the pale of this theoretical orientation" (1975: 461). These deficiencies understandably also characterize our limited fund of information about Filipino compadrinazgo, a study which has been more recent and in less depth.

The scientific study of Christian Filipino society gained momentum around 1950. "Before this date [end of World War II] there was almost a total absence of interest in rural communities of the country on the part of national leaders and scholars" (Pal 1959: 16). Past anthropologists studying Filipinos confined their research primarily to primitive groups.

> The first four decades of Philippine anthropology [1900–1940] are characterized by a nearly exclusive concern for two primary interests, culture history and non-Christian peoples, especially the so-called 'tribal' peoples. A glance at any bibliography of anthropological titles for this period makes these points quite clearly.... Among the 142 titles appearing for dates prior to 1950 [Lynch and Hollnsteiner 1961], 130 (92 percent) deal exclusively with the customs and origins of tribal minorities (Davis and Hollnsteiner 1969: 60).

This once almost exclusive attention to Filipino "tribal minorities" has been drastically modified. "The most dramatic change in Philippine anthropological research strategy in recent years has been the trend toward studies of lowland rural—and lower-class urban—communities.... By returning to the Lynch-Hollnsteiner bibliography it is possible to document how sharp the shift to lowland community studies has been; ... between 1950 and 1960, 50 percent (90 of 181 titles) have concerned lowland peoples" (Davis and Hollnsteiner 1969: 64). The first detailed postwar investigations of Christian Filipino peasant society were made in the Bisayas, i.e., the central Philippines (Hart 1954a; Pal 1956a).

But in spite of the recent attention given to the lowland communities, only two American anthropologists, in addition to the author, have done field research on ritual kinship in the Philippines. Willis Sibley (during a second visit to the Bisayas) has devoted a part of his research primarily to investigation of compadrinazgo. A major addition to the literature on Philippine compadrinazgo is David Potter's investigation of ritual kinship in Dumaguete (1973). One Filipino master's thesis (unavailable to the author) has been written on this subject, with only a small part published (Arce 1961 and 1973). Available sources for Philippine compadrinazgo are, on the whole, scattered articles in which this subject is of ancillary importance. Consequently, earlier cross-cultural analysis of godparenthood excluded the Philippines. This exclusion continues; the most recent general survey of compadrinazgo does not mention the Philippines (Pitt-Rivers 1968).

Although data on this topic were obtained for numerous Filipino cultural-linguistic groups, the author's field research has been limited to Bisayan Filipinos. The best parallel investigation of this type of ritual kinship system in the Philippines was made by Sibley, also in the Bisayan cultural region. Comparatively speaking, our knowledge of Filipino compadrinazgo is best for Bisayans. Data for Tagalogs, Pampangans, and Ilokans are limited in scope but competently collected, while published scholarly sources on compadrinazgo for some major Filipino groups (e.g., Pangasinans and Bikolans) are largely nonexistent or inaccessible (see Map 1).

The Philippine Research Setting

Spanish influence in the Philippines began in 1521 when Ferdinand Magellan discovered the archipelago for Europe. Miguel Lopez de Legaspi established the first permanent Spanish settlement in Cebu in 1565. Spain's greatest impact on the Philippines was to transform the archipelago's population into the only predominantly Christian (Roman Catholic) nation in Asia. Spanish administrators and friars had a lasting influence on many aspects of Philippine culture and society. The process of acculturation was dual, however, for it involved both the Hispanization of much lowland Filipino culture and the Philippinization of diffused Spanish culture.

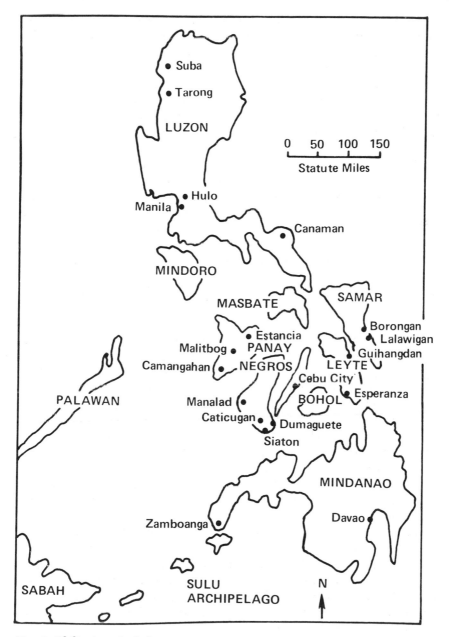

Map 1: *Philippines: Including Approximate Locations of Communities Discussed.*

Spanish rule eventually created a new sense of national identity among lowland Filipinos. The Filipino revolution of 1896 resulted from this combination: a nascent Filipino nationalism that embraced western democratic concepts; Spain's failure to solve crushing tenancy problems; and objections to the continued fusion of church and state. Filipinos later made common cause with the United States in the Spanish-American war of 1898. As a result of the complex events of 1898, the Philipines became America's sole possession in Southeast Asia (Hart 1975a).

The United States, publicly announcing its intention to retain the Philippines only until the people were ready for self-government, quickly shared political power with Filipino leaders. In 1935, after a Filipino plebescite opted overwhelmingly for independence, American withdrawal was planned to occur over a ten-year period. Before this period ended, however, World War II intervened, and the country suffered severely under Japanese invasion and occupation. After Japan was defeated, the nation faced enormous problems of reconstruction. In 1946 the nation became independent, the first Southeast Asian colony to regain its political freedom.

The Philippine population may be divided into three broad cultural categories: Christian, Muslim (Moro), and Pagan (primitive). The term *Filipino*, when used generically, refers not only to lowland Christians but also to highland primitive or "tribal" groups and the Islamized people of southern Mindanao and the Sulu archipelago. When the referent for Filipino is limited to Christians, the cultural diversity of the population is reduced but not eliminated since considerable differences distinguish the various Christian Filipino groups. "The use of a model called 'Filipino' is practicable when attempting to obtain an overall picture of the basic social characteristics of the dominant Philippine peoples, rather than specific knowledge of one or another group" (Eggan 1956 1: 414).

Major Christian Filipino cultural-linguistic groups ranked according to the number of speakers are: Cebuan (Sugbuhanon or Cebuaño), Tagalog (Tagal), Ilokan (Ilocano), Panayan (Ilongo or Hiligaynon), Bikolan (Bicolaño), Samaran (Waray-waray, Samareño, or Samarnon,) Pampangan (Kapampangan), and Pangasinan. A generic name for Cebuans, Panayans, and Samarans is Bisayan (Visayan). All these Filipinos belong to a branch of the Mongoloid race.

Philippine languages are similar in grammatical and phonetic structure, and all belong to the Malayo-Polynesian linguistic family. A preliminary classification of Philippine languages distinguished seventy-five main linguistic groups plus numerous subgroups. But in spite of this linguistic diversity, the mother tongue of the great majority of Christian Filipinos is one of the eight languages previously listed. Until recently, more Filipinos spoke English as a second language than any other tongue. Today, a larger percentage of Filipinos speak Pilipino (the national language based on Tagalog) than English. Spanish is spoken by a steadily decreasing number of Filipinos.

The geographic regions of the Philippines are Luzon, the central Philippine islands (Bisayas), and Mindanao-Sulu. Palawan is the westernmost island of the archipelago. The more than 7,000 islands (many small and uninhabited) have a total land area of 115,600 square miles. With the exception of Luzon and Mindanao, the two largest islands, most major Philippine islands share a similar physiographic pattern. The typical island has a central, usually forested, mountainous highland that gradually merges into rolling uplands and foothills. The coastal margins of narrow lowlands and riverine valleys are drained by relatively short, shallow rivers. Most Christian Filipino peasants live in barrios (villages) located in these coastal lowlands and valleys.

Samar Island and Barrio Lalawigan

The purpose of this section is to sketch briefly the major contours of Filipino society. Since most of the data of this study concern Borongan and Lalawigan, in eastern Samar, and Siaton and Caticugan, in southern Negros Oriental, greater emphasis is given to the geographical features, economic activities, and peasant life of these two regions.

Between Luzon and Mindanao clusters a group of islands called Bisayas. The largest of these islands are Panay, Negros, Cebu, Samar, Bohol, and Leyte. Samar, facing the open Pacific, is the third largest island in the nation. Densely forested central Samar is a maturely dissected highland mass, with scattered small communities. The island's largest continuous lowland follows the coastline from Samar's northwest corner to Catubig valley in the northeast. Catbalogan, once the capital of all Samar and now the capital of Western Samar province, is the island's main port. Northern Samar province's capital is Calbayog.

Eastern Samar province is a series of small, deltaic lowlands, partially separated by mountain spurs that reach toward the Pacific from the central highland. The building of a coastal road has, however, helped consolidate these areas "into what might be considered a single region" (McIntyre 1956: 7). When the island was divided into three provinces in 1968, Borongan became the capital of Eastern Samar province. In 1970 the population of Eastern Samar was 271,000 people (1970 Census: 39).

Historically, eastern Samar has been one of the most neglected and remote regions of the Bisayas. During the research period this isolation of Borongan and Lalawigan continued, owing to poor roads and the lack of an airport or a nearby port for interisland ships. In 1956 one way from Tacloban, Leyte, to Borongan and Barrio Lalawigan was by bus. The bus was ferried across the narrow San Juanico Strait that separates Leyte and Samar. (In 1973 a new bridge was opened connecting the two islands.) The bus then proceeded north to Wright, across the island to Taft on the Pacific coast, and thence southward to Borongan. The trip normally took from ten to twelve hours. One could also take an interisland ship from Tacloban, disembark at Catbalogan, western Samar, and then travel by bus to Wright and the eastern coast of the island. This trip from Catbalogan to Borongan usually took about eleven hours. A road also ran northward to Dolores, the "rice granary" of eastern Samar. During the rainy season the Wright-Taft road sometimes was temporarily closed as a result of landslides or bridges washed out by flooding rivers. Borongan could also be reached by taking an interisland vessel from Tacloban, disembarking the next morning at Guiuan or Balangiga (both in southern Samar), and proceeding north to Borongan by bus. From Guiuan to Borongan was a six-hour ride. Borongan municipality had a population of 28,713 in 1970.

Borongan is one of the largest towns in eastern Samar. In 1956 an occasional foreign vessel stopped in the town's small unimproved bay to load copra (dried coconut meat) and abaca (Manila hemp), two major exports of Samar. In many ways Borongan is a typical Philippine town, with a plaza bordered by an old Spanish stone church, the *municipio* (or "city hall"), a private college, and stores run mainly by the Chinese, Boholans, and Batangueños. The public marketplace is south of the church. A small Catholic college was opened shortly after Liberation. Borongan is now the seat of the Diocese of Eastern Samar, with a resident bishop whose palace adjoins the church. The town has an active if small Protestant congregation that also supports a small high school. In 1970 the city had a population of 5,531 people.

Barrio Lalawigan, a farming-fishing village, is located along the Borongan-Guiuan national road, five miles south of the provincial capital. The village faces a section of the Pacific Ocean that is dotted with small rocky islands that fringe a rugged coastline. In addition to the central part of the barrio, there were two adjacent sitios called Balod and Tubigan.

In May 1956 Barrio Lalawigan had a population of 889 persons residing in 187 households (author's census); all were Roman Catholics. The mother tongue of the people was Samaran; only the school teachers and a few other residents spoke English. In Lalawigan (with the exception of Sitio Balod) the dwellings lined several dirt roads parallel to the national road (Hart 1964: 18). A complete elementary school was located in the community. (Recently a two-year rural high school has been opened in the barrio.) A small chapel has been built by the barriofolk, but in 1956 the nearest priest lived in Borongan. Some years later Lalawigan was made a parish, and a resident priest was assigned to the barrio. Several small stores sold salt, matches, kerosene, canned fish, and a few other essentials. A small Social Welfare building was located across the street from the school. (In 1970 this building was the headquarters for a government medical team.)

Barrio drinking water was obtained from several surface wells plus one artesian well. There was no electricity in Lalawigan. Daytime bus service (and recently Honda pedicabs) enabled residents to travel with some frequency to and from Borongan. The village's economy was based on the production of copra, abaca, and rice and on in-shore, nonmotorized fishing. Fishing was largely a subsistence activity, although some fish were sold in Borongan. (By 1972 most fishermen used outboard motors that extended their fishing range.)

Copra and abaca furnished numerous families with a small cash income. Copra was a somewhat undependable source of income, since the furious typhoons of this region often destroyed both the crop and the trees. (In recent years Lalawignons have stopped growing abaca because of its low price.) Most Lalawignons had their rice fields in the Dolores area. (Although the "miracle" rice varieties were being grown in Dolores in 1972, inadequate irrigation facilities and limited knowledge of the requisite new farming techniques reduced the effectiveness of this innovation.)

Negros Island and Barrio Caticugan

Boot-shaped Negros, the fourth largest island in its nation, is dominated by several volcanic mountains. The island, divided by a densely

forested central mountain range, has a broad western plain, with Baco-
lod as its major port, and an eastern coastal region of fragmented, deltaic
valleys. In southern and southwestern Negros the central range broad-
ens into a dissected hill and plateau area where an extinct volcano
towers. Northern and western Negros were settled by Panayans from
nearby Panay. The eastern and southern parts of Negros are inhabited
by Cebuans (see Map 2).

Negros Oriental, the eastern province of Negros, is thirteenth in
population (715,240) among Philippine provinces (1970 census). Dumaguete, the capital and major port of this province, is also the political
and administrative center of Negros Oriental (Pal 1963: 14). Only part
of the city's 52,000 population (1970 census) can be classified as urban
since the population figure for the city includes people living in villages
within the official city limits.

"Downtown" Dumaguete consists of several major streets of movie
houses and hardware, tailor, grocery, and general merchandizing stores.
The city also has four hospitals and three private colleges and universi-
ties. The local airport provides a frequent schedule of flights to Cebu,
Manila, and cities in Mindanao.

About thirty miles southwest of Dumaguete, on Negros Oriental's
coast, is Siaton poblacion, the municipal center for Siaton municipality.
In 1970 Siaton municipality had a population of 26,963. Today one can
catch an early morning bus from Dumaguete to the poblacion. A paved
road from Dumaguete to Bacong poblacion encourages the driver to
race along the highway. Lining the road are bamboo-walled, nipa-
roofed houses raised above ground on sturdy posts; there are potted
plants on the window sills. Copra, shelled corn, or unhusked rice may
be seen drying along the roadside on mats of woven buri palm leaf.

"The bus halts at the junction with the road to Barrio Bonbonon to
discharge passengers and then continues downhill to the riverine plain
of Inalad. More passengers get off, and empty wooden boxes are left by
the roadside for Malabuhan fishermen. On the return trip the boxes will
be filled with fresh fish from the fish corrals (*bungsod*) for Dumaguete's
market" (Hart 1956: 258). The bus continues, now well into Siaton
municipality, past the "prefab" Inalad elementary school and over the
Canaway river bridge, arriving at Siaton poblacion.

The Catholic church dominates Siaton plaza. At the south end of
the plaza is a two-story concrete *municipio* with a new annex. In this
building are the offices of the mayor, treasurer, and other local officials,
including the telecommunication and post offices. Since 1950 Siaton

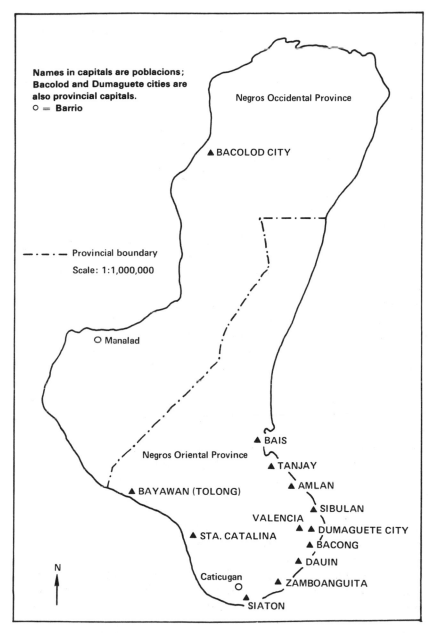

Map 2: *Negros Island: Location of Communities Discussed.*

plaza has been improved, with a fountain with colored lights, play equipment for children, concrete benches (bearing the names of their donors), and lawns and hedges. The former Puericulture building is now the office of the registrar of the Commission on Elections. To the left of this building is the office of the government medical team. Between these two structures is the auditorium for public events, especially the annual fiesta dances. To the rear of this cluster of buildings, facing another street, is the Protestant chapel (United Church of Christ).

The elementary school on the west side of Siaton's plaza is a complex of buildings. Directly in front of the Catholic church is Carmel, the Catholic high school opened in 1963. It occupies the old *convento* (priest's residence). Lining the national road that passes from Dumaguete westward to Bayawan are the commercial buildings of the poblacion, the public market, general stores, tailor shops, bakeries, barber shops, and one drugstore. In 1968 electricity was introduced to the poblacion; current is supplied from six in the evening until six in the morning. A piped water system is a somewhat undependable source of community drinking water.

An attempt was made to determine whom Siaton poblacion residents considered their most prominent citizens, so that selected comparable statements could be made about compadrinazgo for the poblacion and Caticugan. Whenever the Siaton elite is mentioned in this study, reference is primarily to this group that the residents helped identify.

The data on Siaton elite listed in Table 1 were compiled in the following manner. Approximately fifty persons living in the poblacion, selected at random, were asked to name the twenty *dakung tao* (big people) of the poblacion. It was explained that these leaders could be men or women, Catholic or non-Catholic, and engaged, presently or in the past, in any type of profession or business. The informants were merely asked to give their personal nominations of prominent poblacion citizens.

The ranking of the elite in Table 1 is based on the number of times their names were mentioned by the informants. The highest number of votes received by an single person was the present mayor, who received forty-one votes. The last name on the list received only eight votes. (Since one member of the elite was not then residing in the poblacion, the person who was ranked twenty-first was added to the list. When these individuals were interviewed, a former vice-mayor, who was ranked eighth, was ill and could not be interviewed.)

The Siaton elite is predominantly male; only four women were named (all of them teachers). The elite group is largely Catholic, although about one-third are Protestants (either Seventh Day Adventists or United Church of Christ). Their average age is fifty-eight years. The elite are predominantly high-level municipal or provincial government employees or schoolteachers. The few exceptions are an attorney, an engineer, and three local businessmen. Two surprising omissions from the list were the parish priest (assigned to Siaton in 1960) and the government physician, who arrived in the municipality in 1964.

Certain limitations must be stated concerning the information on compadrinazgo obtained from the Siaton elite. The Chinese businessman had no godchildren. Although he was a Catholic, according to him, his business made it impossible for him to sponsor, so his son, an attorney, "takes my place." However, the son was not regarded as a member of the Siaton elite.

Several among the Siaton elite claimed they had hundreds of godchildren—so many that they had forgotten most of their names. (For example, the mayor explained that he had so many godchildren that if he were addressed as "compadre" he could not be sure if he were an actual ritual kinsman of the speaker.) For these elite data were obtained for only a fraction of their godchildren. On the other hand, one of the Siaton elite furnished detailed information for more than fifty godchildren.

In 1965 Caticugan had a population of 732 individuals residing in 145 households (author's census). The Siaton river separates the barrio from the poblacion (Hart 1954a). To get from the poblacion to the barrio one must either ford the river, which often is impossible after heavy rains in the mountains, or walk across the Siaton bridge over which the national road passes to Bayawan. Once across the bridge, one climbs Pangligaran hill and then descends into the tiny floodplain of Caticugan.

The village lacks electricity; the majority of the residents use kerosene pressure lanterns for illumination. The people have a small chapel in Caticugan; the nearest priest resides in the poblacion. Drinking water is obtained from wells and springs at the base of Pangligaran hill. Agricultural land is devoted primarily to corn, although some irrigated paddies are found in part of Caticugan. Irrigation water comes from the springs at the base of Pangligaran hill. An unimproved, rutted spur connects Naga, a sitio of Caticugan, with the national road. No buses

TABLE 1
Elite of Siaton Poblacion: 1972

Occupation	Rank	Sex	Age
Mayor	1	M	46
Attorney	2	M	38
Former Mayor	3	M	64
Retired schoolteacher	4	F	62
Engineer, vice-mayor	5	M	37
Justice of Peace	6	M	47
Municipal employee[1]	7	M	49
Former vice-mayor[1, 2]	8	M	68
School principal	9	M	47
Businessman	10	M	40
Former mayor[1, 2]	11	M	71
Businessman (Chinese)	12	M	70
Schoolteacher	13	M	58
Schoolteacher[1]	14	F	59
Engineer	15	M	47
Former municipal councilor[1]	16	M	45
Schoolteacher[1]	17	F	49
Municipal councilor	18	M	69
Businessman	19	M	42
Municipal employee	20	M	33
Retired schoolteacher[1]	21	F	62

[1]Protestant (Seventh Day Adventist or United Church of Christ)
[2]Ill or traveling, so unavailable for interview

or trucks use this nearly abandoned road. The Caticugan elementary school is located in Naga. There are no stores as such in Caticugan, but in their dwellings several residents sell basic daily necessities.

Comparisons Between Caticugan and Lalawigan

Caticugan and Lalawigan dwellings are similar in design and utilize the same building materials. The houses, raised on poles, are built two to four feet above the ground; the space beneath the structure is used to store firewood and farm equipment. The walls are made of nipa palm tightly pressed between slats inserted in the upright poles. Some dwellings have unpainted wooden walls, but because wood is more expensive, it is used less frequently. Most floors are made of bamboo strips, although some residences have plank floors. The rooves are thatched with nipa shingles or made of corrugated iron sheets. The windows have shutters that are closed tightly each evening when the family retires.

Although the number of their rooms varies from one to four or five, most houses in Caticugan and Lalawigan have a *sala* (a combined living-dining room) furnished with a few straight-back chairs, a table, and some pictures and photographs (Hart 1959). In this room usually is located the family altar with several saint figures (usually including one of the local patron saint) and pictures of the Holy Family. The kitchen has a raised platform covered with earth and ashes; here the food is cooked in cast-iron pots over a wood fire.

Most residences have another room (and some have several) that serves as a combined bedroom-storage space. A wooden or bamboo bed usually is found in this room, although most family members sleep on the floor (sometimes in the *sala*) on mats of woven buri palm. During the day the mats are rolled, with the pillows inside, and stacked in a corner of the room. Room partitions are made of nipa and rarely extend higher than six or seven feet; few residences have ceilings.

Both Caticugan and Lalawigan are primarily villages of single-class subsistence farmers or fishermen. No Protestants lived in Caticugan or Lalawigan in 1956. No drastic social or technological innovations have occurred in these villages since observation began nearly two decades ago. Since 1956 national law has required an elected Council in each barrio, but its achievements in Caticugan have been minimal. The Council in Lalawigan did receive and install seven pumps, improving the community's water supply. Various government community development agencies have assigned workers to the barrios, with slight impact. The barriofolk's agricultural techniques remain basically unchanged, although there has been an increased use by some of chemical fertilizers and insecticides.

In 1972 about one out of every three families in Caticugan and Lalawigan owned transistor radios. The radios increased the barriofolk's opportunity to obtain information about national and international affairs, although music and "soap operas" are the most popular programs. The people's diet remains the same. The only modification in dress is the almost complete disappearance of locally woven abaca skirts and men's shirts.

Over the years there has been a steady increase in individualization of certain aspects of barrio life, e.g., paying workers to do jobs once done by volunteer cooperative labor groups or the growing authority of young people to select their own mates, chosen in the past by their parents. Indeed, the peasants of Caticugan and Lalawigan share many characteristics: most were born in the village they now live in, or in one nearby; mate selection is localized; and kinship organization is bilateral.

Compadrinazgo: A Historical Sketch

Throughout the world, institutions exist that create relationships analogous to kin ties, one of which is compadrinazgo.

> The participants recognize a bond which is likened to, though it is not confused with, kinship. These are commonly defined under the headings of blood brotherhood and ritual co-parenthood, or *compadrazgo*, and they are all best classified as ritual kinship. To refer to them as 'fictive kinship,' as many authors have done, is to invite confusion, since no fiction is involved; these institutions are conceptually distinct from and frequently contrasted with natural kinship (Pitt-Rivers 1968: 409).

This exposition is concerned with ritual kinship resulting from the requirement of the Catholic church that sponsors are necessary for certain rites. The following sections briefly survey the historical and doctrinal development of compadrinazgo, including folk accretions, in Europe, prior to its diffusion to Latin America and the Philippines.

The Christian concept of godparents developed from that of sponsorship, whose origin (it lacks a scriptural basis) is uncertain (Gudeman 1972: 50). *Sponsor* is an adaptation of a Roman term *sponsio*, which refers to a contract enforced by religious sanctions, not by legal ones. The idea of sponsorship may have derived from the Jewish practice of having a witness at a child's circumcision; however, participants in the Eleusynian Mysteries of the Greeks also had sponsors (Mintz and Wolf 1950: 343). It is also possible that the practice of sponsorship originated with the "custom of the early Church (later recognized by Canon law) requiring a sponsor at baptism [for adults] to prevent the entry of bogus 'spy' Catholics during the periods of persecution" (Kenny 1962: 71). At a later date this function was "combined with that of sponsors for infants and that of helper at the baptismal ceremony" (Gudeman 1972: 50).

As discussed by Aquinas and later closely followed by Canon law, adult mentors, or sponsors, in addition to the parents, were needed and duty-bound "to instruct and guide their spiritual children in the Christian faith ..." since the clergy lacked the time to serve (Gudeman 1972:50). Originally, confirmation immediately followed baptism; hence a second sponsor for the former rite was not required. (It is still the practice of the Greek Orthodox Church to confirm a child immediately after baptism, so only one sponsor is needed.)

Crowd outside Borongan church, eastern Samar, before a confirmation ceremony. In the foreground is a statue of Jose Rizal, famous martyred Filipino hero, and the plaza, where local activities take place.

The practice of having multiple sponsors for a child's baptism grew despite the ruling of the Council of Metz (999 A.D.) and local church laws (Kearney 1925: 43–45). The number of sponsors increased "... until general custom admitted between one and thirty baptismal sponsors" (Mintz and Wolf 1950: 348). This latter function explains why compadre often means "neighbor." To stem the practice of multiple sponsors, the Council of Trent (1545–1563 A.D.) ruled that the number of baptismal sponsors would be restricted to one (at the most, two), and only one for confirmation.

At the start, ritual kinship bonds were created between the officiating priest, the child, and its parents and siblings (Mintz and Wolf 1950: 345). All these participants were within the exogamous circle when Emperor Justinian (527–565 A.D.) forbade the marriage of spiritual kinsmen. Shortly thereafter (between 585 A.D. and 595 A.D.) the Latin terms for compadre (*compater*) and comadre (*commater*) became associated with the Western church (Mintz and Wolf 1950: 344).

In 530 A.D. sponsors were prohibited from marrying their godchildren. The Council of Trullo (692 A.D.) forbade the marriage of a godfather and his godchild's natural mother. A synod of Rome (721 A.D.) extended this exogamy to both of the child's natural parents and godparents. Finally the Council of Munich (831 A.D.) halted the custom, from which there had been numerous exceptions, of parents sponsoring their own children.

The Council of Trent (1545–1563 A.D.) limited spiritual bonds resulting from baptism to the priest, child, child's parents, and sponsors. Spiritual fraternity (between the godchild and his sponsor's sibling) was abolished, as were "spiritual relationships between the sponsors themselves, and spiritual relationships arising from catechismal sponsorship" (Mintz and Wolf 1950: 351). Some further changes in this institution were later made by the 1918 Code.

> Spiritual relationships are still said to arise from baptism and confirmation. But they are limited to those between recipient, and minister and sponsors (Canon 768). Parents, and minister and sponsor do not contract spiritual bonds, and there is no matrimonial impediment between co-parents (Canon 1079). While a baptised child and the minister or his godparents may not marry, spiritual parenthood in confirmation no longer gives rise to a diriment impediment (Canon 797) (Gudeman 1972: 53).

Over the centuries various socio-political forces modified the formal structure of compadrinazgo. For example, Mintz and Wolf advanced several explanations for the growth of compadrinazgo, that is, the increased number of occasions for sponsorship, the popularity of multiple sponsors, and the extension of ritual kinship relationships among the participants. They correlate this expansion with the emergence of the nation state, where compadrinazgo was seen as a means to manipulate its increasingly impersonal nature in terms of face-to-face relationships (1959: 346). The widening of the exogamous circle associated with compadrinazgo was the result of three interrelated factors: first, the serfs' effort to maintain their economic position, especially in regard to the inheritance of land; second, their attempt to deal with the increasingly impersonal structure of the state by using familiar mechanisms (e.g., blood brotherhood); third, the Church's struggle to establish itself as an independent landowner.

> In the final analysis, all three factors are but facets of the growing centralization of the feudal structure. This process took place in the main at the expense of the lay aristocracy. In the struggle the Crown attempted to play off Church and serfs against the feudal barons; the Church supported Crown and serfs against its lay competitors; and the serfs looked to both the Crown and Church in their effort to increase their rights on the estates of the lay aristocracy (Mintz and Wolf 1950: 347).

The eventual reaction to this enlargement of compadrinazgo began with the rise of Protestantism and the spreading industrialization of Europe. Not only the Church but also the states imposed restrictions on the selection of sponsors. For example, peasants were prevented from seeking urban sponsors and from asking unknown persons to be sponsors "since rich people were often selected as *compadres*" (Mintz and Wolf 1950: 351). The new Protestant ethic "put a premium on the individual as an effective accumulator of capital and virtue, and was certain to discountenance the drain on individual resources and the restrictions on individual freedom implicit in the wide extension of ritual kin ties" (Mintz and Wolf 1950: 351). As a result of the above factors compadrinazgo was stripped of most of its functions in those parts of Europe where Protestantism prevailed. Its vitality and functions were less affected in Spain, Italy, and the Balkans, where the development of individual capitalism, the rise of the middle class, and the dissolution of the feudal order were delayed (Mintz and Wolf 1950: 352).

Although this brief sketch omits many complexities of the doctrinal foundation and historical development of compadrinazgo, it presents a general basis for differentiating variations that later occurred in Latin America and the Philippines. It was in this basic form that the godparenthood complex diffused from southern Europe (mainly Spain and Portugal) to Hispanic America and the Philippines (Gudeman 1972: 49).

Spiritual or Ritual Kinship Concept

Compadrinazgo, in its basic form, creates three sets of ritual bonds. Traditionally, these ritual ties are achieved through Church-required sponsorship at baptism and confirmation, but not at marriage. The first set of relationships is developed between godparent and godchild. If there is more than one sponsor (co-sponsors), they are ritually linked among themselves and to the sponsored. Second, the sponsor (and co-sponsors) and the parents of the godchild become ritual kinsmen. In many instances, this ritual relationship is diffused to their siblings and other relatives. Third, a ritual relationship is generated between the godchild and the godparents' children.

In much of Hispanic America (and the Philippines), and in contrast to most of Spain, Italy, and Greece, "the compadre ties, in a functional sense, are more important than the godparent-godchild ties, and in some instances the child is little more than a means of establishing a compadrazgo relationship which the adults desire" (Foster 1967: 77;

also Middleton 1975: 465; Manners 1966: 150; Wolf 1966b: 209; Seda
1966: 295). Moreover, wherever godparenthood has been studied, "the
most important of these godparent sets is the one that functions at
baptism" (Rubel 1955: 1038; also Campbell 1964: 222; Madsen 1969:
624; Holmes 1952: 101; Fals-Borda 1962: 197; Nelson 1971: 81; Whitten 1965: 102; Manrique 1969: 74; Gudeman 1972: 56; Redfield and
Villa Rojas 1962: 98; Osborn 1968: 603; Middleton 1975: 464; Moss and
Cappannari 1960: 30; Vogt 1970: 63; Richardson 1970: 83). In one
Guatemalan village

> Baptism is the only sacrament of the Catholic Church which is impor-
> tant to the Chimaltecos and the institution of godparents is linked to this
> Catholic rite; thus in Chimaltenango it is customary to have only godpar-
> ents of baptism (Wagley 1949: 17).

One exception to the general primacy of baptism ritual bonds is reported for the Peruvian community of Aritama, where the most important
compadrinazgo relationships are between marriage godparents and
their godchildren (Nuñez de Prado 1973: 20).

*Main street leading to Borongan. The arch was built in the 1930s during a visit of Manuel
L. Quezon, a famous Filipino statesman.*

Among many folk Catholics "the basic principle of compadrazgo is
ritual sponsorship of a person or persons (occasionally of things) by
another person or persons, with consequent formal ties among a number
of people, which last during the lifetime of the principals" (Foster 1967:
76). This standard definition of the godparenthood complex requires
two revisions. First, sponsorship does not always involve the ritual sponsorship of a person or object. For example, *compadres de voluntad*
become ritual kinsmen in a simple secular ceremony of shaking hands.

Compadres de fogueira (of the fire) sponsor neither a person nor an object but are ritually related after a brief ceremony. (For additional details see Chapter Eight.) Second, ritual linkages do not always result from sponsorship, and if they do the formal ties may not be permanent. As will be later discussed, there are occasions when sponsors for other than Church-prescribed rites do not share any ritual kinship bonds. When these ties are created, including through Church-prescribed rites, the formal relationship and the traditionally associated responsibilities and privileges may cease immediately after the ceremony or at a later date. Lastly, godparents may dissolve their ritual relationships by returning to the parents the baptismal fee they paid; moreover, parents can also transfer this ritual bond to other individuals simply by giving them the same amount of money (Reichel-Dolmatoff 1961: 172). In fact, whether ritual kinship relations continue to be vital may depend solely on the will of the involved principals.

Church and Folk Occasions for Sponsorship: Types and Classification

The Church-prescribed occasions requiring sponsors (or at least witnesses) are baptism, confirmation, and marriage. These are the primary sponsorship events in the Philippines and Europe (Pitt-Rivers 1961: 107; Moss and Cappannari 1960: 30; Maraspini 1968: 200–202; Anderson 1956: 40–48). It is the Latin Americans who have added, with variety and imagination, to the Church-sanctioned occasions requiring godparents.

In Moche, a Peruvian town of 3,178 people, there are fourteen occasions for sponsorship (Gillin 1947: 105); in Huaylas, a Peruvian district, twelve occasions (Doughty 1968: 115–116); in Tepoztlán, eight occasions (Lewis 1963: 351); and among the Yaqui of Pascua (Tucson, Arizona), seven occasions (Spicer 1940: 95–101). In San Lorenzo honorary godparents are chosen for any important social event: "At least once a month there is a celebration that calls for honorary godparents" (Whitten 1965: 111).

Various attempts have been made to classify this almost bewildering variety of occasions for sponsorship. "They can be separated into dogmatically prescribed and nonprescribed categories: baptism and confirmation versus marriage and other ceremonies" (Gudeman 1972: 61). Moche rites have been classified as "Roman" (Christian) or "Pagan" (non-Christian). They have also been grouped into "spiritual" sponsorship of persons and "friendship" sponsorship of things (Gillin 1947: 105). Yet sponsors of religious images and churches in Pascua are regarded by the Yaqui "as being [of] the same kind as the ceremonial sponsors of humans" (Spicer 1940: 111).

There are two types of sponsorship in Tlayacapan, a Mexican town of 3,000 people. The first category is called *de sacramento;* these rites are normally but not always associated with the main occasions for godparenthood, i.e., baptism, confirmation, and marriage. The second category, called *non-de sacramento* ceremonies, are quite similar to Moche's "pagan" or "friendship" rites, except that in some instances they may also be "spiritual," e.g., when parents seek a person (*compadre de la cruz*) to defray part of the cost of a funeral (Ingham 1970: 282–83).

Gudeman comments on past efforts to classify these ceremonies:

> These differences in classification are apparently the result of whether the church's, peoples' or anthropologists' conscious categories are being used. . . . But all such classifications are misleading, for the structure does not lie at the observed level. The issue is not the ways in which the different types of objects and life cycle rites which are brought into the system may be classified but the fact that the *Compadrazgo* Set serves as a model for the variant forms. Viewed in this way the underlying unity of the ceremonies emerges (1972: 61–62).

Gudeman proposes five rules (with several sub-types) that explicate the basic folk variations of compadrinazgo (1972: 61–63). Four of these rules fall into two major categories: those rites involving replication of either structure or position of the participants. A final rule concerns the prohibition of choice reversal. A more detailed analysis of this classification scheme is made in those chapters comparing Philippine compadrinazgo with this institution in Latin America and Europe. Briefly, the Church's call for sponsors does not fully specify who shall serve in this capacity. Local customs establish operative mechanisms for choice, with local social considerations either affecting or guiding the mechanisms.

Replication of Structure

The first variety of structural replication occurs in the folk variations of compadrinazgo when the sets of relationships are "extended metaphorically from the prescribed church rituals of baptism and confirmation to other rites as well" (Gudeman 1972: 61). Their variety defies rigid classification, although most involve some change, physically or socially, in the status of the sponsored person. The phenomenon of structural replication has been noted far more frequently for Latin America than for Europe or the Philippines.

A second variety of replication of structure occurs when in the ceremony objects are substituted for the godchild. "In these instances the objects are not said to be the godchild; they stand in place of the godchild. A personal relationship is formed only between the owner or 'parent' of the object and the godparent" (Gudeman 1972: 61).

A third variation of structural replication involves substitution of the sponsor. The sole example reported for this variant is for rural Portugal where, if an unbaptized child is dying "and no human sponsor is available, a saint may be selected as godparent" (Gudeman 1972: 61). The final variant of structure replication is that of substitutes replacing both the godchild and parent. An individual may "sponsor" an object for an institution, a group, or the community. "The sponsor is said to be the godparent; he may or may not form ties with the other individuals" (Gudeman 1972: 61). An officiating priest may or may not be involved in these ceremonies. Sponsorship for these events may or may not result in ritual kinship bonds.

An additional variety must be added to Gudeman's schema that involves the lack of structural or position replication. This variety has individuals becoming ritual kinsmen without the sponsorship of a person or object. Sometimes no ritual is involved. An excellent example of this variety is *compadres de voluntad* of Puerto Ricans.

> *Compai* [i.e., *Compadre*] Cefo and I had a long talk of becoming *compadres*, but neither his wife nor mine was having a child at the time. After some months, we decided we would become *compadres de voluntad*. We made up our minds while we were talking one night, and we drank beer together. After that, we were *compadres* . . . We are *compadres* just as if *Compai* Cefo were *padrino* to a child of mine, or I to one of his (Mintz 1966: 387–88).

In another instance, *compadres de voluntad* became ritual kinsmen merely by shaking hands (Seda 1966: 294; also see Wolf 1966: 209).

Another example of compadrinazgo that does not involve sponsorship of a person or object is *compadres de fogueira* (of the fire) of Brazilians. During the fiestas of St. John and St. Peter, bonfires are a common part of the festivities.

> Two friends holding each other's hands jumped over the embers of one of the bonfires characteristic of this *festa* [Sao Joao]. They recited to-

Central part of Borongan. Tanks on roof tops store rain for drinking water.

gether the phrase: "St. John slept, St. Peter awoke, let's be compadres as St. John commanded." Repeating this three times, they embraced and said, "*Adeus* compadre" (Harris 1956: 152).

An almost identical rite is described by Wagley, although the participants recite a slightly different oath and hold their clasped hands over the fire three times. It is possible, in this manner, for a youngster to request an adult to become his godparent, in which instance the young person could be considered the one sponsored. However, this rite usually is used to created compadre bonds between two adults (Wagley 1964: 153–54).

Replication of Position

The network of compadrinazgo relationships may be extended or restricted according to the extent of position replication. Repeat sponsorship is one of the three variations of compadrinazgo based on position replication. In repeat sponsorship the same godparent sponsors more than one child of a couple; for example one's compadre may be both the baptismal and confirmation sponsor for several or all of one's children. Repeat sponsorship also occurs when the same godparent sponsors a godchild on more than one occasion. In other words, repeat sponsorship is a "proliferation of children or ceremonies for the same godparents" (Gudeman 1972: 63).

A second variation of compadrinazgo based on position replication is the extension of ritual kinship ties to kinsmen of the principals (Gudeman 1972: 62). This rule also has been described as the "blanketing-in" process. Ritual kinship bonds may be extended, usually to relatives, purposely, automatically, and selectively, with or without a ritual embrace (*abrazo*) in Latin America. (Some of the patterns of extension of ritual kinship have been summarized [Gudeman 1972: 62].) The godchild's grandparents and/or other relatives may become compadres of the baptismal godparents. Ritual kinship terms are also extended to the relatives of the godparents. "Sometimes the godparents for the same or different ceremonies may themselves become compadres" (1972: 62). Individuals who do not share a common compadre or godparent linkage with the principals may become ritually related (for example, the parents and other relatives of a bride and groom).

A third permutation of compadrinazgo results from position replication of the godparent/compadre role. "The number of godparents chosen for any occasion may vary; each godparent stands in place of the other" (Gudeman 1972: 62). The number of sponsors may not be fixed by local tradition but may instead reflect the wishes of the principals.

Choice Reversal

Choice reversal, the final variant of compadrinazgo, is also the rarest. This is the reversal of the parent and godparent roles, where a godfather-giver is also the godfather-taker (Gudeman 1972: 63). Gudeman's explanation of the folk deduction that results in the common prohibition of choice reversal (some exceptions are noted) is similar to the reasoning offered by Caticuganers for the disapproval of repeat sponsorship in general.

> The implicit reasons may be as follows. Natural and spiritual parenthood are conceptually distinct. Just as these two forms of paternity must be kept separate (parents may not become godparents to their own children), so natural and spiritual co-parenthood must be distinguished ... Therefore, if choice were returned from godfather to father, each would be both natural and spiritual co-parents to the other, and each would occupy both a higher and lower status in relation to the other. By prohibiting choice

· reversal this structurally impossible situation is avoided. The two roles are segregated and an individual plays a natural co-parenthood role toward some and a spiritual co-parenthood role towards others (1972: 63).

Chapter Two

Compadrinazgo:
Latin American and Filipino
Cultural Preadaptiveness

Beginning with the sixteenth and continuing into the nineteenth century, Spanish culture "was forcibly exported and brought into contact, in a planned and guided manner, with a variety of very different cultures" (Foster 1951: 311). The differential diffusion and acceptance of Spanish culture in Latin America (and the Philippines) was the result of several factors: (1) the form and content of the recipient cultures; (2) the nature of Spanish domination in these areas; and (3) subsequent external relationships of Hispanic America (and the Philippines) after independence (Foster 1951: 312).

This chapter indicates how various indigenous elements of Latin American and Filipino cultures facilitated the acceptance and subsequent elaboration of the godparenthood complex. These preadaptive indigenous religio-social aspects included religious beliefs and rites, traditional curing practices and shamanism, institutionalized friendships, kinship systems, commercial customs, and blood brotherhood. All of these native traits were typical of societies in both regions. This chapter not only discusses these preadaptive indigenous elements but also frequently indicates how they have been integrated into contemporary practices.

One important "cultural export" of the Spaniards to both Latin America and the Philippines was the godparenthood complex associated with the Catholic religion. The import into Spanish America appears to have come from a focal area; Foster states that "to the extent that a peninsular type of compadrazgo is ancestral to Hispanic American variants, it is Andalusian" (Foster 1960: 231). There are, however, no studies of what regions of Spain contributed culture to what parts of the Philippines.

In other publications the author has explored selected cultural relationships of Spanish origin between Latin America and the Philippines. Considerable similarities and differences occur between the religious or patron saint fiestas of Hispanic America and the Philippines (Hart 1954b; see also Ortner 1967). Humoral pathology, introduced by the Spaniards, became part of the folk medicine of both regions, although less so for the Philippines (Hart 1969). The "plaza complex" (largely of Spanish origin), or the typical spatial arrangement of a town, shares many common features in Latin America and the Philippines (Hart 1955).

Traditional Spanish Catholicism, significantly influenced by North African cultures and the Moorish occupation of Spain, is also typical of both Latin America and the Philippines.

> The first thing that strikes us about the Filipino Christ—that is, the view of Christ most commonly held in the Philippines—is its similarity to the traditional Spanish Christ and therefore also to the Latin American Christ. He appears almost exclusively in two dramatic roles: as the *Santo Niño* (Holy Child) or as the *Santo Cristo* and the *Santo Entierro* (Christ Interred)—the tragic victim on the cross or in the tomb. As with the traditional Spanish image, it is almost as though Christ was born and died but never really lived (Elwood and Magdamo 1971: 5).

It is not surprising, therefore, to find similarities between the Catholic godparenthood complex of Latin America and the Philippines, although all of these diffused Spanish institutions that both areas share are also characterized by some significant differences. One possible cause (others will be discussed later) for similarities between cultural elements of Spanish origin in Latin America and the Philippines, largely undocumented, is diffusion to the Philippines after adaptations had occurred in Latin America. Many Spanish administrators and priests who came to the Philippines had resided first in Latin America. Those who intended to come directly to the Philippines often "recuperated" from the debilitating Atlantic voyage to Latin America before proceeding from Acapulco to Manila. Native Mexican soldiers were sent to the Philippines as part of the Spanish army (Rodriguez 1941: 25). Mexican creoles were imported to staff Augustinian missions in Luzon (Phelan 1959: 36). The Mexican experience "provided the clergy with a galaxy of pertinent models. The sacraments were introduced into the islands with a minimum of controversy largely because of the lessons learned in Mexico" (Phelan 1959: 154). As Bernal demonstrates, more than goods was transported between Mexico and the Philippines by the Acapulco-Manila galleons (1965: 109).

Compadrinazgo in Hispanic America and the Philippines became an established feature of social organization, with significant economic, political, religious, and emotional implications. This variety of ritual kinship assumed far greater significance in these areas than in Spain where "it is (and from all evidence was) of moderate importance, invoked in the baptism and marriage of the individual, usually kept within the family, and relegated to the category of one of a number of routine *rites de passage*" (Foster 1951: 321). This form of ritual kinship, for reasons to be discussed, fulfilled greater needs of Latin Americans and Filipinos than of Spaniards.

Graph 1 schematically diagrams the basic organization and data of this chapter. This graph, illustrating major influences on present-day Philipinne godparenthood, probably is incomplete since it omits possible Chinese influence.

The first section of this chapter discusses why compadrinazgo (in addition to its inherent values of flexibility and choice) was so rapidly and extensively adopted by Latin Americans. Acceptance of the godparenthood complex was facilitated by indigenous concepts regarding ritual kinship, a social structure distrupted by Spanish conquest, and its "congeniality" with native beliefs and customs related to religious and curing rites, friendship, etc. The latter part of this chapter examines similar elements of pre-Hispanic Philippine culture.

Social Structure

Paul proposed that most Latin Americans found the Spanish form of ritual kinship appealing because the Catholic godparenthood complex was congruous with pre-Columbian institutions. The adoption of this form of ritual kinship constituted a change in form but permitted a continuity of function (Paul 1942: 79). Moreover, "Catholic elements seemed to have been accepted or rejected on the basis of their degree of similarity to corresponding [native] elements" (Wisdom 1940: 370). For example, "Zapotec words for padrinos do suggest that a pre-Hispanic form of ritual kinship may have existed" (Nader 1969a: 349). Relationships interpreted as of compadrinazgo origin in Latin America may be indigenous. Although the brother-in-law relationship of the

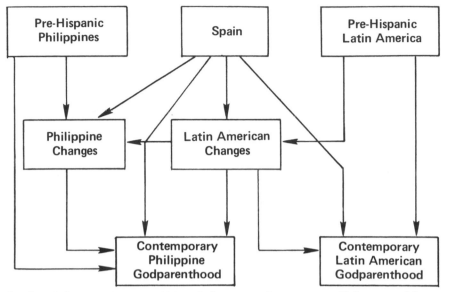

Graph 1: *Schematic Diagram of Major Influences on Contemporary Philippine and Latin American Compadrinazgo.*

Nambikuara Indians of the Western Matto Grosso "could readily be interpreted as a development of the imported Iberian *compadre*" system, Lévi-Strauss argues that actually it was of native origin (1968: 169, 182–83). This relationship presents "a striking example of convergence in which the native and Latin-Mediterranean institutions show numerous apparent similarities overlying important structural differences" (1968: 169).

Compadrinazgo offered many Latin Americans an adjustable institution capable of meeting new needs that Spanish activities and policies brought about in indigenous unilineal social units, the family and community organization.

> It seems probable that crumbling Indian societies, in which aboriginal clan or lineage systems, or other forms of extended family and village organization were breaking down, consciously or unconsciously recognized in the bare form of *compadrazgo* a new device to maintain the social cohesion that was being lost (Foster 1951: 321).

Parsons hypothesized that if the Zapotecans of Mitla ever had a larger kinship group than the bilateral family "it has been substituted for by the *compadre* system which fulfills all the functions that would be expected of a kinship group outside the immediate family" (1936: 69–70). The elaborate godparenthood complex of Tepoztlán supposedly compensates for the weakness of the extended family (Lewis 1970: 395). Goldfrank speculated that among the Cochiti the padrino role was displacing "the clan role of responsibility, mutual aid, and general significance" (1927: 9).

Compadrinazgo usually is less vital in those parts of Latin America where indigenous social units persist. Among the Tzeltal of Chiapas (Mexico) clans are still functional, and compadrinazgo has failed to make any headway (Foster 1953: 23). Yet unilineal systems do not necessarily make a hostile environment for godparenthood. The Zinacanteco Mayas retained their patrilineages (albeit shallow) and also adopted compadrinazgo (Vogt 1970: 38).

Another probable example of the association of the godparenthood complex with agnatic descent groups is found in rural Balkans. In this area peasants who are members of the Orthodox Church inherit from father to son not only property rights but godparenthood obligations (Hammel 1968). Another claims, however, that godparenthood in this region actually "is transmitted through ties of successive filiation. . . . not descent ties" (Rheubottom 1970: 405).

Baptismal Rites

Aztec and Mayan religions had rites similar to Catholic baptism (Madsen 1960b: 30; Tozzer 1941: 102 ff; Orozco y Berra 1880: 170–71). The fourth day after the birth of an Aztec, the midwife, with appropriate prayers and invocations, offered the infant to the gods. The baby was first sprinkled with water (a gift of the goddess of water) and then passed four times over a fire. A boy was given miniature weapons, a girl weaving sticks, gifts symbolic of adult roles. The infant was usually named for the day of its birth, the naming ceremony occurring in the presence of kinsmen and friends (Paul 1942: 80; Madsen 1960a: 124). And, like the Catholic doctrine, it was an Aztec belief that man was conceived in sin that could be symbolically washed away, resulting in a spiritual rebirth (Madsen 1960a: 131).

The Aztec also had an ear-piercing ceremony that required the parents to select a "godfather" and a "godmother" for their child. These sponsors carried their "godchildren" to the temple of the fire god for the ritual. At the conclusion of the ceremony, all participants ate together. Parsons believed these "godparents" continued to sponsor the child in its later ceremonial life (Paul 1942: 82; Parsons 1936: 521). She asserts that present-day Aztec and Zapotec godparents probably have functions once performed by their ancient priests (1936: 524).

Ancient Mayan baptism resembled the Catholic rite so closely that some early Spaniards believed an apostle or his successor must have preceded them as missionaries to the New World. Baptism among the Mayans was compulsory. It occurred between the ages of three and twelve years, and was performed by a priest. During the ritual the boys and girls were separated into two groups. An older man and woman were placed as "godparents," each in charge of the respective sex group. The priest then asked each candidate if he had sinned; if so, confession was required. The children were anointed with perfume and "virgin waters, the latter from an isolated spot unvisited by females" (Paul 1942: 80–81; Thompson 1960: 9; Tozzer 1941: 102–6).

One modern Mayan rite illustrates the tendency of pagan rites to assimilate Christian elements (Redfield 1941: 220; Thompson 1971: 384). When a Mayan child is first carried astride its mother's left hip (at around three or four months old) the *hetzmek* (*hèetzméek'*) is held. The sponsors of *hetzmek* and of Catholic baptism are the same couple. In Quintana Roo, a married couple is chosen by the child's parents. One spouse serves as the baptismal sponsor, the other as the *hetzmek* sponsor. In the latter ceremony the sponsor, holding the child, places in its hand objects symbolizing future skills and capacities that *hetzmek* supposedly assures (Redfield 1941: 220). When *hetzmek* is over, food and drink are enjoyed by the sponsor and family members (Redfield and Villa Rojas 1962: 189). *Hetzmek* is "a kind of pagan baptism" (Villa Rojas 1969 7: 267–68); the presence of godparents may be a Spanish accretion (Thompson 1960: 29).

Other pre-Columbian practices possessed preadaptive elements vis-a-vis the Catholic godparenthood complex. Apparently an exchange of functions occurred between the midwife and godmother. Although the Mitla midwife does not officiate at an infant's baptism, as in the Aztec instance, she does bring the baby to the church for its waiting godmother (Parsons 1936: 80). In the Indian village of San Francisco Tecospa the midwife baptizes the infant shortly after birth. If the baby should die without the midwife's christening, it goes to limbo (Madsen 1960b: 81). In San Pedro de Laguna, the midwife performs several rituals before the new mother reenters secular life, such as bathing the woman in the courtyard of her dwelling.

In Spanish *comadre* means not only "godmother" but, alternatively, "midwife" or *patera* (Cuyás 1940: 113; Kenny 1962: 72). (*Comadre*, however, lacks this alternative meaning in Catlcugan and Lalawigan.) In Huaylas the prominence of the midwife as a sponsor is indicated by her name, *comadrona* (Sp. midwife), or a woman with many comadres (Doughty 1968: 249). In Puerto Rico the midwife (also known as *comadrona*) may automatically become a ritual co-parent or be chosen as a sponsor (*madrina de agua*) at the home baptism of the infant (Mintz 1966: 387; Seda 1966: 295). The midwife in Hualcan is called *pacakumdari* or "comother of the earth." When a child is born the midwife becomes its godmother and also a comadre of the parents, but the ritual relationship is less important than with other individuals who act as sponsors for the child in other life crises (Stein 1961: 132, footnote 32, 154).

A symbolic relationship can be visualized between the roles of the midwife and godmother. The midwife presides at one's physical birth, while the baptismal godmother sponsors one's spiritual "rebirth." Gudeman suggests a similar parallel: "The parents initiate the child into the physical world and household; the godparents initiate him into the spiritual world and community" (1972: 57).

Curing Rites

Congruencies occurred between indigenous healing procedures and the godparenthood complex in Latin America. In San Carlos a sponsor may be secured to pray in the church, often burning a candle or taking a rosary, for the patient's recovery from a severe sickness. These sponsors are called *padrinos del evangelio* (gospel) or *del rosario* (Gillin 1951: 61; Reina 1966: 229; Rubel 1955: 1039). In towns near Cherán, a compadre of the crown (*corona*) may be sought for a child who has been continuously ill (Beals 1946: 103). In Latin America the *padrino de vela* (vigil), also *del Niño Jesus* (child Jesus) or *de iglesia* (church), takes a sick child to church. There a candle is lighted, and the child is given a ribbon or a religious medal (Ravicz 1967: 243; Parsons 1936: 69).

In Tepoztlán there are three forms of sponsorship to protect one against illness. The sponsors are called *padrino de medida* (measurement or prudence), *padrino del evangelio*, and *padrino de miscoton*. The last type of sponsor gives the child a "little sweater" to wear as protection against sickness (Lewis 1963: 351). Among the Mexican-Americans of one south Texas city, a person (usually a woman) whose sickness has not responded to treatment may select a friend to become her *madrina de hàbito* (dress). "The *madrina* purchases for the patient a habit which replicates one worn by a selected religious image. . . . The patient then wears the garment until her condition is remedied or is terminated by death" (Rubel 1966: 83, 198–99). A similar type of sponsorship was once popular in Martineztown (Vincent 1966: 57–58).

Lalawigan village scene. Unhusked rice is drying on palm mats.

Shamans in Latin America had and continue to have some functions congruous with compadrinazgo and its associated rituals. In fact, today in parts of Hispanic America the shaman is called *padrino* (Brinton 1894: 34). Among the Chorti the rain-maker is known as *padrino de agua* (water) and the drought-maker as *padrino de verano* (summer or dry season) (Fought 1969: 473). Brinton reports that when the Quiché shaman prayed to the dead he referred to himself as their self-appointed godparent (1894: 59). The role of godparents as curers in Mitla and Pascua "constitutes a displacement onto godparents of functions normally associated with shamans" (Paul 1942: 84–85). Paul comments that shamans and godparents share a similar function in that they serve as mediums between man and his destiny.

Among the Zinacanteco Mayas of Mexico an exchange of function has occurred between shamanism and baptism. This group believes that "soul-loss" results in sickness. If one or more of the thirteen parts of the "inner soul" is lost, "a shaman must be summoned to diagnose the sickness and to perform a ceremony to recover the missing parts and to place them back into the body of the patient" (Vogt 1970: 10). The most important aspect of baptism for Zinacantecos is not its Catholic function but "to fix permanently in the body the child's soul so that it will not be easily lost" (Vogt 1970: 104).

Other relationships between indigenous religious beliefs and compadrinazgo occur in Middle America. In some parts of this region the spirits of the dead are propitiated by addressing them as comadre or compadre (Wisdom 1952: 122). A Mitla folktale tells of a man who had a ritual relationship with the god of lightning, called him compadre, and, as a result, enjoyed unusually abundant harvests (Parsons 1936:328 –30).

Friendship and Commerce

There was an indigenous Latin American basis "for the compadre aspect of the [godparenthood] complex in the existence of various kinds of formal friendships among native peoples" (Paul 1942: 85–87). Paul claimed that these aboriginal forms of ceremonial friendship were, or are being, incorporated into the godparenthood system (1942: 86). For example, the Carib and Arawak Indians had a friend sponsor a child during its naming ceremony. The parents and the sponsors, as a token of their friendship, exchanged gifts. "While it seems apparent. . . . that compadrazgo was a European import, such a set of practices would find fertile soil among these Indians" (Land 1965: 53).

A form of ritual kinship, primarily based on intimate friendship bonds, used to be practiced in Martineztown in New Mexico. The participants were young adolescents, but sometimes included adult males, who often engaged in drinking bouts. The ceremony was a simple ritual in which two friends joined fingers while reciting a verse. They then became *compadres del dedo* (finger). The ritual relationship was extended, when the couple married, to their spouses (Vincent 1966: 71). It is not known if this form of friendship was indigenous as is *cuatismo.*

Cuatismo (Sp. *cuate,* twin) is a widespread form of male friendship in Mexico (Lomnitz 1973: 45). *Cuate* groups may be composed entirely of kin, mixed kin and nonkin, or nonkin members (Lomnitz 1973: 45). Tepoztecan males of the same age group develop close friendships. After marriage and upon the birth of a *cuate's* child, the ties of the couple are converted to a compadre relationship (Lewis 1963: 292–93). Typically, a Chimalteco boy of twelve or thirteen years has a special male friend of the same age. They eat and sleep together in a sweat house attached to one of their dwellings. They are inseparable until marriage, when, unlike the practice in Tepoztlán, the intimacy of their relationship ends (Wagley 1949: 35). Yet compadrinazgo often is used by Latin Americans to assure greater permanency or stability of original friendship bonds.

Generally speaking, ritual kinship strengthens friendship ties, for it is "not lightly entered into since it is a formal contract, solemnized in public and before God, and once concluded not to be broken" (Boissevain 1966: 21). Since the institution of friendship (*amicizia*) in Sicily frequently is unstable, nonkin friends often reinforce their bonds through godparenthood (Boissevain 1966: 22). In southern Italy (as in Brazil) friends may bind themselves into a pact of friendship and brotherhood on the day or eve of St. John the Baptist to symbolize the religious seriousness of the act (Anderson 1956: 40–46).

Different varieties of ritual kinship have also been associated with trading or commerce. In Africa blood brotherhood may be sought "solely for commercial purpose"; one seeks an ally when traveling in foreign territory (Tegnaeus 1952: 166). Ritual kinship is still used in southern Italy to cement relationships between persons sharing business interests (Maraspini 1968: 205).

Likewise, parallels occur between pre-Columbian trading relationships and compadrinazgo in Latin America. Commercial relations among the Tarahumara (Mexico) created a lasting bond of an intimate character. The Huichol, possessing a similar ritual trading friendship, went one step further by using the word *compadre* to cover these instances. A compadre may also serve the same purposes as a blood brother. Mestizo traders in Colombia depend on the hospitality and assistance of Kwaiker Indians when they visit their communities for commerical purposes. To assure this cooperation, the traders purposely become compadres with some of the Indians. If a trader lacking ritual kinship ties with a Kwaiker visits the community, the Indians hide until he departs (Osborn 1968: 699). In Itá compadrinazgo is used to reinforce "relations between the trader and his collector and farmer customer ... [One] strong commercial man of the community reported one hundred godchildren, and a rural trader had as many as sixty-five godchildren" (Wagley 1964: 159, 157).

Another substitution has occurred, in parts of Latin America, with the replacement of indigenous go-betweens who arranged marriage with ritual kinsmen. For example, in Tepoztlán, "the godfather has taken the place of the professional *cihuatlanque* [marriage broker]" (Redfield 1930: 140). In cases where this displacement has not taken place, "there are native equivalents to function in their stead" (Paul 1942: 85). (This has not happened in the Philippines; in fact, ritual kinsmen, as a whole, are less active in arranging the marriage of their godchildren than they are in much of Latin America.)

Pre-Hispanic Filipino Culture and Compadrinazgo

Pre-Hispanic Filipino religions lacked the baptismal rites, extensive hierarchical organization, and doctrinal complexities of Aztec and Mayan religions. It has been contended often that Filipinos had developed the concept of a Supreme God but that this deity was remote, consigned to the background by a pantheon of lesser gods and spirits. (However, the assertion that primitive groups in northern Luzon had a concept of a Supreme Being prior to the arrival of the Spaniards has been challenged: Scott 1971: 115.) A concept of heaven and hell existed, but there were no public buildings reserved solely for religious functions. Part-time religious specialists directed ceremonies both to spirits and to deceased ancestors; many of their rituals "concentrated on the cure of illness" (Phelan 1959: 23).

The Spaniards' speed in converting most lowland Filipinos to Catholicism is firmly documented. By the end of the seventeenth century, the majority of lowland Filipinos had been baptized as Catholics, "an achievement without parallel in history" (Bourne 1903 1:37). One major explanation advanced for this extraordinary accomplishment is that "Filipinos of the lowlands had a cultural and social heritage congenial with many of the elements of Catholic ritual and belief as introduced by the Spanish" (Eggan 1956 2: 477).

Physical coercion was also, however, a factor in many Filipinos' initial acceptance of Catholic sacraments. For example, Church records indicate that during the Spanish period (particularly at the start of colonization) an "infant had to be baptized within 3 days of its birth or the person bringing the child was flogged" (Nydegger and Nydegger 1966: 68).

There is also considerable evidence that the godparenthood complex was quickly adopted by lowland Filipinos. Pigafetta suggests that Magellan was the godfather of Humabon, a local leader in Cebu who was baptized in 1521 (Phelan 1955: 5). In 1565 Legaspi became the baptismal godfather of Tupas, also a local ruler in Cebu (Zaide 1937: 24–25). The zeal of newly converted Filipino Catholics, as early as the latter part of the sixteenth century, is illustrated by the statement that some searched diligently for poor children "to be baptized [and] . . . as their sponsors, [made] gifts to them afterwards of swaddling clothes or some such thing" (Aduarte 1903 31: 27).

Information on the rapid acceptance of compadrinazgo, and especially its associated secular uses, is indicated by a Spanish edict of 1599 prohibiting Chinese from serving as sponsors. The edict noted that they had

> a great number of godchildren, both Christian and infidel, in order to have them ready for any emergency that may arise, and to employ them as false witnesses—to which they lend themselves with great facility, and at little cost,—and for other evil purposes and intents, exchanging with them favors and assistance in their affairs; . . . it would be advisable, for its reform, to supress this custom of having godchildren, and . . . they should not continue it, under severe penalties . . . (Desquibel 1903 11: 76).

A Chinese often adopted the family name of his Christian Filipino baptismal godfather. For example, the original family name of Sergio Osmeña, a former president of the Philippines, was Go(Wu) (Weightman 1960: 32). (This was also the practice of the Chinese in Huaylas: Doughty 1968: 86.) Undoubtedly, Filipinos became as quickly aware as the Chinese of the secular potential of godparenthood. Indeed, the success of the Chinese in exploiting this aspect of compadrinazgo obviously required Filipino patronage.

Lifelong resident of Lalawigan sitting in front of the entrance ladder to her house, pounding unhusked rice.

Chinese receptivity to compadrinazgo in the Philippines may also have been facilitated by the institution of sworn brotherhood that "is well known and frequently practiced [today] among schoolmates in Manila" (Amyot 1960: 143). Ritual adoption also occurs among the Chinese in Manila.

Two individuals or two families will often seal their bond of friendship by ritually adopting one another's children. A man becomes the *yi fu* ... foster father, sponsor, or special protector ... of his friend's son or daughter who becomes his *yi tze* ... (foster son) or *yi nü* ... (foster daughter). This form of adoption has no religious overtones (Amyot 1960: 143).

Such ritual adoption usually occurs between Chinese families of similar socio-economic standing and entails no marriage restrictions for the persons involved. Although not intended primarily to help the adopted child financially, the foster father may furnish loans that should be repaid. When the foster father dies, the adopted children mourn his death as a sibling or sibling-in-law (Amyot 1960: 143).

According to Amyot, "Christian Chinese often choose the sponsors of their children at baptism in the same spirit as that involved in the *yi tze* adoption. The obligations are understood and practiced much in the same way" (1960: 143). On the other hand, such ritual relationships are rare among the Chinese living in the Ilocos regions of Luzon (Reynolds 1964: 191). Similar adoption occurs among the Chinese in Singapore. Adoptive parents "excercise over their 'adopted' children the same kind of distant benevolence as we associate in Europe with the institution of god-parenthood" (Freedman 1957: 67–68). Freedman suggests that "*godchild*, robbed of its religious connotation, would in fact be a reasonable translation of *khoèkiá* [a child given in nominal adoption]" (1957: 68, footnote 1).

Social Structure

Indigenous Filipino societies were less drastically disrupted by the Spaniards than were those in Latin America (Madsen 1960b: 24). The Spaniards learned numerous lessons in Mexico that they applied in the pacification of the Filipinos. For example, the conquest of the Philippines, compared with the armed subjugation of Mexico, was relatively bloodless (Phelan 1959: 154). The Mexican economic base of maize agriculture was seriously disrupted by the spread of a pastoral economy to parts of the country, with demoralizing social consequences. In contrast, Spanish innovations in Filipino agriculture were more evolution-

ary than revolutionary, more quantitative than qualitative (Phelan 1959:
110, 107). Ecological changes made by the Spaniards often supplement-
ed but did not disrupt the pre-Hispanic Filipino rice agricultural economy (Phelan 1959: 113).

The Filipino community of the Spanish era, although Hispanicized
in many respects, never lost overt "continuity with its preconquest antecedents" (Phelan 1959: 133). For example, efforts to resettle the scattered population into central and larger communities usually resulted in
a compromise "that satisfied the needs of Spaniards and Filipinos alike"
(Reed 1967: 57). Indigenous class structure remained far more cohesive
in the Philippines than in Mexico (Phelan 1959: 120) perhaps because
"no clans or similar unilateral groups" existed in the pre-Hispanic Phil-
lippines or have been reported since (Eggan 1956 1: 415).

In summary, the Hispanization of Filipinos, although probably less
thorough than that of many Mexicans, was accomplished with a "minimum of psychological and physical damage" (Phelan 1959: 159). The
concept of "crumbling" Filipino societies, seeking new techniques to
maintain a social cohesion imperiled by a violent Spanish intrusion, is
not profitable to follow in seeking reasons for the Filipinos' extensive
adoption of the godparenthood complex.

Curing and Baptismal Rites

The fusion of traditional curing rites and folk Catholicism is widespread in Latin America and the Philippines. One factor related to the
Filipinos' rapid acceptance of baptism was their firm belief that this
sacrament not only "wiped away the sins of the soul but also helped to
cure the ailments of the body" (Phelan 1959: 55). Although pre-Hispanic Filipinos had a concept of heaven and hell, it probably was Catholic
priests who introduced the idea of sin, since no evidence has been
found that an indigenous concept of sin existed among Filipinos.

Some of the early priests developed a Christian substitute to replace the healing techniques of the Filipino shaman. The patient first
reaffirmed his abhorrence of paganism and made the sign of the cross.
The priest then blessed him with holy water and requested in a short
prayer that God grant a swift recovery (Phelan 1959: 18). "Since their
pagan cults had stressed the cures of illness, the popular conviction that
baptism was corporeally efficacious did much to attract the Filipinos to
the new religion" (Phelan 1959: 55).

Philippine literature reports a unique local instance of ritual sponsorship associated with the preservation of good health or curing that involves saints (as in Latin America). This is reported for the barriofolk of Cabetican, a Pampangan village in central Luzon. The mother of a child, either to guarantee its future good health or as a cure for sickness, pledges a son to San Nicolas or a daughter to the Lady of Lourdes, this community's patron saints.

For the ceremony parents select sponsors who become ritual kinsmen of both the child and its parents. In fact, the saint also is considered a "kinsman" of the child, who should continue to honor the saint on the latter's feast day. The ceremony is held in the church immediately after the mass on the saint's feast day. For this occasion the son wears a black robe with green piping at the neck, and the daughter, a short white dress with a blue sash. The sponsor gives the child a small gift at the end of the ceremony. The participants regard each other as godparent and godchild or compadre and comadre (Santico 1973: 32–35).

Ritual sponsorship and curing are joined in a ritual held by Ilokans. In Barrio Suba (Luzon) occasionally and under special circumstances, a traditional curer (*herbolario*) may diagnose the illness of a persistently sick child as caused by the spirits (*anitos*). The recommended therapy is the *anak ti digos* (child of the bath) ritual. The *herbolario* gives the Ilokan parents the name of an individual who has recently dreamed about the child. This person is asked by the parents to sponsor the ritual bath that ends with the child temporarily assuming a new name. A ritual washing of the child's head also may take place if the sponsor believes it is necessary. If the sponsor desires, a spirit offering (*atang*) is made at his dwelling's altar. Later, in the poblacion church, the child's parents or the sponsor may burn candles, dedicated either to the person whose name the child has assumed or to the recent dead of the sponsor's family.

The *anak ti digos* ritual creates among two groups the same ritual relationships as does Catholic baptism. The first group includes the sponsor, his children, and the sick child; the second, the sponsor and the sick child's parents (Scheans 1966: 82–85).

Numerous other resemblances exist between the *anak ti digos* ritual and Catholic baptism and associated godparenthood. First, both ceremonies change the status of the principals. Second, both ceremonies require the use of water possessing sanative and supernatural qualities. Third, during the *anak ti digos* rite a placatory offering is made to the spirits, and candles may later be burned in the parent's dwelling during the baptismal meal. What remains unknown is if the original form of *anak ti digos* included sponsorship, with resulting ritual kinship ties.

Name-changing rituals were also a pre-Hispanic practice among various Christian Filipino groups (Scheans 1966: 82; Phelan 1959: 55; Vanoverberg 1936: 113–14). A contemporary practice, with pre-Hispanic elements involving both name-changing and sponsorship, is reported from central Luzon. "In Barrio Anuling, Camiling, Tarlac, the mother of the sick child prepares rice cakes and invites the children of the neighborhood to a party selecting one of them to be *ninong* or godparent [godfather]. The sick baby is seated on a big platter and the *ninong*—perhaps just a few years older than the baptized one—pours cold water on the sick child" (Malay and Malay 1955: 30–31). As the water is poured on the child, all the invited guests shout his new nickname. It is not reported that the parents of the sponsoring children become compadres of the sick child's parents.

Buhos Tubig Baptismal Rite: Pre-Hispanic baptismal rites occurred in the Philippines, although their primary purpose appears to have been protection of the infant from sickness. In this sense they differ from the baptismal rites of the Aztecs and Mayans. (The *buhos tubig* rite shares some elements with folk baptism in the home, or *el bautismo de agua* of newborn infants in Puerto Rico.) Such indigenous rites help explain the Filipinos' quick acceptance of Christian baptism, and their belief in its alleged curative powers, reported by early Spanish priests.

The Puray Remontados of Montalban municipality (Rizal, Luzon) are a group of isolated, illiterate, animist swidden farmers whose Tagalog ancestors fled to the mountains to escape Spanish authority. The nearest Catholic church is in Montalban, the town where the people go for basic supplies. The priest has visited Puray only twice in the memory of local informants. Only three members of Puray, a barrio of about 200 people, regularly attend the Catholic church. Some Protestant missionaries worked in Puray, but they were unable to establish a permanent church (Ramos 1972: 30).

Shortly after birth a Puray infant is "baptized" by a rite called *buhos tubig* (pouring of water). Any man or woman who knows the simple rite may perform it. As water is poured on the infant's head the person in charge says: "I baptize you in the name of the Father, and of the Son, and of the Holy Spirit. Amen." At this time the infant is also given its name. The *buhos tubig* cannot be considered an emergency baptism, permissible by Catholic doctrine, since it is done for all children regardless of their health. Sponsors are selected for the *buhos*

Lalawigan women in front of the village chapel. The chapel was once used only for prayers, novenas, and other informal services, but since the village now has a resident priest, baptisms and weddings may be held there.

tubig rite. Through the "blanketing-in" process, all the members of the sponsor's nuclear family also become ritual kinsmen of the infant's family. Informants claimed that in the past sponsors were not chosen for the *buhos tubig* rite. This addition may have been copied from the Catholic christening.

The *buhos tubig* rite also protects the infant against attacks by the *kayao* (souls of the deceased infants) and prevents an infant, if it dies shortly after birth, from becoming a *kayao* (Ramos 1972: 74–75). One informant explained that "babies who die after the *buhos tubig* rite will become angels, while those without the *buhos tubig* will turn into evil spirits." Ramos states that the people rarely have their children baptized by the priest because it costs money, and those parents who do have their children christened in the church may use the *buhos tubig* sponsors or select new ones.

The *buhos tubig* rite's precise history cannot be unraveled with present data. One can assume, however, that the lowland ancestors of the Puray had been Christianized before they fled to the mountains. This rite's animistic elements were adopted by their descendants after they had settled in their present remote location. Although the present rite closely resembles Catholic baptism, one major function, that of protecting the infant from supernatural harm by the spirits, is of non-Christian and possibly of pre-Hispanic origin. The *buhos tubig* rite illustrates the syncretism of animistic and Christian elements; it might be called a "triumph of animism over Catholicism." The identical ceremony, for almost the same reasons, is currently practiced by Tagalogs in Bay, Laguna, Philippines (Jocano 1970: 291–92). And in Lalawigan it is believed that "an infant who is baptized becomes a *Kristiano* [Christian] and this makes him spiritually stronger to fight the devil and the spirits." Unbaptized infants are believed to be more vulnerable to sickness, especially that caused by spirits.

Friendship

Although formal friendships appear to have been less pronounced among pre-Hispanic Filipinos than they were among pre-Columbian Latin Americans, they existed and could have facilitated the adoption of compadrinazgo's ritual kinship bonds.

Most Filipinos develop close and usually enduring same-sex friendships before or during adolescence. As in Spain (Pitt-Rivers 1961: 138), there is neither ceremony nor formal declaration when two Filipino boys or girls establish a friendship relationship (Hart 1968). In Tarong, during the last years of elementary school, "girls and boys pair off with one of their own age and sex, from whom they are thereafter inseparable. They go everywhere together and share everything; since they are usually *sitio* mates and most often cousins, they may eat and sleep together, alternating between their houses" (Nydegger and Nydegger 1966: 165). Similar friendships occur in Caticugan and Lalawigan, but the participants often are not kinsmen. These friendship groups now are called *barkada* (Sp. *abarcar,* to clasp or embrace), a term that has appeared in Siaton within the last few years.

Compadrinazgo is used not only to intensify same-sex friendships but also to continue into adulthood childhood friendships between the sexes that otherwise might be publicly condemned. Supposedly, married Filipinos have "relatively little time for 'friendship' and when it does develop, the mechanisms of ritual kinship are employed to formalize the relationship" (Eggan 1956 1: 424). A recent study of urban families in Cebu City indicated that married Filipinos, especially males, have rather extensive sex-segregated friendships (Liu, Rubel, and Pate 1970: 81).

In both Caticugan and Lalawigan a number of adult compadres and comadres had been close friends in their early teens. Many barriofolk believe that the "embers of the old flame" between former sweethearts remain aglow after marriage. Ritual kinship extinguishes all "live embers" and removes any possibility of illicit sexual relationships, since marriage, and by extension a sexual relationship, is tabu between principal ritual kinsmen. In Esperanza, a married man and a former sweetheart (who has wedded another Filipino) may become compadres to continue their former friendship. For example, a married Lalawigan escort met her former, still-unmarried boyfriend at the Borongan church. They agreed to serve as co-sponsors of the infant she had brought to the poblacion for baptism "to perpetuate a former friendship." By becoming ritual kinsmen they were freer to associate with each other in public without criticism than if they had remained merely friends.

Commerce and Suki Bonds

Ritual sponsorship appears already to have been a Filipino custom in pre-Hispanic times. The ritualized affirmation of trade relationships among the pagan Gaddang of northern Luzon is an excellent example of an indigenous custom that parallels compadrinazgo in its adhesion to commercial activities. Gaddang may formalize existing trade ties among each other (and Ilokans) through the exchange of gifts. When the exchange is concluded, the new relationship is called *kolak*, the Gaddang term for *sibling* (Wallace 1970: 33). Although *kolak* does not unite the participants (apparently only men) in actual ritual kinship ties (e.g., no associated incest tabus are reported), it does parallel the connection between compadrinazgo and Christian Filipino *suki* bonds that join seller and buyer.

In the Filipino *suki* relationship the seller gives the steady *suki* customer credit and either a slight reduction in the going market price without haggling or a more generous portion for the same price. The buyer, in turn, makes all his purchases solely from this seller of the items; he also recommends his *suki* to friends and relatives (Davis 1968: 13). Some *suki* relationships that are more crucial to the seller than others often are converted to a formal linkage through compadrinazgo.

In the marketplace the formation of compadrazgo bonds has been so frequently preceded by the existence of a *suki* relationship that one must conclude that the former are the results of deliberate strategies intended to replace one interpersonal relationship with another, ideally more obligatory, form (Davis 1973: 234).

This risk-reducing social device is effective, since for most Filipinos violating compadre bonds "involves more of a sense of shame and guilt" than infractions of *suki* norms (Davis 1973: 238).

As Paul has suggested for Latin America, the indigenous Filipino *suki* trading relationship was strengthened by compadrinazgo. Catholic doctrine "tends to bring to bear the weight of public opinion—a third party—to support the relationship. This element is not as prominent in the essentially dyadic *suki* bond" (Davis 1973: 238). Since compadre obligations are less frequently shirked, they become important in stabilizing crucial economic relationships in the marketplace. This additional advantage of ritual kinship bonds probably was quickly realized by shrewd Filipino traders.

Maria Szanton also investigated the complex association of compadrinazgo and marketing activities in Estancia, a Panayan town of 15,000 people (1972). Contrary to Davis, she argues that ritual kinship ties between vendor and customer involved in *suki* association "may be as easily contract-disrupting as contract-enforcing because they involve a much broader set of mutual commitments" (Szanton 1972: 114). For example, although persons involved in the *suki* dyad may initiate compadre ties for economic reasons, they "may be unprofitable for the partner in that they allow noneconomic [e.g., social] reciprocation for economic favors" (Szanton 1972: 112, 114).

Blood Brotherhood

Blood brotherhood appears to have been a widespread pre-Hispanic Filipino practice that anticipated compadrinazgo. Blood brotherhood also has been reported for other Southeast Asians, such as the Karens, Thai, Dusun of Sabah, and groups in Ceram, Indonesia (Tegnaeus 1952: 34, 36, 38). The congeniality between these two types of ritual kinship has been noted by others. In northern Italy a form of godparenthood "flourished that is reminiscent of blood-brotherhood practices" (Anderson 1957: 44). The institution of blood brotherhood does not appear to have been as widespread in pre-Hispanic Latin America as it was in the Philippines.

Although many early Spanish accounts of the Philippines make brief references to blood brotherhood, none was located that presented a detailed description. These sources indicate that blood brotherhood usually was used by the Spaniards in a peace-making ceremony or in establishing a political pact with Filipinos. In essence, based on a synthesis of Spanish sources, ancient Filipino blood brotherhood (Tag. *kasikasi;* Ceb. *sandugo, san,* contracted form of *isang,* one, *dugo,* blood) was a ritual by which two males ended a personal dispute or reconciled two quarreling factions. Blood, drawn from a prick in each one's arm or breast, was tasted directly or mixed in a shell cup with water and/or wine and then equally consumed. The friendship or alliance created by blood brotherhood was "perpetual" and was "not to be broken."

Alzina writes that a variety of *sandugo* was also used by Bisayan Filipinos who were deeply in love. They performed carlet (the rite of drinking each other's blood mixed with wine) as a token that they would never forsake one another. Once a widow came to Alzina offering to serve the Virgin by a vow of chastity for the remainder of her life. She signed her vow using blood obtained by pricking herself over the heart. "Today I know for certain of her constancy and her solicitude in keeping her vow and serving God" (Alzina 1668).

Waterfront scene of Dumaguete, the capital and major port of Negros Oriental province.

Although the two persons linked through this variety of ritual kinship become "blood brothers," the Spanish sources do not state any further extension of this ritual relationship. No information could be found regarding possible marriage restrictions that involved members of their families or associated privileges and responsibilities other than personal fidelity (Chirino 1903 12: 185–86; Legaspi 1903 2: 201; Loarca 1903 5: 161; Zaide 1949 1: 58; Alzina 1668; Hermosisima and Lopez 1966: 508).

Yet we do have some information regarding the extension of blood brotherhood bonds for the Tagbanuas of Palawan. Most men (and a few women) have several ritual brothers. Arrangements for the ceremony usually are made during drinking parties. The behavioral relationships of blood brothers are similar to those of affinal kinsmen. Their duties and obligations are those of brothers-in-law. Moreover, the ritual ties are extended to each other's relatives, who are addressed or referred to only by kinship terms. If a man marries any relative of his blood brother, the pact is automatically broken, and a fine is demanded. Blood brotherhood among the Tagbanuas both expands and extends the number of one's relatives, providing greater security, especially for traders and travelers, who are always fearful of being poisoned (Fox 1971).

Ritual kinship practices occur among at least one Filipino Muslim group, the Tausug of Jolo, southern Philippines. As among Christian Filipinos, Tausug ritual kinship either joins two friends (often from different communities) or ends past hostilities between the participants and their families. The ceremonies may or may not involve the imam, their chief Islamic religious specialist. New ritual kinsmen must not "covet the other's wife," and their children become as "brothers and sisters and cannot intermarry" (Bruno 1973: 61). Kiefer, however, reports that ritual kinship bonds are not extended beyond the participating individuals, for the Tausug are minimally corporate in their conception of social obligations (1972: 105). Blood brotherhood rites also are shared by Muslim Filipinos and the Bagobos of Mindanao (Simpich 1944: 541).

In Dalrymple's eighteenth-century account (1772) of his travels in Jolo, he mentions participating in a blood-mixing ceremony with the sultan. Kiefer writes (in a personal communication) that since such rites today are abhorrent to Tausug Islamic sensibilities, Dalrymple's statement suggests either (or both) that Islam was not then vigorous in Sulu or that blood brotherhood rites were pre-Islamic. He speculates that this concept of ritual kinship was indigenous to Sulu. Fortunately, new data from the Philippines make it possible to be more precise about the preadaptive qualities of blood brotherhood in facilitating the acceptance of the godparenthood complex. This form of ritual kinship is today a viable aspect of life among a small primitive group (the Sulod) living in central Panay. Some of the Sulod appear to have escaped any significant Hispanization, for they reside in the isolated rugged interior of an island distant from Manila. They have two types of ritual kinship: (1)

blood brotherhood (*sandugu'*); and (2) a traditional food-feeding ceremony called *higara* (Jocano 1968c: 92 100, 124).

For the first ceremony blood is taken from the index finger and mixed with rice wine; each participant then shares his cup with the other. Blood brotherhood is used both for economic purposes and as a means of protection in time of danger. The *higara* ceremony requires no sharing of blood among the participants, but the two men ritually feed each other, followed by similar feedings between their wives and among their children. The initiator of the ceremony gives some gifts to his new "kinsmen," who reciprocate at a later date.

Importantly, and for both ceremonies, the ritual kinship ties between the principals are extended to their families and other relatives. Finally, and most significantly for our purpose:

> These practices are disappearing among the younger generation and are being replaced by lowland *compadrazgo* systems in marginal areas where the missionary activities of both the Catholic and Protestant churches have succeeded in converting many Sulod to Christianity (Jocano 1968c: 92).

Most likely, similar substitutions took place elsewhere during the earlier part of the Spanish period in the Philippines.

Blood brotherhood was practiced by pagan groups (locally called "Bukidnons") living in southern Negros Oriental as late as the 1920s. One Caticugan informant who lived among them while stripping abaca in his interior swidden remembers the custom. Interestingly, the principals called each other *igso* (godsibling).

> *Sandugo* is when one man makes a small cut in another man's arm and drinks the blood and the other man does the same thing. Then they call each other *Sandugo* or *Igso*. . . . A *Sandugo* can tell if one of his *Sandugos* is backbiting him. I do not know how. Maybe it is because they have drunk each other's blood (Hart 1954a: 175).

Gudeman claims that classifications lumping compadrinazgo with similar institutions such as blood brotherhood are unacceptable. "Only compadrazgo systems, as forms of the original godparenthood complex, are commensurate" (Gudeman 1972:47). For example, unlike compadrinazgo, blood brotherhood "is rarely found between two women, since the status of women commonly precludes such independence of action" (Pitt-Rivers 1968: 410). (However, women in some African societies do become blood friends: Tegnaeus 1952: 66, 79.)

Both varieties of ritual kinship do share similar functions: mutual aid, hospitality, commercial cooperation, assistance in legal difficulties, and burial aid. Although both blood brotherhood and compadrinazgo bonds supposedly, and usually, are permanent, they can be dissolved. Paul contrasted the two systems by pointing out that while blood brotherhood simulates a sibling relationship, Catholic dogma formally stresses a parent-child linkage, i.e., padrinazgo (1942: 3). Yet compadrazgo, the type of ritual kinship most prevalent in Latin America and the Philippines, also emphasizes bonds described by some as sibling ties. Finally, we must accept with caution in the Philippine context the general statement that blood brotherhood rarely extends ritual kinship bonds to the participants' relatives (Pitt-Rivers 1968 8: 410).

In conclusion, the few available historical sources on pre-Hispanic Filipino society and recent investigations of contemporary Filipino communities indicate that a sympathetic convergence occurred between indigenous cultural traits and the godparenthood complex. In some instances, of course, the lack of reliable and detailed data leaves gaps that future research may at some time close. In other instances, the more precise demonstration of the suggested linkage between indigenous elements and the godparenthood complex described in this chapter may remain forever only informed speculation. At this stage of our knowledge of Philippine society, it is difficult to "reconstruct the historical process by which ritual co-parenthood blended into or destroyed pre-conquest kinship relations or created new kinship ties" (Phelan 1959: 78).

Chapter Three

The Rites of Compadrinazgo

This chapter describes beliefs and practices associated with those Catholic sacraments that establish ritual kinship ties in the Philippines —baptism, confirmation, and marriage. The varied roles of Filipino ritual kinsmen in these various ceremonies are set forth. Emergency baptisms by persons other than priests are reported, as are folk beliefs regarding the assistance deceased godchildren give their godparents. The extension or restriction of ritual kinship bonds through position replication (repeat sponsorhip, the "blanketing-in" process, and multiple sponsors) is presented. Several additional non-Church-prescribed rites that also create ceremonial relationships in the Philippines and in Latin America are discussed, showing a major difference between Latin American and Philippine compadrinazgo—that for the former a plethora of occasions has developed that the folk often believe originate ritual kinship bonds in addition to those the Church requires.

Baptism

All Filipinos regard baptism as the most important of Church sacraments. In the past it was common for Manila newspapers to publish articles describing elaborate christenings. The following announcement, from the former *Manila Bulletin*, is of particular interest because it: 1) indicates how one of the infant's names was selected; 2) gives her age at baptism; 3) notes the selection of a kinsman-sponsor; and 4) illustrates the combining of the baptismal reception with another festive occasion. Except for the late hour of the christening and an officiating bishop, the same pattern occurs throughout the rural Philippines.

> [Name of the infant], one-month-old daughter of Mr. and Mrs. [name of parents] will be christened at five o'clock this afternoon at the San Miguel Pro-Cathedral with Bishop [name] officiating. Wearing the embroidered

piña christening gown worn by her older sisters [names], little [name] will receive three names—[names], the last because she was born on Dec. 22, feast day of St. Francis Cabrini, the first American saint. Godparents will be the baby's great-aunt, Miss [name], [names of two additional male sponsors]. The celebration following the christening will be held at the residence of the baby's grandparents, Mr. and Mrs. [name], who are observing their thirty-first anniversary today. About seventy guests will be attending the *merienda-cena* [buffet] celebrating the double occasion, about fifty of those present being "family" (*Manila Bulletin*, January 1956).

Dumaguete street scene. Today pony-drawn carts have been almost replaced with motorized vehicles.

Caticugan and Lalawigan infants usually do not have a given name before baptism or birth registration. During village census-taking some parents reported: "This child did not have a first name because he (or she) died before baptism." Normally the child is named for a saint on whose birthday it is born, the appropriate name being chosen from lists available at the town hall or the priest's residence.

Before the Council of Trent in the sixteenth century, priests encouraged parents to give their children only the names of canonized saints or angels. The Council made mandatory the use of such names in baptism (Withycombe 1947: xxiii). "A Roman priest is authorized to add a saint's name to those chosen by the godparents, if those are unscriptural and not taken from the calendar" (Withycombe 1947: xxvi).

Priests in the Philippines may refuse to baptize an infant unless both the personal and middle names, especially the former, are those of a saint. Recently, it has become popular to give one's child a "modern" or "American" name. One informant in Boroñgan explained how this problem is solved. "Our eldest daughter could not be christened with the name Laurie. So we added the name Maria. On her baptismal certificate her name is Maria Laurie. But she only uses Laurie, even at school."

Caticuganers state that most infants are baptized several weeks after birth. In 1951 (but not today) a municipal clerk in Siaton went to the priest's residence to register births, after which baptism certificates were issued. During that year a baptismal certificate could not be secured until the child's birth had been registered. About 69 percent of the 316 reported births in Siaton municipality in 1951 were registered by the end of the fourth week after birth, and 86 percent by the end of the eighth week.

Although precise data were not collected on this topic in Lalawigan, children are typically baptized younger than they are in Caticugan. About thirty informants in the barrio estimated that infants were christened when about one week old and sometimes only a few days old. The reason for their early christening is the belief that the sacrament of baptism spiritually, and hence physically, strengthens an infant. An unbaptized child is more vulnerable to sickness, especially illness caused by the supernaturals. In Lalawigan "an infant who is baptized becomes a *Kristiano* [Christian] and this makes him spiritually stronger to fight the devil and the spirits." In another Bisayan village in Panay unbaptized children "are viewed as constitutionally weak and . . . susceptible to illness. They do not yet enjoy the protective concern of their guardian angels" (Jocano 1969: 15).

For many Filipinos baptism, in addition to its function as a Catholic sacrament, has certain magical qualities. Most rural Filipinos believe that christening protects an infant from ill health resulting from natural causes. This ceremony also is said to shield the child from supernatural harm—not only from malignant Christian preternatural entities but also from the indigenous environmental spirits (Ceb. *ingkanto*). The parents' personal and family prestige may be a more important consideration, however, for baptisms often are postponed, sometimes for months after the infant's birth. One reason for delaying the christening is to permit the parents time to accumulate funds to hold an elaborate christening feast.

Baptisms may also be delayed, particularly in villages remote from the priest's poblacion residence, until the annual patron saint's fiesta is celebrated. The fiesta usually is the only time during the year that most parish priests are able to visit many interior barrios to hold mass in the local chapel. Another reason for postponing baptism until the annual fiesta, in communities where easy accessibility to the church is not a problem, is that sponsors can be entertained more lavishly during this event, since almost everyone prepares a fancy meal to serve his guests. Among Ilokans, Pampangans, Bikolans, and Tagalogs, and in Manalad, Caticugan, and Lalawigan, in the Bisayas, the child's baptism may be postponed to coincide with the fiesta (Eggan 1956 2: 646; Santico 1973: 24; Sibley 1958: 67). "In some barrios distant from the poblacion church of Siaton, as many as 30 babies were baptized by the priest when he visited the community for its annual fiesta [during 1951]" (Hart 1954b: 28). During the 1956 Lalawigan fiesta the visiting priest christened six infants in the barrio chapel. One child, the sponsor, and friends were preceded to the chapel by the village string band. In Tarong baptisms usually are delayed "until a convenient date, often until after the rice harvest" (Nydegger and Nydegger 1966: 68), while in Canaman the christening may be postponed so that the parents can accumulate the money required to hold this "essential meal" (Arce 1973: 52–53).

Sunday morning after mass is the regular time established by most priests for baptisms in the rural Philippines. A dozen or more infants may be christened at these mass baptisms, although a separate baptism may be arranged by the infant's parents or sponsors at a time selected by them. Regular baptisms may be held at the side altar (for example, in Cabetican); a special christening is performed at the main altar. Since the church fee for a special christening is greater, the rite is uncommon; for example, only fifteen persons in Cabetican had been christened in this manner (Santico 1973: 23–24).

Sunday morning after mass is also the established time for multiple baptisms in Siaton, Lalawigan, and Boroñgan churches. A dying custom is this: shortly before baptism some Caticugan parents cut a few strands of hair from the top of the infant's head and trim its fingernails. The hair and nail clippings are put inside a guitar, a book, or the hollow top cover of a fountain pen. This *lihi* (an imitative magic inaugural ceremony) supposedly guarantees that the infant will mature into a highly intelligent, industrious adult; moreover, the infant will speak early and will not be shy. Others help the infant take three faltering steps before going to the church for christening so that it will walk sooner than normal.

For a Sunday morning baptism in Siaton all the sponsors assemble in front of the massive wooden altar of the church, holding their future godchildren. (The ritual in Boroñgan and Lalawigan is almost identical.) The infant wears a gaily colored baptismal dress, normally furnished by a godparent, who often rents or borrows it. The dress is blue for boys and pink for girls. When there is more than one sponsor, the co-sponsors flank the person holding the infant. If there are co-sponsors, the infant is alternately held or touched by each during the christening. In Hulo, co-sponsors (*katuwang*) must touch the infant briefly during the ceremony. As in Caticugan and Lalawigan, they are considered as much godparents as the primary sponsor (Hollnsteiner 1967: 201).

The priest begins the christening by reciting the appropriate words, anoints the infant with oil, and makes the sign of the cross on its forehead, nape of neck, and pulse spots of the inner arms. A tiny pinch of salt is placed on the infant's tongue, symbolizing the preservation of the faith. Next the sponsors move to the large stone baptismal font where they stand in single file. The child, with a white cloth over its face, is baptized as each sponsor holds a lighted candle. After all the infants are baptized, the sponsors return to the altar of the church where they kneel and recite the Lord's Prayer.

Residence of an elite Dumaguete family facing the waterfront. Photo by Dan Doeppers.

Upon completion of the prayer, the sponsors stand while the priest briefly instructs them regarding the obligations of a godparent. The sponsor is now a spiritual parent of the child and must see that the godchild is married and buried within the Catholic faith. (In Siaton the priest's explanation of the duties of godparenthood was always brief and perfunctory.) The formal baptism ceremony now ends. The sponsors and friends, with the exceptions noted, return to the godchild's dwelling for a meal prepared by the parents. The sponsor's spouse rarely comes to the christening but is considered a godparent.

The custom (called *bolo* in Latin America) of the departing godfather giving candy or small change to children waiting outside the church was once practiced in Caticugan but was unknown in Lalawigan, although in Cabetican the sponsor throws small coins to the gathering outside the church after the christening. It is believed that this custom (*pasabog*) ensures the future prosperity and success of the newly baptized infant (Santico 1973: 26–27).

A primary sponsor does not have to attend the christening to become a godparent. In Siaton the use of stand-in is called *pakaytan sa uban* (to hold for a friend). An individual may agree to sponsor a child and pay the baptismal fee but be unable to attend the baptism. In such a case he requests a friend to stand as his substitute. The absent sponsor's name is recorded on the baptismal certificate, and the obliging proxy is not considered a godparent. One Siaton poblacion baptism included a stand-in for a man living in the United States. He had mailed the required money to the godchild's parents, who selected his substitute for the christening.

In some instances a stand-in for an absent sponsor is not required if there are several sponsors. One Boroñgan informant's brother wanted his sweetheart, who lived in Guiuan, to be a sponsor of his sibling's daughter. The girl wrote, requesting permission to be a sponsor, and enclosed the baptismal fee. The baptism occurred without her presence or that of a stand-in, but her name was written on the certificate as one of the child's sponsors.

Parents' Attendance at Baptism

In the rural Philippines the child's parents rarely attend the baptismal ceremony. The Filipino infant usually is taken to the church by the sponsor or escort. In Canaman the infant is brought to the church by a female (*nag-abít,* or "the one who carries") who usually is a kinsman, neighbor, or friend of the parents. "The *nag-abít* takes the place of the recently-delivered mother, who would still be discouraged from any task requiring physical strength" (Arce 1973: 52; also see Lynch 1959: 54). At the church the *nag-abít* gives the infant to its sponsor.

In Cabetican, the traditional midwife attends the ceremony to care for the infant in case of a sudden illness. Her participation is also regarded as recognition by the parents of her previous services. It is the midwife who gives the infant to the sponsor before baptism begins (Santico 1973: 26).

A baptismal meal usually is served to the sponsor and other guests in Caticugan. The father stays home to kill and dress chickens or, for a larger feast, a goat, pig, or cow. The mother does not participate in the baptismal ceremony for numerous reasons. First, her physical recovery from delivery may be incomplete. During delivery the woman's "grave opens wide," i.e., her life is endangered. The trip to and from the poblacion church might result in a postnatal relapse. Second, she has the responsibility to act as the hostess of the meal and would be blamed if preparations were inadequate.

Another important reason a Caticugan mother does not attend her child's christening—also reported for Spain, Italy, and Mexico—is that she may not yet have been ritually purified from the "contamination" of birth. Several female informants said they would be "ashamed" to mix with people in the Siaton church shortly after delivery "because we are still malodorous." The Siaton priest claimed that "church regulations" require that the mother have her first postnatal bath before entering the church after delivery. This "regulation" was not mentioned by any Caticugan informants.

The Catholic church provides for but does not prescribe "churching," a purification ceremony for a woman who has recently delivered (Eggan 1956 2: 650–51). "Churching" is known in Latin America as *sacamisa,* or the Purification Mass (Eggan 1956 2: 650; Foster 1960: 120). Ideally, this special mass should occur within forty days after the birth of the child. A ceremony similar to this mass is known in the two villages, but it is rarely practiced today in Lalawigan. This ceremony was called *paghalad* in Lalawigan and is called *vindision* (Ceb. *bendisyón,* Sp. *benedición*) in Caticugan. The baptismal sponsor did not participate in the *paghalad* but occasionally is present for the *vindision.* The *paghalad* was held "about 40 days after the birth of the first child." The mother and child went to the rear of the church before the mass. The priest came to them with a cord tied to his waist. The mother took hold of the cord and followed him to the altar where she knelt with her child during most of the mass. The *paghalad's* purpose was to ask God to bestow good health and a long life upon the child. No celebration was held after this ceremony.

The Caticugan *vindision* takes place when the child and mother come to the church about forty days after the christening. The sponsor rarely attends this ceremony and in the past never made a gift of clothing. If the sponsor attends, after the *vindision* each returns to his own residence, and neither serves either a meal or drinks. These ceremonies differ from the *sacamisa* in that they are not the obligation of the godparents, gifts are never given the infant, and they exclude a festive meal. A difference in degree is that one ceremony has been abandoned and the other's popularity has waned.

"From two to three weeks elapse between the delivery and the bath that ends the Caticugan puerperium" (Hart 1965a:73). The bath water includes herbs believed to be sanative. The mother's first postnatal bath has one function similar to "churching." An additional objective is to "purify" the woman whose unique body odor during pregnancy is inordinately attractive to harmful supernaturals. Later she passes through the "contamination" (e.g., bleeding and other discharges) of delivery. If the mother's recovery is delayed, baptism of an infant may occur before the former's first postnatal bath. (Moreover, a sickly child may be baptized when only a few days old, weeks before the mother is able to take this bath.)

Many Caticuganers believe that after a new mother's first bath she should attend church for three successive Sundays. Others claim that forty days after delivery the mother and child should go to church. Participation in church services "purifies" the mother, while the child receives a blessing. There are no sponsors for this event.

Today, Lalawigan parents attend their child's baptism. This is an innovation the priest made when he began to live in the barrio. At present, if the mother is weak from delivery, she is excused from the ceremony. The father, however, must be present. When christening was done in Boroñgan, Lalawigan mothers rarely attended for the same reasons, with one exception, that Caticugan mothers gave. Lalawignons reject the idea that there was time when a new mother did not attend her child's baptism because she was still "contaminated" by her earlier pregnancy and delivery.

Emergency Baptism

"The notion that anyone (presuming the proper intention) can baptize in an emergency is an ancient tradition, and its first appearance as an enactment is at the local council of Elvira in Spain at the beginning of the fourth century" (Bullough 1963: 79). In the pre-Reformation period "it was the custom for a midwife to christen premature children before birth when it was feared that they might not be delivered alive" (Withycombe 1947: xxx).

In the Philippines the traditional midwife may baptize a newborn infant that appears to be dying (Malay and Malay 1955: 31). Among Tagalogs an emergency baptism is called *buhos tubig* or "pouring of water." Reportedly, "in many rural areas of the Philippines, this 'emergency' baptism is routine at the birth of a child" (Eggan 1956 2: 645–46). Emergency baptism in Lalawigan and Caticugan may be by the attending midwife, although any knowledgeable person may serve. In some instances a sickly or dying infant may be baptized by a *manalabtan* (a person, usually a woman, skilled in folk Catholicism, e.g., able to lead novenas, etc.). However, such baptisms are not "routine" in these two barrios. In such crises the sponsor is the person most easily available, and the ritual relationships thus created are considered as valid as those established by church baptism. A recent publication describes the procedure for an emergency baptism (*Ritwal sa Bunyag* 1971).

In the past, but not today, stillbirths in Caticugan were buried near the dwelling. One reason for this practice was that unbaptized persons could not be interred in the municipal cemetery. One instance was remembered in Caticugan of parents whose two-month old infant had died without church baptism. "The parents explained that their child was not baptized because they had no money and no one requested to sponsor its baptism." The child was secretly buried in the cemetery. The priest later learned of the irregular burial, called the parents to his *convento*, and told them they had "made a great sin" in not having their child baptized. He did not, however, require them to rebury the infant outside the cemetery.

A Lalawigan or Caticugan child that dies after christening, and before reaching the age of reason (four to five years old), is believed to go directly to heaven. In Malitbog a dead but baptized child is known as *Santo Anhil*, or "Saint Angel" (Jocano 1969: 15). Filipino children of the same age group who die unbaptized either wander around the world as spirits or must first pass through limbo before reaching heaven

(Jocano 1969: 15). In Malitbog the time an unbaptized child's soul must spend in limbo is dependent upon the seriousness of his parent's original sin. (Some Caticuganers thought limbo was not in the sky but was a dark cave.) Informants claimed that an unbaptized infant who had nursed before death (and nursing begins the day after birth) must pass through purgatory on its way to heaven.

Elsewhere in the Philippines it is believed that an unbaptized child who dies goes directly to hell or becomes a malevolent spirit (Malay and Malay 1955: 24; Jocano 1970: 292). Baptized children who die after they have reached the age of reason must pass through purgatory as do adults before gaining entrance to heaven. According to the folk, heaven is obtainable only after a man's original sin is removed in purgatory.

According to Lalawignons, an unbaptized child's soul (*kristobig*) roams either with the clouds or in limbo. The *kristobig* blames its parents if its death occurs before christening. One song sung to a dying child has him thanking his parents and godparents for baptism. A short folktale collected in Lalawigan illustrates this aspect of local folk Catholicism. One day an abandoned dead infant was found in the public toilet built over the river running at the edge of Boroñgan. It was rumored that the infant had been left there by its unmarried mother. Since the infant was not christened, its soul wandered in the sky. After her death the repentant mother asked God's forgiveness, but He refused. She then asked God where she could find her infant's *kristobig*, and God pointed to a distant cloud. The mother went to the cloud and cried out to her infant's soul. "Forgive me!" But the child's soul replied: "No, mother, I cannot forgive you. You failed in your duty to see that I was baptized before my death."

Lalawignons explain that their dead children and godchildren become their "lawyers," pleading to God for their remission from purgatory. Godchildren, however, are more eager and effective "advocates" since their sponsors made it possible for them to become Christians, but their willingness to argue their parents' and godparents' "cases" with God also depends on faithful remembrance in prayer.

In Manalad "It is universally believed ... that upon death, the deceased's *igso-un* [godsiblings] are the ones first seen in Heaven, followed by the blood sibling group, or *otud*, then by the parents and other relatives" (Sibley 1958: 63). Some, but not all, Caticuganers said that in heaven one's "children" are godchildren, not one's real children. One informant had heard this belief and when asked if it were true, replied: "I don't know. I've not been to heaven."

Caticugan barriofolk also believe godchildren are the first to welcome their sponsors to heaven, but their role as "lawyers" was not mentioned. Some Caticugan informants explained that people like to sponsor a sickly or dying infant during an emergency baptism: "Since the infant is innocent it will surely go to heaven. Later it can help its godparents come to heaven." A dying person with three deceased godchildren (for whom he has furnished shrouds) will have one each at his feet, side, and head to "guide his soul to heaven."

Central part of Siaton poblacion showing the public marketplace. The road connects Tolong in the west with Dumaguete to the north.

Confirmation

"In Catholic teaching Confirmation is a true sacrament. . . . At baptism a person has become a friend of God; at confirmation (as the name suggests) he is made into a *firm* friend" (Bullough 1964: 86, 89). Even so, peasants in Catholic countries usually regard confirmation as less important than baptism (Service and Service 1954: 72; Madsen 1960b: 95); in some Latin American communities it is skipped (Wagley 1949: 17; Laughlin 1969a: 169; Redfield and Villa Rojas 1962: 189).

The Council of Florence (1438) stated that "Holy Baptism holds first place among all the Sacraments because it is the door of the spiritual life" (*New Catholic Encyclopedia* 1967 2: 62). This definition explains the greater importance of baptism in the minds of most Filipino (and Latin American) peasants, since the early missionaries emphasized this sacrament and enforced it more vigorously than marriage (Redfield 1941: 219–20; Mintz 1966: 387). For example, in Mexico friars taught that an uncoverted person was a witch or warlock, and an unbaptized

Mitla child was believed to have the power of turning into an animal (Parsons 1936: 80). The fact that both in the past and today baptism is believed by most Filipinos to protect the infant from sickness and supernatural harm reinforces its primacy among sacraments. Although the same belief is associated with confirmation in the Philippines, it is less intense and widespread.

The attitudes and practices associated with confirmation in Caticugan and Lalawigan are similar to those described for Manalad and Camangahan.

> In both Camangahan and Manalad, the informants were in agreement that the confirmation sponsor is far less significant in the total range of social dealings than are the baptismal and/or marriage sponsors. Because the confirmation must be done at the time of the approximately biennial appearance of the bishop, rather than at a time of the parents' choice, frequently the confirmation sponsor is chosen among those conveniently at hand. Often, apparently, this sponsor is even chosen among persons with whom the chooser is not especially intimate, and with whom longstanding reciprocal relations may or may not hold (Sibley 1965b: 11–12).

One Lalawigan claimed she did not refer to her children's confirmation sponsors as compadres, but most of the residents do. In both Caticugan and Lalawigan the people claimed that they do not "feel as close" to compadres through confirmation as to those created by baptism. Confirmation godparents generally are, indeed, a "pale reflection" of godparents through baptism (Eggan 1956 2: 652).

This attitude expressed by Bisayan Filipinos toward confirmation is widespread throughout the Philippines as one Filipino writer expresses:

> Confirmation is not quite so important to Filipinos as baptism ... Even the confirmation fee is only a fraction of the baptismal fee. And to be asked to be a sponsor for a confirmation is not considered so great an honor as to be asked to be a sponsor for baptism (Mallari 1954: 14).

However, upon death the soul of a Filipino who is also confirmed is said to go "directly to heaven [without passing through purgatory], there to be received by the singing cherubim" (Jocano 1969: 16).

Church fees associated with baptism and confirmation provide another explanation as to why many Filipinos (and Latin Americans) consider the latter a less important rite. The costs also reflect how social class differences may be reinforced by the degree of elaborateness of the ceremony. Table 2 lists the different fees for baptism and confirmation for San Cristobal (Van den Berghe and Van den Berghe 1966: 1238) and Lalawigan (Hart). In Lalawigan both *Ordinario* and *Extraordinario* baptisms are also called *Yano*. The popular name for a *Solemne* baptism in this barrio is *Special*. Unlike in Mexico, there is only one category and fee for confirmation in Lalawigan and Caticugan. Individual confirmation in these villages is exceedingly rare.

In Lalawigan there is no difference in ceremonies between an *Ordinario* and *Extraordinario* baptism except that *Ordinario* refers to group baptism, while in *Extraordinario* only one infant is christened. For a *Special* baptism the priest, wearing a cape, meets the infant and its sponsors at the church door. When the water is poured on the infant's head during the ceremony, the church bells are rung. Finally, when the baptized infant and its sponsors leave the church, the bells peal again. If there is more than one sponsor, each pays the same fee. Only the well-to-do in Lalawigan and Caticugan can have a *Special* baptism since such a ceremony normally requires multiple sponsors and an unusually elaborate baptismal meal.

TABLE 2

Different Categories and Cost (Pesos) of Baptism and
Confirmation in San Cristobal and Lalawigan

Category	San Cristobal		Lalawigan	
	Baptism	Confirmation	Baptism	Confirmation
Ordinario	5	2	5	
Extraordinario	11	10	6	1
Solemne	35	25	15	

In rural Philippines confirmation may be delayed because the sacrament requires the participation of a bishop. The first post-war visit of a bishop to Siaton municipality was in 1954. Until this year parents who wanted their children confirmed took them to Dumaguete. Today the bishop tours the province every odd year, holding confirmations in communities along the national road. In 1965 the bishop visited Siaton. The Siaton priest had announced the bishop's pending visit in letters to all the barrio captains in the municipality. A "welcome" arch was erected in front of the church, and a large crowd gathered in the open courtyard. Here vendors sold food and drink from portable stalls, mainly to persons from outlying barrios.

Since Boroñgan now is the residence of a bishop, confirmation is held monthly in the town. It is also held in barrio chapels during the annual village fiesta if the people can pay for a pontifical mass, presided over by the bishop. In 1970 Lalawignons raised 1,000 pesos for such a mass during their fiesta.

Potter's investigation of compadrinazgo in Dumaguete indicates that the median age at which children are confirmed is about two years.

> Catholic officials are distressed by this practice, preferring that the custom be changed to conform to the theological purpose of the rite.... Local Filipino clergy explain infant confirmation as a Spanish tradition that had to be altered. In their opinion colonial priests had instilled a belief among the people that without infant confirmation, evil will befall the child (1973: 196–97).

At one confirmation observed by Potter, thirty-seven of the forty-one children to be confirmed were so young that they could not stand or walk (1973: 306). The frequency of infant confirmation in this city may be because it is considered a perfunctory obligation, to be fulfilled as soon as possible. Early confirmation may also reflect the desire of parents to expand quickly their ritual kinship network.

Confirmation, according to Caticugan and Lalawigan residents, is less impressive than baptism; it is a briefer, more hurried ceremony. "It is not like baptism with papers to be signed." Frequently, as many as twenty or thirty children line before the altar for this sacrament. Confirmation starts with a prayer by the bishop. He anoints each child with holy oil, making the sign of the cross on the top of each child's head, forehead, and pulse spots of the inner arms. Finally, the bishop lightly pats the right side of the child's face with his right hand. None of the barriofolk in these two villages could explain the significance of this action. In Dumaguete this light pat on the cheek by the bishop is said to be "a custom originating in the twelfth century and borrowed from the dubbing of knights: through confirmation one becomes a 'knight of Christ'" (Potter 1973: 305).

One Filipino may sponsor several children during the same confirmation: "you just put a hand on the head of each child." Some Lalawigan mothers sponsored their own children's confirmation, a practice not reported elsewhere in the Philippines. Since many sponsors once were obtained at the Boroñgan church shortly before the ceremony, numerous informants said neither their children nor they remembered the names of their sponsors "picked up at the church." This practice in Siaton, called *pamonit ug pagkugoson* (to select anyone handy), is more common for confirmation than for baptism. Sponsors secured in this fashion usually agree to serve only if the parents pay the confirmation fee.

Before the bishop moved to Boroñgan, confirmation was only an occasional event that took place whenever the bishop arrived in town. Then the catechist who prepared the children for the sacrament often was their sole sponsor. He notified the parents of the pending confirmation, collected the fee (one peso per child in 1971), and sponsored all the children in his instructional group. For this reason several children in one family shared the same godparenthood through confirmation. Caticugan and Lalawigan baptismal godparents rarely serve as confirmation sponsors for their godchildren.

After confirmation in Spain and Middle America, the child's parents often serve refreshments or a small meal to the sponsor (Kenney 1962: 63; Ravicz 1967: 245). This is not the practice in Caticugan and Lalawigan. However, confirmation in other parts of the Philippines "takes place almost invariably during the town fiesta" so that the sponsors can also enjoy the fiesta banquet prepared by the child's parents (Eggan 1956 2: 651–52). Some parents in Cabetican serve a "snack" after the confirmation of their child; in Dumaguete a feast (*kumbira*) following confirmation is less common than for baptism (Potter 1973: 315).

Marriage

Canon law provides for "no true sponsors for matrimony. There are 'official witnesses' provided (usually the best man and maid [or matron] of honor) whose presence is deemed essential to the valid performance of the ceremony. However, this man and woman contract *no* spiritual relationships and no obligations other than that of testifying to the fact of the marriage if asked to do so by competent authority" (Eggan 1956 1: 425). The decreased sacramental importance of marriage sponsors often, although not always, is reflected in the lack of or reduced social significance of the ritual bond between sponsors.

Marriage sponsorship in the Philippines normally creates the same formal compadrinazgo relationships as baptism and confirmation (Pal 1956a: 356; Santico 1973: 31; Nurge 1965: 67; Hollnsteiner 1967: 201; Malay 1957: 78). In Suba and Caticugan informants often explain that marriage sponsors are "merely witnesses." Unlike for baptism, some

Municipal officials of Siaton in front of town hall (municipio) *wearing the Filipino* barong Tagalog *shirt. They are assembled to welcome a visiting politician from Manila.*

Caticuganers stated that marriage sponsorship creates "no brotherhood through God." Several Caticuganers reported, although others disagreed, that the children of marriage sponsors and those born to the bridal pair had no ritual relationship and could marry one another. They were not godsiblings. Yet marriage sponsors are invariably referred to and addressed as compadres. Most Caticuganers probably would agree that ritual kinship bonds are created by marriage sponsorship, but, as one informant explained, "they are lighter." Yet in Canaman the reverse is true. The relationships between marriage godparents and their godchildren are more vigorous and intimate than with the latter's parents (Arce 1973: 69).

If the godparents of a child in Suba are living, they are expected to be his marriage sponsors, although they must be asked. The major reason for repeat sponsorship is explained as, "It is the Christian way." Hence, in Suba, marriage sponsorship is not regarded to be as "close" as baptismal sponsorship because "when the child gets married I am supposed to take him to be godchild again."

Wedding sponsors in Caticugan and Siaton are selected in numerous ways. They may be chosen in these two communities and in Cana-man by the couple, individually or together, with parental approval (Arce 1973: 53). They may be selected by either the bride's or the groom's parents, usually with each other's approval. In one instance the groom's parents selected both sponsors, who were approved by the bride's parents. The bride's parents ("they were better educated") se-lected the wedding sponsors for a couple residing in Barrio Bonbonon. Sponsors may also be selected by persons other than the bride and groom and their parents, e.g., a municipal councilor or relative. In one instance a marriage sponsor was chosen because he owned an automo-bile that could take the bridal pair to the church and bring them home after the wedding.

In Payabon (a poblacion in Negros Oriental) the couple's parents usually select the marriage sponsors (Vailoces 1952: 106). In Bulacan province, Tagalog marriage sponsors once were, and perhaps still are, chosen during the marriage negotiations and later were formally noti-fied by the boy's side (Malay 1957: 78). Marriage sponsors in Alicia, a Bohol poblacion, should be elderly men and women who can advise the young couple; nothing, however, is reported about their relationship to the couple or the method of their selection (Iyoy 1950: n.p.). In Zam-boanga City the wedding sponsors typically are the bride's father and the bridegroom's mother (Enriquez 1956: n.p.).

An eighty-five-year-old Caticuganer reported that "in the old days" baptismal godparents usually sponsored their godchild's wedding "to finish what they started." Today some Caticugan informants consid-er it courteous to give baptismal godparents an opportunity to sponsor their godchildren's weddings, but no one's feelings are hurt if the god-parents refuse. One woman was asked to be the wedding sponsor of her baptismal goddaughter but declined "because I had a small infant to nurse." Some said they might ask a deceased godparent's sibling to serve as a marriage sponsor of the former's godchild. A Caticugan in-formant cited a case in which her child's baptismal sponsor was already dead when the daughter was to marry. So the mother asked a close relative of the deceased sponsor. She believed close kinsmen of a deceased baptismal sponsor have priority over others.

Actually, Caticugan baptismal (and confirmation) sponsors normal-ly do not serve as wedding sponsors for their godchildren (see Table 3). When they do, they usually do not volunteer but must be asked. Siaton elite, according to the survey made, never are repeat sponsors for their godchildren, and weddings in Siaton, according to the priest and obser-

vation, never include more than four sponsors, two for the groom and
two for the bride.

The Wedding and the Wedding Feast

In the Philippines "the wedding ceremony follows the Mozarabic
(Toledo) rite which was introduced by Spanish missionaries in the sixteenth century. It is essentially the same as the Roman rite used in most
of Europe, in the United States and Canada" (Eggan 1956 2: 656). The
following description of the wedding is for Siaton, although it is quite
similar to the regular ceremony as performed in Boroñgan and Lalawigan. A recent Catholic publication describes the marriage rites (*Ritwal
sa Kasal* 1971).

If the couple lives in a barrio, they spend the night before the
wedding with friends in Siaton poblacion. The bridal pair is escorted
to the church by their sponsors and friends. The couple's parents rarely
attend, since they are busy at home preparing the wedding feast. The
bride and groom, dressed in white, assemble in front of the altar with
their sponsors, backed by friends and relatives. With joined hands they
agree to marry, and the priest sprinkles their clasped hands with holy
water. He then puts a ring on the groom's left finger. He gives the groom
another ring that he places on the bride's same ringfinger. As the rings
are put on the priest prays. The rings are later returned to the priest.

The bride now cups her hands under the groom's cupped hands.
The priest lets thirteen silver coins (Sp. *arras*, earnest money) fall into
the groom's hands. He, in turn, permits them to tumble into the bride's
hands. The coins then fall from the bride's hands into a plate held by
an acolyte. The coins are church property. The *arras* is "a sign of
fidelity bestowed irrevocably and a symbol of the completion of the
marriage contract" (Quisumbing 1956: 68). (In parts of rural Spain the
bride retains the *arras* that the marriage sponsors have furnished. In
Madrid the groom provides the *arras:* Kenny 1962: 72, 181.)

Next the priest recites additional prayers over the couple. Usually,
but not always, a nuptial mass is held. In the part of the mass called the
Sanctus (when the bell rings), a veil is placed over the groom's shoulders
and the bride's head. A *yugal* (Sp. *yugo*, nuptial tie), a cord made of silk
or of strung white flowers, is entwined around their necks in the form
of the mathematical symbol of infinity. Caticuganers could not explain
the meaning of the cord, but the veil is said to be a symbol of modesty
and an invitation to the bride to be humble and obedient to her husband.

After the wedding, the bride, the groom, and their sponsors sign the necessary papers. A group picture may be taken of the bridal party, often including the priest. If the couple lives in a barrio the party takes a light breakfast at a friend's residence in the poblacion. When this snack is finished, the bridal pair returns to the wife's dwelling, often followed by a local string band. In Siaton a newly wedded barrio couple may be accompanied to or be met in the bride's village by several adults dressed in the clothing of the opposite sex. They laughingly make bawdy remarks about the sexual union to occur that evening. In the past, the men stuffed cloths in their dresses, simulating breasts. A woman may have had the long neck of a squash protruding from the open fly of her trousers.

Caticugan fields being being plowed by carabao *(water buffalo) for the planting of corn.*

The wedding day is completed by feasting at the residences of the parents of the wedded couple. In Caticugan and Lalawigan, as in Tepoztlán (Lewis 1963: 409), the new godparents may give marital advice to the married couple before the elaborate meal begins. In Lalawigan (but not in Caticugan) the newlyweds perform a stylized wedding dance called *ado* after arriving at the bride's residence. The couple's relatives and friends throw money at their feet, an act known as *gala* (Sp. ostentation; Sp. America prize, present, or reward of merit). Marriage sponsors are expected to make the largest contribution to the *gala*. A similar dance is done by newlyweds in the Ilocos with their relatives and friends competitively tossing money on the floor as "bets." The couple's wedding sponsors are expected to lead in the "betting," that is to give the most money (Agnir 1966: 9). The newly wedded couple first returns to the bride's residence; in the late afternoon the group goes to the groom's dwelling for another feast.

Possibly one reason why most Filipino parents do not attend their child's wedding reflects the persistence of the greater relative importance associated with the nuptial feast in pre-Hispanic Philippines. At least this is one explanation offered as to why the bride and groom's immediate family among the Cochiti Indians never participate in the wedding ceremonies.

This has been interpreted as an indication of the relative importance between the Church ritual and the feast—a survival of pre-European practices—in the minds of these Indians (Lange 1959: 414).

As the preceding pages demonstrate, sponsors (or witnesses) are required by the Church for baptism, confirmation, and marriage, although the method of their selection is not doctrinally prescribed. One means of obtaining sponsors is repeat sponsorship, or the use of the same godparents for two or more ceremonies. While the Church has tried to limit the number of sponsors for any rite, Filipinos often exceed this favored number through multiple sponsorship. Finally, Filipinos frequently extend ritual kinship bonds linking the sponsors (and their kinsmen) and the godchild's parents (and their kinsmen) beyond the scope recognized by the Church. The discussion of these three topics concludes this chapter.

Repeat Sponsorship

When asked why repeat sponsorship was so rare, Caticuganers explained that baptismal (or confirmation) godparents might be dead, sick, or moved away when their godchildren married. Their priest believed repeat sponsorship undesirable, "since if the godparent dies, the child is left without any spiritual guidance." He did not directly state that it was prohibited by the church. Several informants thought the priest discouraged repeat sponsorship because it created a "double responsibility" for the godparents. Still others said repeat sponsorship would result in *doble* (Sp. double) or *magdaug* (*daug* also is a verb meaning "to overcome" and, in this sense, "to defeat": Wolff 1972: 207–8). *Magdaug* involves this concept: all informants agreed that it is improper for parents to sponsor their own children. Since godparents are "spiritual parents" of the godchildren, repeat sponsorship creates a situation where "parents" sponsor their own "children."

However, this belief prevents repeat sponsorship only for confirmation; it is permissible for a baptismal godparent to sponsor a godchild's marriage. The reason for this exception is that ideally baptismal godparents should sponsor their godchild's wedding. The vigor of this belief may be the reason that only one repeat sponsorship for confirmation is reported in Table 3.

Repeat sponsorship in southern Negros is called *tahos* or *tapus* (Ceb. to end or finish); there is no special Samaran term for this practice. Actually repeat sponsorship is a rarity not only in Caticugan but also among the elite of Siaton poblacion. As Table 3 indicates, only two Caticugan residents and none of the Siaton elite were repeat sponsors.

TABLE 3

Repeat Sponsorship for Caticugan Residents and Siaton Elite: 1972

Events	Number of Persons		
	Caticugan[1]	Siaton Elite[2]	Totals
CONFIRMATION			
Baptismal Sponsor	1 (R)	—	1
New Sponsor	78	92	170
Don't know	1	—	1
MARRIAGE			
Baptismal Sponsor	1 (R)	—	1
Confirmation Sponsor	—	—	—
New Sponsor	29	17	46
Don't know	1	—	1
Eloped	1	—	1
Totals	112	109	221

[1]N=15 informants   [2]N=18 informants   (R)=repeat sponsor

Few sources on Philippine compadrinazgo discuss repeat sponsorship. However, in both Camangahan and Manalad, tradition states that baptismal sponsors should be asked to sponsor their godchild's wedding. In Camangahan about 60 percent of baptismal sponsors were also their godchildren's marriage sponsors, but in Manalad only 20 percent sponsored both events. Repeat sponsorship occurs less frequently in Manalad, since there it is common to seek marriage sponsors among persons of higher status than those who served as baptismal sponsors.

(Elite sponsors are believed more capable of helping a newly wedded couple find employment, etc.)

"Blanketing-in" Process

The extension of ritual kinship beyond the principals varies in the Philippines, although data on this topic are scarce and often superficial. The majority of Caticuganers do not extend ritual ties to the principals' kinsmen. Only the child's parents and sponsors "who face God during the rite [of baptism]" are ritually related. This is also true for confirmation and marriage. Yet a minority of informants claimed that ritual bonds could be extended to other relatives since the sponsor and the godchild's parents become "like brother and sister." In practice, however, this extension is rare. Lalawignons, and other Samarans in eastern Samar, are more emphatic that ritual kinship relationships are never extended beyond the principal sponsors.

The "blanketing-in" process among other Filipino cultural-linguistic groups may be automatic or depend on previous contacts and role behavior. In some Tagalog communities, compadrinazgo is "further enhanced by the fact that the direct 'compadre' of a family becomes 'compadre' also by diffusion to one's brothers, sisters, and even cousins" (Samson 1965: 518). The Tagalogs of Hulo diffuse ritual kinship ties only if the persons "perform the roles expected of a compadre" (Hollnsteiner 1967: 205). In Malitbog, terminology and ritual bonds are extended to the co-parent's siblings, and the godchild bond is also diffused to the godparent's siblings' children (Jocano 1968b: 28; 1969: 93; 1972: 69).

The Ilokans of Suba reciprocally, if in a highly variable and situational manner, extend the ritual bond to the siblings and their spouses and the cousins of both the sponsor and the godchild's parents (Scheans 1963: 220).

Multiple Sponsors

Multiple sponsors are uncommon in Caticugan. Of the 414 Caticugan godchildren surveyed, only 8 percent had two primary sponsors (excluding spouses of married individuals), 2 percent had three primary sponsors, and one child (of the most prominent village family) had four such sponsors. In Siaton poblacion the number of co-sponsors increases as the parents' social position rises. One municipal official had twelve officials as primary sponsors for his infant's baptism, including the visiting candidate for the Philippine presidency.

As mentioned earlier, having multiple sponsors for a child's christening or wedding is regarded by the barriofolk of Caticugan as an upper-class custom of the Siaton elite. Social status among many of the elite can be measured by the number of sponsors chosen, particularly for the person's baptism or marriage. Multiple sponsors, of course, testify to the family's affluence, since a larger and more expensive feast usually follows the ceremony.

Multiple sponsors for baptism or marriage were uncommon in Lalawigan in the past, but since a resident priest was assigned to the village, co-sponsorship for baptism has increased. Since the ceremony is now performed in Lalawigan, and not Borongan, multiple sponsorship by local residents can be more easily arranged. Another reason is that more Lalawignons today can afford the additional cost. "Having more than one sponsor is an indication of a more stable living [higher income] since one has to prepare a bigger party." Caticugan and Lalawigan data indicate a direct relationship between co-sponsorship and income.

Co-sponsorship is reported elsewhere in the Philippines. The Suba sample (Table 11) indicates that most godchildren in this Ilokan village had more than one baptismal sponsor; one child (not included in the sample) had twenty-nine sponsors for its christening. In Suba parents believe that the first-born should have more godparents than subsequent children, and that the sponsors should be even in number and paired male with female (Scheans 1963: 227). Among Tagalogs co-sponsors (*katuwang*) generally are nonrelatives, while the primary sponsors are kinsmen. "The *katuwang* are sometimes not recognized as official sponsors by the church" (Jocano 1972: 67).

The mayor of a large town in the Ilocos (northern Luzon) had 200 sponsors for his son's wedding. In this same region there were 40 sponsors for the marriage of a minor official of the United Church of Christ. The marriage sponsors each made a donation of two pesos to the church, and most of them also gave a wedding gift to the bride and groom (Reynolds 1964: 119).

Surveys in Caticugan indicate that women average ten baptismal sponsorships, and men six, while men and women average five confirmation sponsorships apiece. Data were not collected on marriage sponsorship, but the number is an estimated average of five. If these godchildren are counted, including those of one's spouse, most middle-aged barriofolk would have scores of godchildren, and double this number of compadres.

Precise figures could not be obtained from many of the Siaton elite regarding the number of their sponsorships, since those with numerous godchildren could remember the names of only some of them. Several counted their godchildren in the twenties and one woman "had more than fifty godchildren." One Siaton municipal official had so many godchildren that he kept a notebook with the names of thirty-one godchildren. He proudly commented that "not one of my godchildren has died." In Dumaguete Potter found that the average respondent in his survey sponsored about eight baptisms or marriages. However, the average for individuals who served as a godparent more than twenty-one times was sponsorship of fifty-one baptisms, forty-nine confirmations, and sixty-five marriages (1975: 7).

Those familiar with the basic structure and functions of Latin American compadrinazgo will recognize its striking similarities to Philippine godparenthood. Moreover, identical folk beliefs and practices

Typical Caticugan dwelling of bamboo and nipa. The space under the house is used for storage.

adhere to both complexes. The major differences characterizing this aspect of compadrinazgo in the Philippines (as in Latin America) are the varying emphases different Filipino groups make regarding possible alternatives—the frequency of repeat sponsorship, whether and how extensively ritual kinship bonds are extended beyond the principal participants, etc. A more detailed comparison of Philippine compadrinazgo with Latin American (and to a lesser extent, European) ritual kinship is made in Chapter Eight.

Chapter Four

Filipino Compadrinazgo Terminology

This chapter presents a comparative analysis of the compadrinazgo terminology of seven Filipino cultural-linguistic groups: Ilokan, Pampangan, Tagalog, Samaran, Cebuan, Panayan, and Aklan (see Table 5). As an introduction to Table 5, Table 4 indicates, for the groups surveyed, their geographical location and the number of communities furnishing terminology. It is believed, given the basic similarity of compadrinazgo for these groups, that the data are sufficient to establish patterns for Christian Filipinos in general (see Table 4). Graph 2 illustrates the basic Filipino godparenthood relationships and lists the associated terminology in both English and Spanish.

TABLE 4
Filipino Groups Furnishing Compadrinazgo Terminology

Cultural-Linguistic Groups	Geographical Location	Number of Communities
Ilokan	Northern Luzon	1
Pampangan	Central Luzon	1
Tagalog	Greater Manila	1
Samaran	Eastern Leyte and eastern Samar	2
Cebuan	Southern Leyte and southern Negros	2
Panayan	Central Panay and western Negros	2
Aklan	Northern Panay	1

Godparenthood vocabularies offer but limited insights into the actual functions of this ritual kinship system. In some instances, the terms are used to address persons with whom one has no ritual relationship. Social distance between ritual kinsmen may also result in asymmetrical usage of the terminology. Nevertheless, a first step in a comprehensive

TABLE 5
Godparenthood Terminology for Seven Filipino Cultural-Linguistic Groups

Categories	Suba[1] (Ilokan)	Cabetican[2] (Pampangan)	Hulo[3] (Tagalog)	Lalawigan (Samaran)
Godchild to godfather	Ama ti (R); Tatang (A)	Ninong (R); Tanang (A)	Iná-amá and Ninong (R&A)	Pangamayon (Tatay (A)
Godchild to godmother	Ina ti (R); Nanang (A)	Ninang (R); Inang or Inda (A)	Iní-amá and Ninang (R&A)	Pangiroyon (P Nanay (A)
Godparent to Godchild	Anak ti (R); Barok or Balasangko (A)	Nainac (R); Name or nickname (A)	Ináanák (R); nickname (A)	Pinanganak (I Nickname (A
Godchild's parents & godparents	Compadre-Comadre (R&A)*	Cumpadre-Cumadre (R&A)*	Kumpare-Kumare (R&A)*	Padi-Madi (R
Gobsibling	Kabagis ti (R); nickname or respect term (A)	Quinacapatad (R); nickname or respect term (A)	Kinákapatíd (R); nickname or respect term (A)	Ugto (R); nickname or respect term (

*Means term often is followed with a nickname; R means reference term, and A, address term.

+Used only in Camangahan.

[1]Suba is a barrio of 496 persons, about eight miles from Laoag, the provincial capital of Ilocos Norte (Scheans 1962 and 1963: 216).

[2]Cabetican is a community of approximately 4,000 people about 50 miles northeast of Manila (Santico 1973 and 1974).

[3]Hulo is a poblacion of about 12,000, about 15 miles from Manila (Hollnsteiner 1967: 200).

[4]Guinhangdan is a barrio of 1,200 individuals, about 11 miles south of Tacloban, Leyte (Nurge 1965: 16).

[5]Esperanza is a barrio of about 2,000 persons in Matalom municipality, Leyte, about 30 miles south of Baybay (Pal 1956a: 337).

investigation of compadrinazgo in the Philippines is a complete colla-
tion of its known terminologies for all Christian Filipino groups.

Compadrinazgo terminology for Filipino cultural-linguistic groups
represented in Table 5 is quite uniform, in part because some terms are

TABLE 5 *(Continued)*

Guinhangdan[4] (Samaran)	Esperanza[5] (Cebuan)	Caticugan[6] (Cebuan)	Camangahan and Manalad[7] (Panayan)	Aklan[8]
ompadreh (R); atay (A)*	Ama-on (R&A); Ninoy (A)*	Ama-on (R); Tatay (A)*	Padrino and Maninoy+ (R); Paninoy and Maninoy+ (A)	Maninoy (R); Itay and Tay (A)
omadrah (R); anay (A)*	Ina-on (R&A); Ninay (A)	Ina-on (R); Nanay (A)*	Madrina and maninay+ (R); Maninay (A)	Maninay (R); Inay and Nay (A)
	Anakon (R&A); nickname (A)	Inanak (R); nickname (A)	Ihado-Ihada (R); nickname (A)	Oñga or inanak (R); Anak or nickname (A)
ompadreh-omadreh (R); adi-Madi (A)	Pari-Mari (R&A)*	Pari-Mari (R&A)*	Compadre-Comadre (R&A)*	Compadre-comadre (R); pare-mare (A)
gto (R&A)	Igsô (R & A); nickname or respect term (A)	Igso or Igso-Igsà R); Igs, nickname or respect term (A)	Igsô-un (R); nickname or respect term (A)	Egsô-on or Igsô (R); nickname or respect term (A)

Quijano reports the same terms for Cebu as those used in Caticugan. The same terms for father and mother are used for godparents to which are added the occasion, e.g., *sa bunyag* (baptism), etc. Godchildren and the children of their godparents refer to each other as *igsoon sa Dios* (Quijano 1937: 359–60).

Camangahan is a barrio of about 900 persons in Guimbal municipality, Panay; Manalad, in southwestern Negros Occidental province, has a population of about 600 persons (Sibley 1965b: 1–2). For additional godparenthood vocabularies for Panay see Jocano 1969 and Gonzalez 1965. Gonzalez states that a godchild's siblings call the former's godfather *tiyo* (uncle) and godmother *tiya* (aunt).

Terminology in this source is incomplete (Tuason 1937; 552, 571). Tuason's vocabulary was augmented by an interview with an Aklan informant. *Oñga* is also a term for child. To indicate the type of godchildren, one may say *oñga sa bonyag* (baptism), *sa pirma* (confirmation), and *sa casal* (marriage).

derived from Spanish. (In South America both Spanish and indigenous terms are used for ritual kinsmen, while in Middle America all terminology is Spanish: Holmes 1952: 111.) Reciprocals for the sponsor and the godchild's parents (*compadre* and *comadre*), or their local varia-

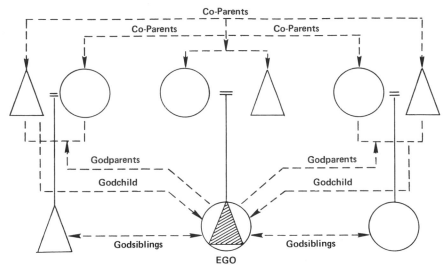

Graph 2: *Basic Compadrinazgo Relationships and English and Spanish Compadrinazgo Reference Terms.*

English	Spanish
Godfather	Padrino
Godmother	Madrina
Godson	Ahijado
Goddaughter	Ahijada
Co-parent (male)	Compadre
Co-parent (female)	Comadre
Godsibling (Ceremonial or Co-sibling)	No term

tions, are identical for all groups. *Pare* (*padi*) and *mare* (*madi*) are shortened forms of *compadre* and *comadre*. The use of dimunitives (i.e., *compadrito* and *comadrito*) apparently does not occur in the Philippines, although these forms are frequently heard in Latin America (Romanucci-Ross 1973: 82). In Mexico *patrón* also refers to a ceremonial sponsor (Foster 1963: 1282). This usage of *patrón* is not reported for the Philippines.

Only Panayans (in Manalad and Camangahan but not Malitbog) use the Spanish-derived *ihado* and *ihada* for godchildren. *Ninang*, or *godmother*, (*ninay*, etc.) is derived from the word for *mother* (Tag. *ina*; Ceb. *inahan*; Ilok. *ina*). There are two exceptions to the rule that godchildren refer to godparents by derivatives of words for parents. In Camangahan and Manalad the terms used are *padrino* and *madrina*. In Guinhangdan godchildren refer to godparents as *kompadreh* or *komadreh*. These terms are not Samaran referentials for godparents in Lalawigan or elsewhere in eastern Samar. This reported usage may be a form of reverse teknonymy or an ethnographic error.

In Caticugan *padrino* and *madrina* are referentials used only by marriage co-sponsors in referring to each other. The groom's witness refers to the bride's witness as *madrina*, and the latter refers to the former as *padrino*. These words are never used as vocatives. In Caticugan and Siaton *padrino* and *madrina* are used only in this context—and perhaps this usage is also true for some Tagalogs (Eggan 1956 2: 656). In Canaman marriage sponsors are referred to as *madrina*, female, and *padrino*, male (Arce 1973: 53). In Suba the groom and his witnesses refer to one another as *maninoy*, while the bride and her witnesses use *maninay*. A baptismal or confirmation godparent is also known as *nikugos* (Ceb. *kugos*, to hold a child or to sponsor a baptism or confirmation). Those who sponsor a wedding are also known as *nusunud* (Ceb. *sunud*, to stay behind, follow, or to be the next one). *Sunud sa kasal* is a wedding sponsor (Wolff 1972 2: 939).

Godsiblings

There are no Spanish or Portuguese terms for godsiblings (ceremonial or co-siblings). Latin Americans have no special term for this ritual relationship that they usually recognize. Godsiblings in Los Boquerones are called "political brothers-sisters" (*hermanos politicos*), also the word for step-sibling (Gudeman 1972: 62). ("Political 'siblings' are close to being prohibited partners, [but] sexual relations are not proscribed between them": Gudeman 1972: 58. Lewis and Reina state that godsiblings cannot marry each other since they are ritual siblings: 1963: 76; 1966: 196, 233.)

Since a godsibling may serve as a godparent substitute in case of the death of the original sponsor, he is also called *padrino*. Sometimes a godsibling is referred to as "*segundo papá de mi papá* [second father of my father]." The godparent's offspring and his godchild may also refer to one another by the sibling term, or derivatives of it (Ravicz 1967: 247). Some sources for Latin American compadrinazgo do not indicate any ritual relationship between the godparent's children and their godchildren (Foster 1967; Beals 1946). Gillin's schematic presentation of Moche compadrinazgo terms omits any ritual linkage between godsiblings (1947: 106).

Filipinos refer to godsiblings by using derivatives of the word for sibling. "Among Tagalogs the term *kaka* or *nana/* personal names are sometimes used [as vocatives by godsiblings]; sibling terms *kuya* or *ati/* personal names are often used when the *kinakapatid* are older and personal names when they are younger" (Jocano 1972: 69). Only in Cebuan do the terms indicate the sex of godsiblings: *igsô*, (male godsibling) and *igsâ* (female godsibling). In Caticugan godsiblings may address each other as *Igs.* One Bisayan (Cebuan)-English dictionary lists both terms: "*igsá igsoon* [*babáye?*] *sa bunyag,* n. God-sister, and *igsó, igsoong lalaki sa bunyag,* n. God-brother" (Hermosisima and Lopez 1966: 246). Wolff's Cebuan dictionary gives only *igsù* (1972 1: 365).

Some Caticuganers insisted that *igsâ* referred to both male and female godsiblings. The "mountain people" (inhabiting isolated communities in the interior of Siaton municipality) use *igsô* as a friendly address term for both sexes, including nonritual kinsmen. *Igsô* is also used, with the identical meaning, between itinerant Muslim Filipino traders and their customers in Siaton. (Also see Wolff 1972 1: 365). Yet other informants in Caticugan and Siaton claimed that *igsô* and *igsâ* were the appropriate terms for godsiblings. A few believed these terms were used in this manner largely by young people.

The greater terminological attention given to godsiblings may reflect the intense sibling solidarity of Christian Filipinos. More so than in Latin America, "the sibling group ... is a basic building block in Philippine society" (Eggan 1968: 31). Whatever the reasons, Filipinos give far more importance to this relationship than do most Latin Americans.

Vocatives for Filipino ritual kinsmen, reflecting both age and sex, are the address terms for consanguines. Table 5 lists only the most common terms of address. Godparents normally are addressed by godchildren as *father* or *mother* (*tatay* [*tata*] or *nanay*). Among Tagalogs (at least in Hulo), *ninong* or *ninang* are both referentials and vocatives; *iná-amá* and *iní-amá* (*iníiná*) are considered more formal than *ninong* and *ninang*.

In the Southern Tagalog region, *ninang* and *ninong* are used most often for godparents or sponsors in baptism and confirmation; sponsors in matrimony are *amáng-kasál* [Sp. *casal*, marriage] and *ináng-kasál* [Tag. *kasal*, marriage]. The reciprocal is either *ináanák* or *anák sa kasál*. In Bata-an, the pattern is extended: *amáng-binyág*, "godfather in baptism"; *ináng-kumpíl*, "godmother in confirmation," and so on (Lynch and Himes 1967: 33).

Parallels to the Tagalog use of godparent terms as both referentials and vocatives also occur in Esperanza and Camangahan but are culturally-linguistically Cebuan and Panayan respectively. In an affective situation, however, most godchildren in Esperanza address godparents as *ninoy* and *ninay*. In Canaman godchildren address their godparents as *papá* (Spanish) or *tio* (uncle) and *mamá* (Spanish) or *tia* (aunt), followed by the familiar form of their first name (Arce 1973: 53; also see Edmonson 1957: 29).

Caticugan residence kitchen. Cooking is done over a wood fire built inside a clay horno. A bamboo river fish trap hangs on the wall.

Except in Suba godparents address their own children and godchildren by nicknames; there are no data for Guinhangdan. In Esperanza, when *anakon* is used as a term of address, it usually indicates a less intimate relationship than when godparents call their godchildren by nicknames. In this Leyte village and Guinhangdan *igso* or *ogtu* are used as vocatives; *igso* may also be used along with the nickname.

Godsiblings, in addressing each other, use terms of address that indicate both age and sex. If two godsiblings are of the same age group, they usually call each other by nicknames. If one is younger, the older one uses a nickname, and the younger responds with a respect term that depends upon the speaker's sex.

Compadre and *comadre* are both referentials and vocatives. Sometimes they are also used with a person's nickname, e.g., Pare Coring or Madi Day. Caticugan and Canaman parents-in-law address one another as compadres, a usage that also prevails in Spain (Arce 1973: 54; Pitt-Rivers 1958: 426). Although the closest functional relationships among ritual kinsmen for most Filipinos are those of compadres, for some Tagalogs

> close ritual kinsmen are those who must participate in the rite which creates the following relationships: "godfather," "godmother," and "god-child." *Kumpadre* and *kumadre* here are considered intermediate ritual kin terms since, although the relationships they denote are created by the rite at the time that it is performed, it is not the purpose of the rite to create them. *Kinákapatíd*, on the other hand, is taken to be a distant ritual kin term since one's "god-sibling" need not even have been born when the causative rite was performed (Himes 1967: 132–33).

Compadre and *comadre* often are used as forms of address for nonsponsor friends and strangers. This extension of the original meaning of *compadre* and *comadre* has been interpreted as a technique outside the Philippines "to solidify social relationships horizontally among members of the same ritual neighborhood" (Mintz and Wolf 1950: 348). In parts of Spain and Italy, *compadre* and *comadre* are used for any acquaintance or stranger, accomplice, gossip, "protector," or "benefactor," or for one who has cuckholded a husband (Mintz and Wolf 1950: 348; Kenny 1962: 71–72; Moss and Thompson 1959: 38; Maraspini 1968: 202).

In Latin America these terms are "to some extent synonymous with neighbor" or close friend, or indicate a desire for a more intimate association (Watson 1952: 20; Harris 1956: 152; Whiteford 1964: 181; Gudeman 1972: 62; Redfield 1941: 222; Reichel-Dolmatoff 1961: 172; Redfield and Villa Rojas 1962: 99; Riley 1969; 826; Van den Berghe and Van den Berghe 1966: 1238). Contrarily, in San Lorenzo "a man must be careful about who calls him compadre as there is a tendency to attribute the faults and debts of a person to those in compadrazgo relationship with him" (Whitten 1965: 108–9). In Tobatí people are quite strict about the correct use of godparenthood terms of address (Service and Service 1954: 177).

Filipinos also use *compadre* and *comadre* as amiable terms of address (in Caticugan, Lalawigan, Manalad, and Camangahan) for non-sponsor friends and strangers of the same age and status group. In the Ilocos regions of northern Luzon members of teen-aged "gangs" call members *pari* or *mari* as a sign of their intimate friendship (Agnir 1966: 10). Supposedly, this use of these terms began in the Philippines after World War II (Cortez 1965: 22).

Linguistic usage often distinguishes interclass and intraclass compadrinazgo, although the formal ceremonial bond uniting members of different classes is identical. In parts of Hispanic America compadres of equal status are formal with one another, replacing the familiar *tú* with the formal *usted*. Client compadres are equally formal with patron compadres, but "patron compadres, almost without exception, address their village compadres with the familiar '*tú*,' so that the relative status of the two partners is never in doubt" (Foster 1967: 231). One explanation for this usage of *tú* and *usted* is that where functional relationships are desired for long periods of time, they are best maintained at the "midrange of intimacy" that minimizes the possibility of emotional disruptions (Kearney 1972: 79).

Yet in Erongaricuaro, a community of 2,000 people about 250 miles west of Mexico City, the use of the formal or informal form of *you* does not always indicate the degree of closeness felt by the speakers. "The use of *Tú* can indicate both *confianza* (closeness) and lack of respect. *Usted* can be used to connote distance as well as respect. Both terms depend upon the situation and the person using them" (Nelson 1971: 78–79).

An apparently unique usage of *compadre-comadre* occurs in Aritama. Compadres and comadres address each other with these vocatives only if one of them is the biological parent of the child. "When they are padrinos of a child who is not related biologically to either of them, they do not use these terms and are not considered to be ritually related to each other" (Reichel-Dolmatoff 1961: 172).

Similar social distinctions in the use of godparenthood terms are made by Caticugan barriofolk. On those occasions when an infant has a locally prominent (usually poblacion) sponsor, parents may not tell other barrio co-sponsors until the christening since the latter might be "hesitant" to establish a ritual bond where the more important individual should be called compadre or comadre.

Furthermore, if a child's godparents are considerably older or more socially prominent than the parents, the latter may not address them as compadres. The district school supervisor is the godfather of a child of an elementary school teacher in Siaton. Although he eats lunch in this teacher's home when visiting Siaton, she never calls him "compadre" but always addresses him "Sir" (Snyder 1971: 169–70). One sponsor of the Siaton mayor's son's baptism later became the president of the Philippines, but the mayor would never address him as "compadre" since "we met only once."

In a Brazilian and a Mexican village, and also in San Lorenzo, godparenthood terminology supplants kinship terms previously used for most relatives (Pierson 1951: 142; Whitten 1965: 102, 105, 108, 120; Romanucci-Ross 1973: 80). A similar practice is reported for late eighteenth-century Puerto Rico (Mintz 1966: 386). In Aritama when a father and son or brothers are ritually related, compadrinazgo vocatives frequently replace kinship terms (Reichel-Dolmatoff 1961: 172). On the other hand, in Chan Kom compadrinazgo terms are not used to address near relatives because one is "first a father or brother, and then only the godparent of one's child" (Redfield and Villa Rojas 1962: 99).

This latter practice is also common among many Filipinos; where ceremonial principals are kinsmen, the associated vocatives are not used in Caticugan, Lalawigan, Esperanza, and Suba. "To address a close kinsman as pare," commented a Caticugan resident, "would be awkward. We already have a way to call him." In Cabetican compadrinazgo vocatives are limited to ritual kinsmen who are friends or affines. Consanguines never address each other as compadre-comadre or as godparent-godchild. For this category of relatives, informants claim it is "useless" to use ritual kinship terms when there are "available kinship terminologies for them" (Santico 1973: 36). This is another example of how compadrinazgo reinforces but does not replace basic functions of Filipino kinship.

Although the data for all major groups are incomplete, some general comments can be made regarding Filipino godparenthood terminology. The terms are based almost entirely on consanguineal kinship terms. The godparenthood terminologies among the various Filipino groups are quite similar. This terminological uniformity reflects, in part, the adoption of Spanish terms, although other Spanish godparenthood

Caticugan woman weaving a grain storage bag of buri *palm strips in front of the family altar.*

words are replaced by terms of identical or similar meaning from various Filipino languages.

Future research may uncover significant variations in the affective or connotative meanings of some godparenthood terms. Filipinos emphasize compadrazgo that stresses the importance of the parent-sponsor relationship. Hence, *compadre-comadre,* with exceptions noted and to be discussed later, signify a more intimate association than other compadrinazgo terms. Yet Himes found that some Tagalogs regarded *compadre* and *comadre* as "intermediate kin terms," indicating less intimacy than godparent and godchild (1967: 132). Perhaps the meaning of these two terms varies situationally as well as according to whether the stress is on compadrazgo or padrinazgo.

The explanation offered by Mintz and Wolf for the custom of addressing nonritual kinsmen as *compadre* and *comadre* also applied to Filipinos. In this instance, terminological extension is horizontal. Vertical extension (e.g., an adult referring to a younger nonritually related person as a godchild) does not occur in Caticugan and Lalawigan. This usage is also supported in the literature on Latin America. Finally, the parent-sponsor ritual linkage is the only godparenthood relationship for which Filipinos lack vernacular words.

In conclusion, as the result of either Filipino participation or indirect involvement in these basic Catholic rites, both the sponsor and the sponsored (and sometimes but not always many of their kinsmen) gain new privileges and assume additional responsibilities in relation to one another. An initial step in the assumption of these new roles is to meet the sponsorship qualifications imposed by the Catholic Church or set by folk Catholicism for godparenthood.

Chapter Five

Ritual Kinsmen:
Their Qualifications and Procurement

This chapter discusses the ideal and actual qualifications of potential Filipino godparents, as defined by both Canon law and folk Catholicism. The various means of obtaining sponsors are described—the circumstances governing selection or volunteering, the importance of the christening meal in the selection process, and the use of intermediaries. The Lalawigan escort system and the Caticugan baptismal *union*, unique Philippine ways by which sponsors are selected or volunteer, are reported. Since the sponsors' places of residence may influence whether they are chosen or not, this factor is examined. The chapter ends with a brief survey of Protestant or non-Catholic compadrinazgo in Siaton.

Qualifications of Godparents

The following statement summarizes important qualifications of baptismal sponsors according to Canon Law:

> For valid sponsorship, the godparent must be baptized, have the use of reason and the intention of acting as sponsor, and conform to several other more technical qualifications. The godparent must not be the mother, father, or spouse of the person baptized, or his parents or guardians, or the priest baptizing. During the baptism, the sponsor must personally or by proxy hold, touch, raise or receive from the baptismal font or from the hands of the priest the person baptized. For lawful sponsorship, in the eyes of the Church, the godparents should be [at] least fourteen years of age and know the rudiments of the faith, in order to be able to teach them, should the need arise (Eggan 1956 2: 647).

A recent statement of baptism, revised by decree of the Second Vatican Ecumenical Council, published by authority of Pope Paul VI, and printed in the Philippines, states it is an "ancient custom of the

Church that an adult is not admitted to baptism without a godparent [who] as occasion offers ... will be ready to help the parents bring up their child to profess the faith and to show this by living it" (*Rite of Baptism for Children* 1971: iii). This source reiterates that a godparent should be sufficiently mature to assume the responsibility of sponsorship, have received the three sacraments of initiation (baptism, confirmation, and the eucharist), and be a member of the Catholic Church, canonically free to serve as a sponsor.

In Caticugan and Cabetican a pregnant woman cannot be a sponsor; this custom may be common throughout the Philippines (Santico 1974; Malay and Malay 1955: 29). In Esperanza, if a sponsor is pregnant, both the unborn child and the child held in her arms (or by the husband, if he is the sponsor) will "claim" the baptismal sacrament. "If the child in the womb is the one who gets the sacrament, then there is no ceremonial bond established between the sponsors and the child [she or] he holds in [her or] his arms" (Pal 1956a: 379, footnote 33).

Although most sponsors are adults, unmarried Filipinos in their late teens may become sponsors of baptism, confirmation, or marriage; adult unmarried Caticuganers and Lalawignons may also be sponsors, as is true in Peru and Mexico (Gillin 1947: 105; Foster 1948: 262). In Cabetican wedding sponsors usually are married, since if one is unmarried this is considered "proof that one's character and reputation are questionable" (Santico 1974: 31). Generally, since most Filipinos favor compadrazgo, baptismal and confirmation sponsors (as in Canaman) are of the parents' generation and are married (Arce 1973: 64). Wedding sponsors, however, often are close friends of the bride and groom and frequently are in their age group.

In one Mexican village the priest served as a sponsor; in fact, he was ritually related to almost the entire village (Nelson 1971: 85). The only located reference in Philippine literature to priestly sponsorship is a prewar account of village life in Luzon in which the informant states he was named after his godfather "who happened to be a priest living in another town" (Parsons 1940: 441). The Siaton priest had two godchildren, one each through baptism and confirmation. He explained that a priest might serve as a sponsor if he had the prior approval of his bishop. But sponsorship by priests apparently is extremely rare in the Philippines.

In the past some priests assigned to Siaton prohibited both sponsorship by proxy and baptismal sponsors standing for the opposite sex. In one instance a Caticugan woman asked to be the sponsor of an unborn child of a close friend. When a male infant was delivered, the Siaton priest would not permit this sponsorship, so her son served instead. In 1972 the Siaton priest raised no objection to these two kinds of sponsorship.

Inside the Caticugan chapel. It is decorated for a mass to be held by a visiting priest for the annual fiesta honoring the village patron saint, San Isidro.

Kinsmen serve as baptismal sponsors in Caticugan and Lalawigan, but parents never and real godparents rarely. In several intances a Lalawigan mother sponsored her child's confirmation but never its baptism. Many Caticuganers also believe that no permanent member of the godchild's household, whether relative or not, can be a sponsor. Sponsorship by these relatives or persons is called *umay* (tabu) and results in *magdaug*. In this context, *magdaug* refers to supernatural though unconscious competition caused by God between any two persons (in this case the sponsor and the child) in which the loser sickens and eventually dies.

Lalawigan informants claimed that in the past, but not today, one could not sponsor the baptism of any relative. The "old people" believed that sponsorship of a kinsman resulted in a "double relationship" that was preternaturally dangerous. When the sponsor was a relative, particularly a close one, a supernatural competition (*abong*) was created between the two. The person "overpowered" in this struggle eventually became ill and sometimes died. This belief parallels the Caticugan concept of *magdaug*.

Sex and Sponsorship

There is a predominance in Caticugan of women over men as primary baptismal sponsors. Table 6 indicates that for this barrio, based on a sample of 414 godchildren, women participated as baptismal sponsors nearly twice as often as did men. Godparents, whether male or female, have substantially the same pattern of relative frequency of sponsorship of kin and nonkin godchildren. About 37 percent of the godchildren were related to their godfather, and 41 percent were related to their godmother. The difference in the percentages is statistically insignificant.

Where godsons are concerned, more men than women act as sponsors, but in the sponsoring of goddaughters, women predominate by over four to one (Table 6). The greater percentage of same-sex sponsorship by women probably is a function of their keener sense of responsibility that a child be christened. When there are two primary baptismal or wedding sponsors in Lalawigan, one is always a male, the other female.

TABLE 6

Sex and Relationship of Caticugan Baptismal
Sponsors to Their Godchildren: 1965

	Godfather			Godmother			
Godchildren	Kin	Non-Kin	Σ	Kin	Non-Kin	Σ	*Totals*
Godson	40	72	112	40	50	90	202
Goddaughter	17	22	39	67	106	173	212
Totals	57	94	151	107	156	263	414

Most Filipinos are more active participants in their church than all but relatively few men in Caticugan and Lalawigan, Siaton, and Borongan. Women dominate the local Catholic sodalities in Caticugan and Siaton poblacion and are more supportive of various folk Catholic practices.

> Any Siaton male beyond adolescence, and not yet considered an old man, who participates as actively in Catholic ritual, official or folk, as most women would cause some doubt to be cast on his masculinity. . . . Prayers and novenas recited at the family altar in Caticugan are always led by the

wife or another female household member. *Manalabtan*—lay specialists who lead prayers for the dying, novenas for the dead, and individual saint devotions—almost invariably are women. The only male *manalabtan* observed, of two reported by informants, was an aged effeminate resident of another barrio (Hart 1968: 119).

Men would accordingly not seem to be ideal "spiritual" sponsors, for they have a more limited knowledge of the formal doctrines of Catholicism and are less active participants than women in routine church services. But given the Filipino stress on compadrazgo, the religious knowledge and inclination of males is not of overriding importance to most barriofolk.

Selectees and Volunteers

Published Philippine sources are almost devoid of detailed information on the selection of sponsors. Existing data on this topic suggest, however, that the same criteria are used by Filipinos and Latin Americans. A common and general comment for the Philippines is that it is an honor to be asked to be a godparent, particularly for baptism. Moreover, "the feeling of honor and satisfaction on the part of friend asked in intraclass compadrazgo is perhaps greater than in the cross-class case since he knows that real friendship and a desire to cement further their mutual attraction had precipitated the request rather than any ulterior motives" (Hollnsteiner 1967: 205).

It is "bad luck" in Hulo to refuse a request to sponsor a baptism (Hollnsteiner 1967: 206). Rarely, if ever, in Barrio Suba is a request by parents or an offer by a volunteer refused. The person declining would be criticized as having "no shame," and the infant might sicken or its life be shortened (Scheans 1963: 227). In Estancia, a town in Panay, refusal to be a sponsor is difficult and therefore rare. Normally, sponsors are individuals with whom the parent already has an informal relationship. Rejections by a status equal would indicate "pretensions to superiority" that might result in retaliation (Szanton 1972: 112). If the individuals involved were clearly status unequals, refusal to be a sponsor would mean repudiation of the mutual obligations of the traditional patron-client dyad. In either instance, Szanton argues, declination violates basic Filipino norms.

The intimacy of adult social relations in Caticugan and Lalawigan and basic Filipino values make it difficult, but not impossible, to reject a volunteer sponsor. Some parents boldly lie, saying that a sponsor has already been selected. Then they hastily find one. If the volunteer presses to be a co-sponsor, the excuse in Caticugan may be offered that the first sponsor wishes to "solo." Some Caticuganers refused the request of a volunteer sponsor who was not a close relative by explaining they would be embarrassed to accept since they could not hold a "fancy baptismal party." In Camangahan and Manalad, some persons who frequently volunteer are assiduously avoided, since it is known that they probably will take advantage of the obligatory relationships involved.

One important Siaton elective municipal official said it was almost impossible to refuse a request to be a sponsor. However, another town official said he had refused some requests for sponsorship. "This discourages others from asking me." One member of the Siaton elite had only one godchild. He was known as "difficult to approach because when he is not working he is always in his house." As a consequence, people were hesitant to ask him to serve as a sponsor since he was not "socially approachable."

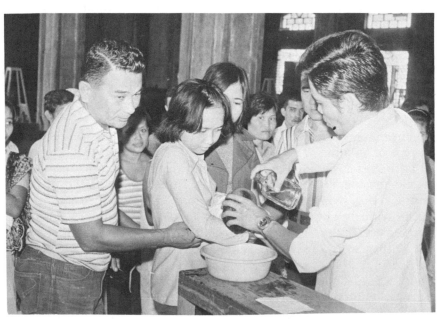

Baptism in Boroñgan church. The godmother is holding the infant, while the godfather touches the child during the christening.

Volunteer sponsors normally are welcomed by Lalwigan parents who have children to be baptized. When a volunteer sponsor has been considered undesirable (e.g., believed to be either an *aswang* or a sorcerer), rejection is never direct. Parents may explain that a sponsor has been selected or may have their child baptized when the volunteer is away from the barrio. Several residents claimed they had no godchildren and wanted none, "for they are too much trouble." They had rejected requests to be godparents. In the Ilocos region a Chinese storekeeper must accept if a Filipino customer asks him to be a sponsor. "If he refuses, and later the child gets sick, the Chinese is blamed" (Reynolds 1964: 191).

It is unwise for a pregnant Bisayan to refuse a sponsor's offer; her action can result in *gaba* (a curse). As a result of *gaba* she may suffer an abnormal delivery, or her infant may be born with a physical deformity. (*Gaba* is also defined as "sacrilegion, punishment, retribution": Hermosisima and Lopez 1966: 184).

For some Filipinos intraclass compadrinazgo ideally requires that the baptismal sponsor be a volunteer. Parents are honored by the unsolicited selection of their child, the volunteer by their gratitude. The necessity of seeking a sponsor, even at their own socioeconomic level, may honor the selectee, but it often embarrasses the parents. This attitude was particularly prevalent in Caticugan. Caticugan parents were so loath to admit they had to seek baptismal sponsors and were not sought out by volunteers that most of them did not tell the full truth when asked. In the initial stages of our first survey, 98 percent of the sponsors for several hundred godchildren were, according to their parents, volunteers. Bias was recognized when the survey began to produce known inaccuracies, such as parents claiming that compadres had been volunteers when actually they had been sought out.

A second survey, using a different sample, was made in which informants were asked if they had volunteered or had been asked to serve as baptismal sponsors. It was reasoned they would not be embarrassed to report honestly that they had volunteered or hesitate to state that they were asked to be godparents. This second survey showed that sponsorship of nearly 25 percent of these informants' godchildren (44 out of 180) was the result of parental requests. Another reason most Caticuganers were reluctant to report that many compadres were selectees was that nearly one out of every two baptismal sponsors was a kinsman. Ideally, kinsmen should volunteer their assistance and not have to be asked. As might be expected, three out of every four of the

Siaton elite who served as baptismal sponsors had been requested by the child's parents (see Table 7).

TABLE 7

Means of Procuring Siaton Elite as Baptism and Marriage Sponsors: 1972

Persons Requesting	Baptism	Marriage
Parents	102	—
Groom	—	27
Groom's Parents	—	37
Bride	—	6
Bride's Parents	—	11
Volunteer	29	—
Others	—	10*
Totals	131	91

*For groom includes municipal councilors (4), barrio captain, groom's sister, cousin of bridal pair, bride and groom, and for an eloping pair the municipal judge. One bride secured a male sponsor by asking the sponsor's wife.

For marriage sponsorship, none of the Siaton elite volunteered. However, Caticugan informants said marriage sponsors often volunteer. In the barrio the decision regarding marriage sponsors is made during the *integral,* the period after the dower has been delivered to the bride's family and before the banns are posted at the poblacion church.

The reluctance of Caticugan parents to admit that they often had to seek baptismal sponsors for their children generally was not shared by Lalawigan residents. Several reasons may explain the latter's willingness to disclose their need to seek godparents. First, only occasionally did relatives sponsor children in Lalawigan. Second, a smaller percentage (16 percent) of parents had to seek sponsors for their child's baptism than in Caticugan. Lastly, Lalawignons had another alternative for obtaining sponsors—the escort system. A survey indicated that 40 percent of the sponsors were secured through this impersonal technique (see Table 9).

Lalawigan Escort System

In the recent past, escorts (*upod*) were used by Lalawigan parents not only to take their child to Boroñgan for the christening but also to seek sponsors at the church before the ceremony. These escorts were always women ("for they know how to feed the baby") and usually were close friends or relatives of the child's parents. Once at the Boroñgan church, the escort obtained a sponsor in one of several ways. Some sponsors were secured by "trading," with each of two escorts agreeing to sponsor the child the other brought. A sponsor might also be obtained by the escort's promise later to return the favor. Others became godparents because they "pitied" a child whose escort was having a difficult time finding a sponsor, or because they were an intimate friend of the escort.

Lalawigan parents paid the bus fare of the escort and gave her money for the baptismal fee in case she was unable to find a sponsor and had to serve herself. This system was stopped when the present parish priest established residence in Lalawigan. Today he also requires at least one of the parents to be present at their child's baptism in the barrio chapel.

The escort system was an impersonal means of obtaining sponsors and had certain advantages for Lalawignons. First, if no volunteer appeared, one did not have to seek locally for a sponsor. Sponsors obtained at the church by the escort rarely returned to Lalawigan with their new godchild. This saved the parents bus fare and the cost of a fancy baptismal party. Some food was always served the escort, even if she was not the child's sponsor, but the repast might by merely a few glasses of *tubâ* and a dish of *kinilaw* (raw fish mixed with strong vinegar and chopped onions).

Second, the escort system helped restrict the proliferation of compadre relationships. In many instances the child's sponsor and its parents were strangers; they might never meet one another. As in Mexico, persons were "selected [as sponsors] with whom no real functional ties are anticipated, i.e., who fulfill the letter but not the spirit of the institution" (Foster 1969: 274).

Lalawigan's Pinalit Nga Relacion

A unique way to secure ritual kinsmen in the Philippines (at least it is unknown in Siaton and unreported in the literature) occurs in

Lalawigan and is called *pinalit nga relacion,* or "purchased relationship." This ritual bond is created when a "sponsor" who is also a close
friend returns to the parents all or part of a child's baptismal fee years
after the christening.

Bride in front of the Siaton church immediately after wedding.

Several examples from Lalawigan will further clarify the concept
of *pinalit nga relacion.* Two Lalawigan men, Peping and Valentin, were
good friends: "We always attend the cockpit together." They wanted
to be compadres, "so we can call each other *padi.*" Yet all their children
had been baptized. Peping volunteered to be a sponsor for another
person's child, and Valentin helped him with the baptismal fee, although he did not go to the church. In this manner, Peping and Valentin
became "real *padi.*"

In another instance an itinerant peddler regularly stayed with one
family when passing through Lalawigan. After several years, the peddler and the householder became close friends and wanted to be compadres. The peddler, however, had no children, and the host's children
were already baptized. The peddler gave the father of the child money
equal to the original baptismal fee for the boy, purchased a little *tubâ*
for a small "drinking party" (limited to the peddler, the householder,
and his wife), and the two began addressing each other as *padi.*

Similarly, one woman said that four of her children had "purchased" godparents; one *pinalit* sponsor returned one-third of the baptismal fee; each of another two returned half of the fee; and the fourth
sponsor gave nearly twice the original amount. The purpose in returning part or all of a child's past baptismal fee to the parent is that this
gift binds the ritual kinship relationship. By giving back all or part of
the baptismal fee, the compadre relationship is "sealed."

Several Lalawigan *pinalit* compadres had been sweethearts but had not married one another. They became compadres to continue their former friendship and to raise it above suspicion after their marriage. The ritual linkage with the godchild, or the godchild's parents in the case of co-sponsors, was of minor importance compared with the significance of their compadre bond.

Pinalit compadres are regarded in Lalawigan as "regular" compadres. In fact, some informants claimed such compadres were more intimate with one another than selectees who "are not real compadres in the heart, for they had to be asked." The affectionate nature of this *pinalit* relationship appears similar to the Latin American *compadre de corazón* (of the heart) "reserved for relationships of true friendship" and "usually ritualized by one of the more serious forms" (Pitt-Rivers 1968: 412).

Caticugan's Baptismal Union

Catholic sodalities are the most numerous, stable, and active non-kin-based voluntary associations in Lalawigan and Siaton. In Siaton their members predominantly are female residents of the poblacion, although people from Caticugan and other nearby barrios also belong. Several community improvement clubs were also organized in the poblacion, but after a few meetings they faded into inactivity. There are also three Siaton burial associations. An individual contribution of twenty five to fifty centavos is made on the death of a member, member's spouse, or child. In 1950 the total membership (both men and women) of these three burial associations was 172 persons. About 65 percent of the members lived in the poblacion, 9 percent in Caticugan, and the remainder in other nearby barrios.

The only active barrio-based nonelective association in Caticugan is the *union* (Sp. *union*), a largely nonkin association of both married and single men and women. The *union's* sole aim is to help its members sponsor baptisms at a reduced cost. Before the Second World War the Siaton baptismal fee was one peso ($.50). In 1951 the fee had doubled, and by 1964 it was 3.50 pesos ($.90). If a baptism is held at other than the usual time (after high mass on Sunday morning) the fee is increased to 5.00 pesos.

The first *union* was organized in Caticugan as one direct result of this christening fee increase. Normally a *union* is started by a person who wishes to sponsor a child but needs financial assistance. A *union* has from four to as many as ten members. Each person contributes an equal amount toward the cost of sponsoring a baptism. The money is given to the member who sponsors the child. Only this member attends the christening. None of the others is considered to be a godparent of the infant. Once every member has sponsored a godchild, the *union* is *tangkô* (Ceb. completed or finished). The group either disbands or begins another cycle of individual sponsorships. Sometimes the members contribute more than the cost of a baptism. The extra money may be used to buy *tubâ* for a small informal party for the members.

Some Caticugan barriofolk disapprove of the *union* since sponsors do not always tell the parents of their membership. Although only one *union* member goes to the church, some parents feel obligated to invite the others to the baptismal meal. Sometimes the surprised host is embarrassed by unexpected *union* guests. As in Moche, "non-invitees are not encouraged 'just to drop in' at this baptismal meal" (Gillin 1947: 106). Several informants claimed they rejected the request of a volunteer sponsor because of *union* membership. (*Unions* are not formed to sponsor a confirmation or marriage, and there are none in Lalawigan.)

Another technique for reducing the cost of sponsoring a baptism was reported by an Ilokan informant. When two persons wish to sponsor the same child, the given name of the first sponsor and the family name of the second sponsor are recorded on the baptismal certificate. As a result, only one sponsor pays the fee, but the parents consider both to be godparents of their child and compadres.

Baptismal Meal and Sponsor Selection

Providing the traditional meal following a christening is a primary responsibility of the child's parents. The amount of money they can or are willing to spend for this event has an important—often determining —influence on the selection of the baptismal sponsors. One Filipino sociologist has described the importance of the baptismal feast in the Philippines.

> The christening of a baby boy will be looked upon as a crisis which will necessitate all kinds of sacrifice. . . . The feast ended, the host finds himself three or four hundred pesos in debt, which usually is transformed into a life debt. . . . When the days have passed and lingering memories of his hospitality are waning, with pride and air typical of our country folk, he

explains: "When my boy was baptized, I fed the whole neighborhood"
(Macaraig 1929: 52–53).

Today, more than forty years later, the elaborateness and cost of the
typical baptismal meal in Caticugan and Lalawigan are less. Some celebrations, however, approach this ideal. In 1965, one Caticugan family
killed a cow and several pigs and purchased enough beer and *guhang*
(a mild alcoholic beverage made from the buri palm's sap) to serve about
seventy-five guests, including the Siaton mayor. In Siaton one financially pressed elite family delayed their child's baptism for nearly a year
until they were able to serve a large feast commensurate with their
social standing. In Canaman the christening may be delayed for the
same financial reasons (Arce 1973: 53).

*Bride and groom, sponsors and friends, with string band, returning to Caticugan after
wedding in Siaton.*

The baptismal meal's importance in Siaton is symbolized by its
name, *bautismo* (Sp. baptism). In Samaran there is no special term for
the baptismal party. *Panagtawo* is the general Samaran word for feast
or party; the phrase *panagtawo han pabunyag* is used to indicate a

baptismal party. In Tagalog the baptismal meal is called *handaan* (Eggan 1956 2: 649). However, *handaan* appears to have the same meaning as *panagtawo; pabinyag* is a more appropriate Tagalog term.

As in Latin America, godparents in Manalad often help with the baptismal feast (food donations) or later entertain their new compadres (Sibley 1958: 67). But such assistance is a custom neither in Caticugan nor in Lalawigan, nor apparently elsewhere in the Philippines. New Filipino godparents also do not entertain their new compadres after the christening meal as frequently is done in Latin America.

The baptismal meal in the Philippines does not have the formal legitimizing function (e.g., the *abrazo*) it has in parts of Latin America. The only information on a similar practice was related by a Siaton informant who was born and reared in Tanjay. In Tanjay the sponsor returns from the church to the child's house after the christening. On entering the dwelling, he is met by the parents. Kneeling in front of the child's mother and father, he offers the infant, saying: "*Pare* and *mare*, here is our child who has just received the Holy Baptism." One of the parents replies, on accepting the child: "May the Lord bind our relationship so close that from now on we shall feel as brothers and sisters do."

The expense of a fancy baptismal meal is also one important reason relatives become christening sponsors in Latin America. In Cherán kinsmen rarely are sought as sponsors. When they are, "the reason usually is a desire to save money, as between relatives there need be no ceremony or expense" (Beals 1946: 103). Tzintzuntzan parents normally have friends as the baptismal sponsors for their first several children. However, relatives may sponsor these children if the parents are poor because "it is more economical to have relatives rather than friends" (Foster 1969: 275).

In the past, more than today, the baptismal meal was almost an absolute requisite for the christening in both Lalawigan and Caticugan. Although the ideal baptismal meal today is an elaborate feast, some are simple affairs, attended only by the godchild's immediate family, the sponsor (and spouse, if married), and a few intimate friends and relatives. Some Siaton sponsors are bought an inexpensive meal in a poblacion cafe, particularly when the parents live in a distant barrio and the sponsor resides in the poblacion or a nearby village. Spiraling prices were given in 1972 as a major reason why an increasing number of Caticugancrs were omitting the baptismal meal. A meal rarely follows confirmation in the rural Philippines, but nearly every marriage ends with an elaborate wedding feast—in Caticugan at the residences of both the bride and the groom.

On Luzon, "among the poor [Tagalogs], relatives are usually chosen because in such a case the expenses entailed [for the baptismal party] need not be so great as when outsiders are asked to take part" (Cruz 1958: 214). Similarly, the embarrassment that results when Lalawigan or Caticugan parents can serve only a simple baptismal meal is lessened when relatives are sponsors. One can offer a sparing meal to a kinsman-sponsor that served to a nonkin sponsor would mean loss of self-esteem. In fact, some sponsors remarked that they volunteered to sponsor a kinsman because they wanted to save the family the cost of an expensive baptismal party. Demands on the ceremonial funds of peasants are great, and their material resources are extremely limited (Wolf 1966a: 7). And as in other peasant societies, kinsmen are a major resource in the rural Philippines.

About 40 percent of the baptismal sponsors for a sample of Lalawigan godchildren were obtained by the escort at the Borongan church (see Table 9). Since these sponsors often were strangers to the child's parents and lived in other communities, they normally did not return to Lalawigan for a baptismal feast. The parents were spared not only the cost of this meal but also the sponsor's bus fare to the barrio. This saving was a major factor that encouraged many parents to secure sponsors in this impersonal manner.

The same pattern regarding frequency of social celebrations following the major sacraments exists in Dumaguete. Most parents (62 percent of all the respondents) had a baptismal party, but only 13 percent had a meal after confirmation. "For marriages reported in the questionnaire, an impressive 91 percent were followed by a *kumbira* [party with food and drink]" (Potter 1973: 15). Although not all Caticuganers today have a baptismal feast, this party is more essential to them than to many residents in Dumaguete.

In Caticugan, as reported, kinsmen-sponsors often are sought so the christening party could be less elaborate, reducing its cost for the parents. Potter found that "about one-fourth of all rites include relatives as sponsors; yet only one-fifth of the rites without *kumbira* include kinsmen-sponsors" (1973: 317–18). Apparently Dumagueteños do not regularly seek kinsmen-sponsors to eliminate the baptismal feast. However, what was not investigated in Dumaguete was whether the *kumbira* for non-kinsmen sponsors was more lavish than the party the parents held for sponsors who were relatives. It is possible that Dumagueteños do not need to seek kinsmen sponsors to reduce the cost of the christening since cash is more available in the city than in Caticugan. This is also one possible explanation for the scarcity of kinsmen-sponsors in the Ecuadorian city of Manta (Middleton 1975: 466).

Another group of Filipinos who participate in christening and marriage ceremonies and the subsequent parties are known as *damas*. They usually are close friends who are selected by the baptismal and wedding sponsors; some sponsors may have as many as ten *damas*. They assist the sponsors during the rite and also share part of the cost of sponsorship. Although they are regarded as witnesses, no ritual kinship ties are created between the *damas* and any of the participants in the ceremonies. The only instance of the use of *damas* reported in the literature is for Cabetican (Santico 1973: 26).

Intermediaries

Intermediaries often are used in Latin America by parents seeking a baptismal sponsor (Nader 1969b: 410; Gillin 1947: 107; Ravicz 1967: 245; and Redfield and Villa Rojas 1962: 185–86). In Hulo and Esperanza intermediaries are employed to approach possible elite baptismal sponsors (Hollnsteiner 1967: 206–7; Pal 1956a: 380). In Esperanza a child's "kinsman-spokesman" may indirectly suggest to a higher status person the possiblity of sponsorship ("to kneel for the child"). The suggestion is delicately phrased, implying that the request comes from the speaker, not the child's parents. Consequently, if the higher status person does not accept the hint, no one is embarrassed. In Suba an intermediary may be used if a desired sponsor is "hard to talk to." Another reason for the use of an intermediary in Suba is that most sponsors are poor, and acceptance requires payment of the cost of the formal baptism. This indirect approach makes it easier for the person asked to reject the request, and it also protects him from feeling "ashamed" of his poverty.

Caticugan and Lalawigan parents rarely use intermediaries in seeking sponsors. When intermediaries are employed, the parents usually seek a prominent member of the poblacion elite as a sponsor. (A Lalawigan escort was not regarded as an intermediary since she sought a sponsor in her own name.) But since intermediaries are a common feature of intraclass marriage negotiations in Caticugan and Lalawigan, their use does not always indicate interclass relationships.

Villagers carrying bride across Siaton river to Caticugan.

Parents may also extend to others the privilege of selecting sponsors. In Estancia the primary sponsor may be permitted to suggest or to select additional sponsors. For example, the parents may let the first sponsor ask others to act as co-sponsors. Or the primary sponsor may suggest to the parents names of additional persons whom they ask to serve as sponsors. In either instance this enables the primary sponsors, selected by the parents, to choose persons with whom they personally wish to have a ritual kinship relationship (Szanton 1972: 112). Extending this privilege to primary sponsors not only honors them but also assures their acceptance. Primary sponsors in Cabetican may also select their co-sponsors (Santico 1973: 25).

Residences and Sponsor Selection

Most people seek the persons to become their ritual kinsmen almost entirely among members of their own community. Others, however, purposely seek sponsors at some distance from their village to protect their ritual relationships from possible abuse or disruption through overly intimate daily contact or to secure patrons who usually reside in towns. (This aspect of compadrinazgo is analyzed in greater detail in Chapter Eight.) The following section documents the residential patterns of ritual kinsmen of the inhabitants of the three communities studied. Further, it explains why most lived outside Lalawigan, Caticugan, and Siaton poblacion. For these Bisayan communities, compadrinazgo is largely a centrifugal social force, not a centripetal one (see Table 8).

TABLE 8

Where Ritual Kinsmen of Lalawignons, Caticuganers,
and the Siaton Elite Resided[1]

Lalawignons		Caticuganers		Siaton Elite	
Where Ritual Kinsmen Resided	*% of Total*	*Where Ritual Kinsmen Resided*	*% of Total*	*Where Ritual Kinsmen Resided*	*% of Total*
Boroñgan Municipality		Siaton Municipality		Siaton Municipality	
Lalawigan	31	*Caticugan*	38	*Caticugan*	4
Poblacion	16	*Poblacion*	27	*Poblacion*	34
Other localities	20	*Other localities*	24	*Other localities*	35
	67		89		73
Other Municipalities, Eastern Samar Province	32	Other Municipalities, Negros Oriental Province	9	Other Municipalities, Negros Oriental Province	22
	99		98		95
Outside Eastern Samar Province	1	Outside Negros Oriental Province	2	Outside Negros Oriental Province	5
	100		100		100

[1]All percentages are rounded. In 1956, Samar was a single province. However, all ritual kinsmen of Lalawignons resided in what today is Eastern Samar province except those living in Catbalogan (Western Samar province). Data for Table 8 are based on Tables 9 and 10.

Lalawigan

According to sample surveys in these communities, most of the ritual kinsmen of the residents of Lalawigan, Caticugan, and the Siaton elite did not reside in their respective communities (see Tables 9 and 10). Sixty-nine percent of the 281 ritual kinsmen (through baptism) of Lalawignons lived outside the village, while 36 percent lived in other communities but in Boroñgan municipality (see Map 3). The three communities furnishing the most sponsors were, in rank order, Boroñgan, Dolores, and Maypangdan. (The last two localities are north of Boroñgan municipality.)

There were numerous reasons why a substantial share (16 percent of the total) of these ritual kinsmen lived in Boroñgan. Boroñgan was the place where most of the essential services and goods required by the people were concentrated. *Suki* bonds were sought with vendors in the public marketplace and with town merchants. These dyadic relationships often were strengthened through compadrinazgo. The sponsors whom escorts found were mostly town residents, since baptisms in the municipality, at this time, were ordinarily held only in the poblacion church. Most of the potential elite sponsors for Lalawignons resided in Boroñgan.

Moreover, if one wanted sponsors from other barrios or towns, the logical time and place to seek them was at Sunday baptisms in Boroñgan. For example, one Lalawigan woman said that she had no kinsmen in Maydolong, a village eight miles south of Lalawigan, and that she "felt uncomfortable visiting this barrio." One Sunday she searched before baptisms began at the Boroñgan church until she found a child from this barrio and volunteered to be its sponsor. "Now I won't be hesitant to go to Maydolong, particularly during the fiesta."

It might seem surprising that so many sponsors (7 percent) of Lalawignons lived in distant Dolores, nearly forty-five miles north of the barrio. (Dolores is the name of both the municipality and its poblacion.) However, Dolores is the place where most Lalawignons who own agricultural land have their rice fields. Other Lalawignons go there annually to help, on a share basis, in the rice harvest or to buy new rice. Furthermore, many barriofolk who live in Lalawigan were born in Dolores, while the spouses of others came from this municipality. The Dolores fiesta is a gala event for these Lalawignons. Thus, there were many social and economic reasons for seeking sponsors in this municipality, although it was a five-hour bus ride north of Lalawigan.

Sponsors (7 percent of them) were also sought from Maypangdan, a barrio about nine miles north of Lalawigan, because this community is locally noted for its nipa shingles. Having a compadre in Maypangdan made it easier, and often cheaper, to purchase shingles that frequently were in short supply in Lalawigan. Six percent of the ritual kinsmen of Lalawignons resided in Suribao, south of Lalawigan; the residents of this village raised excellent vegetables and were the local suppliers of rattan and lumber. As one informant explained: "Lalawignons often prefer sponsors from these two villages [Maypangdan and Suribao] so they can buy these products at lower prices—sometimes they may get them free from their *padi* or *madi*."

There are various reasons for the relatively large number of sponsors from Locso-on. Locso-on is the nearest community south of Lalawigan; its fiesta is locally popular, so many visiting Lalawignons "pledge to be sponsors at the drinking sprees that occur during this celebration." Locso-on residents also fish off the coast of Lalawigan, and many of their farms are adjacent to the fields of Lalawignons. As a result, they have many occasions for interaction and many opportunities to be asked or to volunteer as sponsors.

TABLE 9

Baptismal Sponsors: Their Residences and Means
of Procurement: Lalawigan: 1956

| Sponsors' Residence[1] | Population 1960 | Selectees | | Volunteers | Total |
		Parental	Escort		
Bato	894	2	3	5	10
Boroñgan+	3,970	6	23	17	46
Cabong	583	2	4	5	11
Can-abong	392	1	2	3	6
Can-avid*	2,209	1	—	—	1
Catbalogan+	14,274	—	2	1	3
Divinubo	386	7	5	1	13
Dolores*	4,151	3	7	9	19
Guiuan*	5,865	1	—	—	1
LALAWIGAN	1,225	14	20	53	87
Liboton	667	—	2	—	2
Llorente*	5,079	1	5	5	11
Locso-on	631	2	9	5	16
Maybacong	150	—	3	—	3
Maydolong*	2,502	—	1	3	4
Maypangdan	782	2	10	6	18
Omawas	750	2	2	—	4
Punta Maria	—	—	1	—	1
Santa Fe	787	—	—	1	1
Suribao	—	1	11	4	16
Tabok	772	—	—	6	6
Tabunan	832	—	2	—	2
Totals	—	45 (16%)	112 (40%)	124 (44%)	281 (100%)

[1]Communities followed by (+) are provincial capitals and by (*) poblacions. The remainder of the communities are either barrios or sitios. Census data are unavailable for sitios.

Most baptismal sponsors of Lalawignons were nonresidents of the community; 36 percent of these sponsors lived in communities within Boroñgan municipality. Lalawigan, in this regard, was oriented primarily northward and to the nearby east (Divinubo Island) if one judges by the total number of sponsors per 1000 population for the localities indicated on Map 3. High ratios persisted as far north as Maypangdan, waned, and then peaked again with Dolores; to the south they continued high only as far as Locso-on. This northward orientation is explained by the overwhelming local importance of Boroñgan, Maypangdan, and Dolores. Furthermore, the national road to the north is the only land route to the urban centers of Catbalogan and eastern Leyte (Tacloban). With a few exceptions, all of the communities listed on Map 3 are located along this national road.

Caticugan

Residential patterns of the godchildren (through baptism and confirmation) of Caticuganers reflect basically the same trend reported for Lalawigan. Sixty-two percent of 541 ritual kinsmen resided outside the village, while 51 percent lived in other communities but in Siaton municipality (see Table 10). In this regard these ritual kinsmen are somewhat more heavily concentrated in Siaton municipality than those of Lalawignous are in Boroñgan municipality.

The four communities furnishing the largest percentage of ritual kinsmen for Caticuganers were, in rank order, Siaton poblacion, Sandolot, and Datag and Mantuyop (each the same number). These communities are adjacent to and surround Caticugan (see Map 4). Only the shallow Siaton river divides Caticugan and Datag, while a smaller river separates Caticugan and Mantuyop. Many spouses of Caticuganers came from these communities, especially Datag and Sandolot. Their annual fiestas—the occasion for mass baptisms in their local chapels— were popular with the residents, since they were easily attended and all had kinsmen or close friends living in these villages.

About 55 percent of the godchildren of Caticuganers who lived in Negros Oriental municipalities other than Siaton resided in either Zamboanguita or Dauin. (Zamboanguita is fourteen miles from Siaton, while Dauin is twenty-one miles; both are along the national road to Dumaguete.) But only two godchildren lived in Sta. Catalina and Bayawan, two municipalities west of Siaton, and also bisected by the national road. (Sta. Catalina is twenty-one miles and Bayawan is thirty-one miles from Siaton poblacion.) Public transportation was equally available to all four of these localities. (Sometimes a bus originated in Siaton poblacion for trips to and from Dumaguete, but most bus routes were round-trips between Dumaguete and Bayawan. Occasionally, however, buses from Dumaguete were so crowded that they did not stop at Siaton poblacion enroute to the western municipalities).

Why did Caticuganers have more ritual kinsmen in the two eastern

Residences (at Time of Sponsorship) of Godchildren
of Caticuganers (1965) and Siaton Elite (1972)

| | | Numbers | | |
Residences[1]	Population 1960[2]	Caticugan Baptism-Confirmation	Siaton Baptism	Marriage
Siaton				
Municipality				
Apoloy	277	—	1	—
Balanan[+]	—	3	—	—
Bonawon	4,179	1	8	9
Bonbonon	1,117	3	2	4
Bugwal[+]	—	1	—	—
Cabangahan	1,001	3	4	7
Canaway	1,305	3	1	2
Candugay[+]	—	1	—	—
Casala-an	1,010	3	—	1
CATICUGAN	910	205	2	4
Danao[+]	—	1	—	—
Datag	665	23	—	1
Dulog[+]	—	3	—	—
Giliga-on	1,751	1	1	5
Inalad	1,201	5	3	1
Lamtok[+]	—	4	—	—
Lico-Lico[+]	—	3	—	—
Malabuhan[+]	—	2	9	—
Maladpad[+]	—	1	—	—
Maloh	899	2	4	—
Mantuyop	1,304	23	5	4
Nagba[+]	—	3	—	3
Nahunyod[+]	—	1	—	—
Naloy[+]	—	1	—	—
Nasig-id[+]	—	3	—	—
Odlum[+]	—	1	—	—
Omanod[+]	—	—	2	—
POBLACION	2,862	145	56	20
Salag[+]	—	1	1	—
Sandolot	617	29	—	—
San Jose[+]	—	2	—	—
Somolok[+]	—	2	—	—
Sumaliring	1,517	—	2	—
Tagima[+]	—	2	—	—
Tampaga[+]	—	1	—	—
Tayak	528	1	—	—

TABLE 10 *(Continued)*

Residences (at Time of Sponorship) of Godchildren
of Caticuganers (1935) and Siaton Elite (1972)

Residences[1]	Population 1960[2]	Numbers		
		Caticugan Baptism-Confirmation	Siaton Baptism	Marriage
Other Negros *Oriental* *Municipalities*[3]				
Amlan	1,532	1	—	—
Bacong	1,671	2	—	—
Bais	5,058	1	—	3
Bayawan	6,204	1	4	1
Dauin	1,606	11	—	—
Sibulan	1,755	1	—	4
Siquijor	696	—	—	1
Sta. Catalina	3,733	1	9	1
Tanjay	12,355	1	—	2
Valencia	955	1	—	—
Zamboanguita	4,099	13	1	—
DUMAGUETE	35,282	11	9	12
Other Provinces, *Cities, and* *Islands*				
Bacolod	119,315	1	—	—
Cebu	—	3	—	2
Luzon (and Manila)	—	1	5	—
Mindanao	—	—	1	3
Residences unknown	—	8	—	1
Totals	—	540	130	91

[1]Sign + indicates a sitio; with the exception of the poblacion all other communities for Siaton municipality are barrios.
[2]Census data are not collected for sitios.
[3]Population figures are for poblacions.

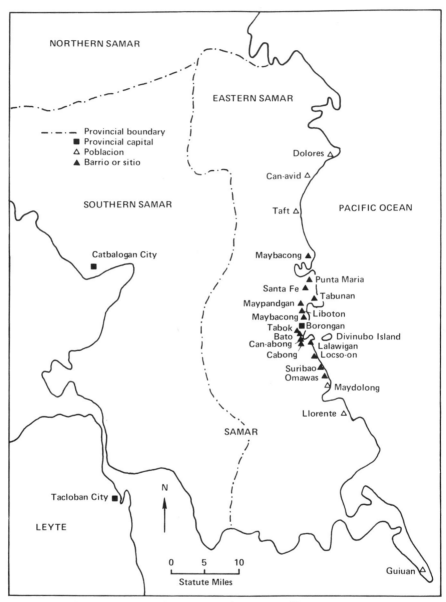

Map 3: *Residences of Baptismal Sponsors, Lalawigan: 1956.*

municipalities than in those to the west? The annual fiestas of Zamboanguita and Dauin are traditionally popular with Caticuganers—and with residents of the poblacion. They attract far more visitors from Siaton than do the fiestas of St. Catalina and Bayawan. As mentioned earlier, fiestas are occasions for baptisms in these communities. Zamboanguita and Dauin are also more important spouse-furnishing communities for Caticuganers than Sta. Catalina and Bayawan. For this reason the villagers have more kinsmen in these localities to visit, not only during the fiestas but for other ceremonies, e.g., anniversary celebrations for the dead, funerals, etc.

Moreover, many people from Zamboanguita and Dauin come to Siaton, including Caticugan, for the annual corn (and rice) harvest. Since they stay in the area until the end of the harvest, they may during this time be asked to serve as sponsors. Local baptisms often are arranged to coincide with the harvest period when food is more plentiful. This seasonal interchange of people during the fiesta and harvest times is less extensive between Sta. Catalina and Bayawan. Bayawan is the "rice bowl" for southern Negros. A labor shortage usually occurs during harvest, but outside, temporary workers come mainly from Sta. Catalina.

Compadrinazgo is almost totally ineffective in ritually relating the peasants of Caticugan and Lalawigan to inhabitants living beyond their home provinces. Only 1 percent of the ritual kinsmen of Lalawignons lived outside eastern Samar, and all were obtained when the latter once resided in Catbalogan. This situation is duplicated for Caticuganers, for whom only 2 percent of their ritual kinsmen lived outside Negros Oriental province. In every instance when a godchild lived in another province (or island), the godparent once worked (e.g., as a maid or laborer) in that locality or lived there before moving to the village.

Siaton Elite

About the same percentage (36 percent) of 221 godchildren of the Siaton elite resided in the poblacion. There is also a similar geographical dispersion of these godchildren, for 39 percent lived in Siaton municipality and 95 percent in Negros Oriental province. It was thought that the elites in other municipalities frequently might seek Siaton elites as sponsors, but this was not true.

There are, however, two major differences between the distribution of residences of the ritual kinsmen of the Siaton elite and Caticuganers. First, the elite's godchildren (living in Negros Oriental) are

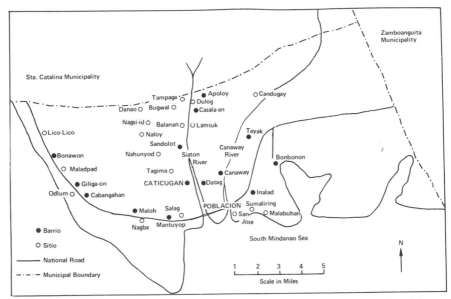

Map 4: *Siaton Municipality Residences of Godchildren of Caticuganers (1965) and Siaton Elite (1972).*

concentrated in fewer communities. Their godchildren live in twenty-six barrios and poblacions; the ritual kinsmen of Caticuganers resided in forty-three different communities. Second, nearly one-half of the godchildren of Caticuganers lived in twenty different sitios (a small cluster of dwellings, usually isolated from the national road), while the ritual kinsmen of the elite lived in only three such communities.

Since nearly all of the elite's godchildren resided either in barrios or in poblacions along the national road, their parents were more easily able to have frequent contacts with the elite in Siaton poblacion, for buses daily passed through their communities. It is also reasonable to assume (although no specific data were gathered on this topic) that most of these parents were more prosperous, socially prominent, and politically active than the majority of the ritual kinsmen of Caticuganers who resided in barrios and sitios, the latter usually isolated from the national road.

This residential pattern can be vividly illustrated by examining the compadrinazgo relationships of Caticuganers with those of the residents of the Siaton river valley. The narrow Siaton river valley extends northward ten miles toward the mountainous forested interior of southern Negros. No road parallels this valley. Movement north or south in the valley is by foot; during the rainy season travel is extremely difficult, for the flooded river must be forded in a dozen places between Apoloy in the north and Caticugan. Yet in this valley, fourteen communities, mainly sitios, were the residences of seventy-five godchildren of Caticuganers but of only three godchildren of the Siaton elite.

Caticuganers often visited these more remote communities to obtain forest products (rattan, bamboo, house posts, etc.) or to tend their swiddens in the hills in both sides of the river. They were frequently volunteer workers for the corn harvests of the valley. There were numerous advantages in having compadres in these barrios and sitios, e.g., a place to stay overnight when securing forest products, assistance in obtaining and hauling bamboo and logs to the village, etc. Their fiestas were well-attended by Caticuganers.

Most residents of the more remote communities in the valley rarely visited the poblacion. Their fiestas were not popular with the elite, for they were relatively simple and one had to walk to them, not ride. Only a handful of their children graduate from the complete elementary school (grades one through six) in the poblacion. A frequent sight was a small group from the northern part of the valley carrying their dead in bamboo coffins—regarded by many as symbol of their poverty and "backwardness"—to the poblacion church for burial services. Their residences were humble (often thatched with cogon grass, not nipa palm), and their annual cash income was pitifully meager.

Undoubtedly, the lack of transportation facilities in the Siaton valley explains, in part, the few ritual kinsmen the elite had in this region. The valley residents, however, would have been extremely reluctant to approach the more sophisticated elite to sponsor their children. Moreover, the elite had few economic or social interests in the valley that made ritual kinship with valley-dwellers desirable.

How typical the residential patterns of ritual kinsmen to the people of these three Bisayan communities are of the rest of the Philippines is unknown for lack of data. For Canaman the pattern would appear to be different since most sponsors resided in this town, and often were neighbors (Arce 1973: 68). However, since the upper class in Canaman is small, they often had to seek elite sponsors in other towns—sometimes as distant as Manila. Most sponsors of the barriofolk of Camangahan were kinsmen-residents, although in Manalad the desire for patron sponsors for weddings required looking for ritual kinsmen beyond this village.

The ideal and real contribution of compadrinazgo in developing significant social networks in southern Negros and eastern Samar may be broadly illustrated by a series of expanding concentric circles. The center, the smallest circle, is the village or poblacion. About one-third of the ritual kinsmen of the inhabitants of the three communities studied are also local residents. Outside this circle (an oval for eastern Samar) is a larger one, composed of sitios and barrios in the same municipality. For Lalawignons and the Siaton elite, an additional one-third of their ritual kinsmen live in these communities. The exception is that slightly more than one-half of the ritual kinsmen of Caticuganers resided in this intermediate region. This asymmetry is largely the result of Caticuganers' contacts with the people in the Siaton river valley; west of Lalawigan's boundaries are rugged, thinly inhabited uplands. Lastly, the final and largest circle, encompassing other municipalities of the province, is more variable. About one-third of the ritual kinsmen of Lalawignons lived in this outer ring, about one-fifth of those of Caticuganers, and slightly less than one-tenth of those of the Siaton elite. Beyond their provinces, Lalawignons and Caticuganers had only a few scattered ritual kinsmen (most likely of little or no functional importance); the number for the Siaton elite is somewhat larger, but not significantly so.

It is difficult to explain with certitude some asymmetrical features of the spatial distribution of ritual kinsmen of the people of these Bisayan communities. Probably the larger number of godchildren of the Siaton elite (in comparison with those of Caticugan) residing outside Siaton municipality and Negros Oriental province is the result of the former's greater mobility and increased sociopolitical contact. (Four of the five godchildren living in Manila were sponsored by an elite member when he resided in the capital.) Possibly the reason Caticuganers had a larger percentage of godchildren living in Siaton poblacion (in comparison with Lalawignons for Borongan poblacion) is that the town is near the village. One can walk from Caticugan to Siaton poblacion in about twenty minutes. From Lalawigan to Borongan (in 1956) was a thirty-minute, twenty-five centavo fare ride, with buses running only infrequently between the two communities and never at night.

Yet ease of contact with external communities is not always the determinant of multiple compadrinazgo relationships for these peasants. For example, Zamboanguita and Dauin, Sta. Catalina and Bayawan are localities each approximately equally accessible to the barriofolk of Caticugan. However, for reasons already cited, Caticuganers have many more ritual kinsmen in the first pair of places than in the latter pair. Finally, the relatively large number of ritual kinsmen of Caticugan-

Bridal pair leaving the church after their wedding. When strings attached to the bell were pulled, pigeons flew outside.

ers in many an isolated sitio of the Siaton river valley is not because such places can be reached by a quick, inexpensive bus trip.

Normally, most Bisayans do not select (and the sponsors do not volunteer to be) ritual kinsmen for a single motive. Age, sex, kinship, friendship, economic and political advantages, residential location, and traditional ties among communities are often important factors in influencing the spatial distribution of ritual kinsmen. However, motivation is so complex that in many instances none of these qualities is of any importance, as evidenced by the former escort system of Lalawignons and the practice of Filipinos in all these communities of obtaining sponsors, often strangers, shortly before baptism and confirmation ceremonies at the church.

Compadrinazgo's primary importance for Lalawignons, Caticuganers, and the Siaton elite is not to increase their economic security or to reaffirm their social status among members of their own communities. Instead, its most significant function is to establish ritual ties between themselves and individuals in nearby sitios and barrios who control desired economic resources. Other functions are to strengthen traditional bonds of intercommunity cooperation and hospitality and to create or maintain bonds for the other purposes already stated. Compadrinazgo in these three Philippine communities is municipality-oriented; most ritual kinsmen evidently are more valuable when they live outside one's own village but close enough to be helpful when the occasion or crisis arises.

Middleton explains that in urban Manta the spatial extension of ritual kinship ties beyond one's immediate residence is also more important than their intensity. "The value of social and spatial extension is that it transforms interpersonal relationships in the wider society into predictable social ones, through which various exchanges of respect, information, and economic tokens take place" (1975: 472). As the previous information indicates, this is a major function of compadrinazgo for most Catucaganers and Lalawignons. In Manta, as in one Guatemalan city, these extended "linkages are likely to decay because changes in status, residence, and occupation occur regularly" (Middleton 1975: 472; also Roberts 1973: 14). However, with the greater stability of socioeconomic conditions in southern Negros and eastern Samar, and the decreased mobility of the residents, these compadrinazgo bonds are more constant and dependable.

Non-Catholic Compadrinazgo in Siaton

The godparenthood complex is associated not only with the Catholic church but also with some Philippine non-Catholic and Protestant churches. Ritual kinship is an essential aspect of social relations in Malitbog, a Panayan barrio of over 1,000 peasants who are predominantly Protestants (Jocano 1969: 12, 192–93). Elsewhere in the Philippines, non-Catholic Filipinos have retained compadrinazgo. Aglipayans (or members of the Philippine Independent Church) have preserved compadrinazgo rites (Szanton 1972: 114). One brief comment is made that this ritual kinship system differs among the various Protestant denominations (Cortez 1965: 20). Unfortunately, published information about the ritual kinship system of Protestant (and non-Catholic) Filipinos is almost nonexistent.

Whether non-Catholics in the Philippines are permitted to be sponsors of Catholics appears to depend largely upon each local priest, with more permissiveness now than in the past (Eggan 1956 1: 429). The publication of the baptismal rite, as recently revised by decree of the Second Vatican Ecumenical Council, states that "a baptized and believing Christian from a separated church or community may act as a godparent or Christian witness along with a Catholic godparent, at the request of the parents and in accordance with the norms for various ecumenical cases" (*Rite of Baptism for Children* 1971: iii).

Although prohibited in the past, today non-Catholics serve as baptismal and wedding sponsors in Boroñgan. One Protestant member of a provincial government agency is a popular sponsor in Boroñgan. The Siaton priest permits Protestant sponsors so as not "to hurt the feelings of the child's parents" or for "social [and political] purposes," but he asks the Protestant sponsors not to touch the child during the christening, so "they are only honorary sponsors."

Since little is known about non-Catholic compadrinazgo, the association of this ritual kinship with the three different religious groups in Siaton poblacion was examined. The purpose was to discover whether these churches had sponsors for their various rites, how they were selected, and if sponsorship created ritual kinsmen. On the whole, relations between Siaton Catholics and non-Catholics are amicable. Several mayors have been members of the United Church of Christ or were Seventh Day Adventists. Prominent Siaton Protestants are baptismal, confirmation, and marriage sponsors of Catholics. Typically they sponsor children of elite poblacion families. The author, a Protestant, has several godchildren, both Catholic and Protestant.

There are three Protestant or non-Roman Catholic churches in Siaton municipality: the Seventh Day Adventist (whose members are also known as *Sabadistas*, i.e., Sabbatarians), the United Church of Christ in the Philippines, and the *Iglesia ni Kristo* (Church of Christ). According to one aged informant, the first Seventh Day Adventist church was organized in Negros Oriental in 1918 when this informant (living in Siaton) returned home after conversion in Borneo (Sabah). At present there are three churches in Siaton municipality: the poblacion church with about sixty members; the church in Giliga-on with twenty-five members; and a third church located in Maiton (Bonawon), with forty-two members. The first chapel in Siaton poblacion was built in 1948. The present wooden chapel was constructed in the poblacion in 1964.

Seventh Day Adventists in Siaton do not participate in the godparenthood complex. Baptism does not require sponsors, and there is no confirmation ceremony, since baptism makes one a full-fledged member of the church. Marriage is their sole occasion for sponsorship, and the only function of these sponsors is to stand as legal witnesses that no impediments bar the couple's wedding. Since no ritual relationship is created between the couple and their marriage sponsors, compadrinaz-go terminology is not used. Marriage sponsors may be chosen by the couple, their parents, church elders, or the pastor. Volunteer sponsors are rare; individuals volunteer only when a wedding is about to occur and no sponsors have been selected. No incest tabus prevent the later marriage of these persons. Marriage sponsors may give the pastor a small gift of money or help in the cost of the wedding meal.

Guests at wedding in Caticugan. They are eating on the floor of the bride's residence in front of the dais where the newly wedded couple were received earlier.

The *Iglesia ni Kristo* was founded in 1914 by Felix Manalo, who claimed to be a "messenger from God." This indigenous Filipino off-shoot of Christianity synthesizes both Catholic and Protestant doctrines into a tightly-knit authoritarian church with a strong nationalistic appeal. Church officials claim a membership of over two million (Gowing 1967: 212–13).

The first house meetings of the *Iglesia ni Kristo* in Siaton began in 1956. The present small, bamboo, dirt-floored chapel was built in 1958. All but a few members (in 1964) resided in the poblacion. Members of this church often are regarded by other Filipinos as aggressive in promulgating their faith. They are viewed with more covert hostility in Siaton than any other religious group.

In the *Iglesia ni Kristo* the only sponsors are the legal witnesses required for marriage. Baptismal sponsors are unnecessary, since one is not baptized until he is an adult (twelve to fifteen years old). The church does not confirm its members. No compadrinazgo terminology is used by the marriage sponsors and the wedded couple, and no incest tabus prevent their future marriage. Although church members address each other as "brother" and "sister," it is as brother and sister in Christ.

The United Church of Christ in the Philippines was founded in 1948 with the merger of various denominations, e.g., Presbyterian, Congregational, Evangelical United Brethren, Methodist, Disciples of Christ, etc. (Gowing 1967: 196–98). Protestantism in Negros Oriental has a relatively early history, since Silliman University in Dumaguete City was founded in 1901 by the Board of Foreign Missions of the Presbyterian Church of the United States. The first Protestant church in the province was within the university. In 1918, such a church was established in Siaton, although the members had no permanent minister or chapel; a minister from Dumaguete came each Sunday to preach. A number of Siaton elite are members of the United Church of Christ, including the local congressman and several municipal officials.

There is little difference between the ritual kinship systems associated with the Catholic Church and those of the United Church of Christ in Siaton. The major difference is that the Protestant Church has no confirmation, since a person is not baptized until he is an "adult" (twelve to fifteen years old) and is "capable of confirming his faith on his own." Baptismal sponsors ideally should be "second parents" to their godchildren, and marriage sponsors act primarily as witnesses, although they may also later be "advisers" to the couple. Sponsors may be single or married, preferably members of the Church, and must be at least eighteen years old. Marriage sponsors should be older than the bride and groom.

Sponsors in the Church of Christ may be asked or volunteer. For baptism, the parents pay fifty centavos for the baptismal certificate; the baptismal party is also their responsibility. Baptismal gifts may or may not be given the child by his new godparents. Compadrinazgo terminology associated with the godparenthood complex of these Protestants is identical with that of Catholics as already described. The godchild usually addresses his godfather as "Papa" and his godmother as "Mama." Marriage sponsors usually are addressed as *maninoy* (godfather) and *maninay* (godmother) since they are "more witnesses than parents." The "blanketing-in" process does not occur. Godsiblings cannot marry (and no instances of such marriages could be recalled) since they are like "siblings," but unlike the Catholics in Siaton, there is no prohibition against the marriage of compadres.

The official service book for the United Church of Christ makes provision for sponsors.

> When [baptismal] sponsors are chosen they are expected to take a
> special interest in and foster the spirtitual growth of the child. Sponsors
> should not be selected because of any material or social advantage which
> they may give the child (*The Book of Common Worship for Pulpit and
> Parish Use* 1961: 20).

Since United Church of Christ baptism need involve no cost (although
donations are usual), some informants believe these Protestants often
have more sponsors than do most Catholics. In the case of co-sponsorship, the papers are signed only by the "chief" sponsor. Although coun-
seled against the practice, Protestants and non-Catholics in Siaton and
Boroñgan also select patron sponsors. The elaborateness of the Filipino
baptismal feast or wedding reception probably depends less on denomi-
nation than on family socioeconomic status. No special attention was
paid in the research to the possible relationship between compadrinazgo and Protestantism in Latin America. However, Protestants (Assem-
bly of God and Jehovah's Witnesses) in Huaylas do not participate in
compadrinazgo (Doughty 1968: 227).

Conclusion

The purpose of the minimal qualifications for sponsors established
by the Church is to obtain godparents who can assist in, if not guarantee, the godchild's proper Catholic rearing. However, Filipinos (and
other folk Catholics) have set additional requirements for sponsors.
Some of these folk qualifications do not conflict with the Church's
criteria, while others are in opposition to them.

For example, for many Filipinos, pregnancy, certain kinship relationships, or permanent residence in the godchild's household disquali-
fies one as a sponsor. These folk qualifications are not antithetical to
those promulgated by Canon law, and they are not publicly condemned
by the Philippine church. Repeat sponsorship, however, is prohibited
by Canon law (Gudeman 1972: 62), while the practice of some Filipinos
of selecting Protestant sponsors is contrary to the major purpose of
sponsorship insofar as the Church is concerned. It is this opportunity
to add to or to oppose Church qualifications defining eligible sponsors
(according to the occasion) that partly explains the extraordinary plas-
ticity of compadrinazgo.

While the Church's primary reason for sponsors is to contribute to
or, when necessary, to continue the child's Catholic education, this

purpose often is of secondary importance to many Filipinos. For example, a child's baptism may be purposely delayed for months until the parents have sufficient funds to have a christening appropriate to their social position in the community. Strangers may be selected as sponsors, either by the parents shortly before baptism or confirmation or by the person taking the child to the church for the rite. Their religious qualifications, outside of being Catholic, and their sincerity as responsible godparents often are of little importance. Multiple (or patron) sponsors are chosen by the parents primarily for socioeconomic or political reasons. A repeat sponsor's death may leave an adolescent godchild without godparental guidance and support. Most Filipino sponsors know that rarely, if ever, will they be required to assume parental responsibilities for an orphaned godchild. It is this ability of parents to seek sponsors for numerous reasons, in addition to the religious qualifications, that enhances the utility and maintains the viability of compadrinazgo for most Filipinos.

While folk traditions extend the range of potential sponsors, they also restrict choices. The Church decreed certain basic qualifications for sponsors, but it did not establish their means of selection. As a result, the parents' ability to select sponsors often is restricted by folk traditions. As indicated earlier, it is usually difficult, if not impossible, for most parents to refuse an undesirable volunteer sponsor. Parents permit primary sponsors to select co-sponsors for their child's baptism or confirmation. The selection of sponsors by impoverished parents may be limited to close kinsmen to reduce the cost of the almost mandatory baptismal party. As a result of these and other folk practices, the parents' choice of godparents is restricted in ways not intended by the Church.

Although the Church defines the spiritual relationships sponsorship generates among the participants, Filipinos are able to manipulate this fundamental feature of the godparenthood complex. If they wish to minimize their ritual kinship bonds, repeat sponsorship is available for this purpose. The impersonal selection of stranger-sponsors is another way to fulfill the requirements of the Church without creating meaningful and effective ritual kinship relationships. On the other hand, if socioeconomic and political benefits can be promoted by multiplying their ritual kinship ties, they have use of the "blanketing-in" concept. On the whole, repeat sponsorship and the "blanketing-in" process appear to be more a matter of choice for most Filipinos than for Latin Americans. The fact that Filipinos can make individual decisions

Bride and groom seated in front of the family altar in the bride's house. The couple has returned from Siaton after their wedding.

about whether to restrict or extend their ritual kinship bonds gives Philippine compadrinazgo greater flexibility than is possible when repeat sponsors are mandatory and the extension of ritual kinship bonds is automatic.

While the formal and folk qualification of sponsors, their methods of selection, and the occurrence of repeat sponsorship and the "blanketing-in" process varies in the Philippines, their basic patterns are remarkably similar. It seems as if there is no occasion—or need—that the godparenthood complex cannot adjust to in accommodation to the Church and the needs of Filipinos. Finally, this protean characteristic of compadrinazgo is seen in another form by its adoption by non-Catholic religions in the Philippines.

Chapter Six

Responsibilities and
Privileges of Ritual Kinsmen

This chapter presents an analysis of the responsibilities and privileges of Filipino ritual kinsmen, distinguishing, whenever possible, their ideal and normative roles. A general summary is made of the typical mutual assistance patterns of godparents, godchildren, and compadres. Following this section is a more detailed description of the specific duties and rights associated with ritual kinsmen through baptism, confirmation, and marriage, including the financial obligations of ritual kinsmen. The religious responsibilities of a godparent toward a godchild are noted, with comments on the rarity of inheritance from or adoption by a godparent.

Discussing Erongarícuaro, a community of 2,000 people about 250 miles west of Mexico City, but generalizing for other Mexican villages, Nelson states that the godparenthood system is a major mutual assistance unit in the community that in other societies may be a lineage, clan, or voluntary association (1971: 86). Christian Filipino society does not include lineages and clans, while voluntary associations, although numerous, often are transitory. Yet compadrinazgo in the Philippines does not appear to be "a major mutual assistance unit" in the rural regions investigated in the Bisayas. Numerous ritual kinsmen of these Bisayans are individuals from whom no aid or assistance was ever expected, and, in many instances, they are persons who were before and remain after the sponsorship ceremony total strangers. Compadrinazgo's most important, if limited, function is to create a mutual assistance network for Lalawignons and Caticuganers with persons residing outside their villages. A few of these ritual kinsmen may be helpful during a serious crisis, and most of them offer hospitality and assistance to visiting compadres, but their contributions to the minor emergencies of daily living probably are minimal since most of them are not neighbors.

Elite wedding of Siaton school teachers in the Catholic Church. One sponsor of the bride was a local congressman.

Yet this aid and assistance must not be discounted, for the personal resources of most of these Filipinos are meager. The presence of ritual kinsmen in external communities must make movement for Lalawignons and Caticuganers throughout their municipalities easier and "safer," for they come not as strangers but as godparents or compadres. In major crises, however, it is one's close, intimate relatives, rarely ritual kinsmen (whether they are village inhabitants or reside elsewhere in the municipality), who usually give major and lasting assistance, e.g., loans, adoption of godchildren, etc.

Mutual Assistance Among Ritual Kinsmen

Most of the published information on mutual assistance among Filipino ritual kinsmen is of a general nature. For example, when large-scale cooking is required for a wedding or funeral, one's compadres and godchildren often contribute some food or assist (as in Hulo) in the preparation and serving of the meal (Hollnsteiner 1967: 208). Economic considerations are crucial when Filipinos select Chinese sponsors in the Ilocos region, since Chinese godparents often contribute food to the meals following baptism and marriage.

> Personal friendships have had a place, but the usual reason for inviting Chinese to accept these ritual positions rests on wealth and position. Ilocanos speak of the Chinese friends as kind and generous. Such qualities are useful to the Ilocanos when they give a feast (Reynolds 1964: 191).

More specific information from Cebu City is available on compadres as a source of economic assistance. Informants in this second largest Philippine city were asked what kinsmen or other persons they would first seek out for aid in marketing, approach to borrow a small sum of money, or request to help them during sickness or other emergencies. Ritual kinsmen were found to be one of their less frequent choices. For example, in requesting a small loan, informants say they would seek out their compadres only if they could not approach first their siblings, parents, siblings-in-law, unspecified relatives, cousins, parents-in-law, or aunt or uncle (Jacobson 1969: 192). In fact, for seeking a small loan from any source, only 1.5 percent of the informants would go first to a ritual kinsman.

In discussing social relations in Estancia, a town in Panay, the poor judge horizontal bonds as of limited value among them. Since they exist at a subsistence level, they have little to share with others. Moreover, the poor often are in competition with each other for support and assistance from more prosperous individuals. "In periods of crisis ... there is usually little that family or neighbors of similar status (and resources) can do to help. At that point it is almost entirely the vertical ties which spell survival, enhancement, or extinction" (Szanton 1971: 87). In addition, as indicated earlier, the economic value of *suki* relationships reinforced by compadrinazgo in Estancia has been questioned (Szanton 1972).

Most Lalawignons and Caticuganers do not seek ritual kinship ties to establish patron-client relationships. When these vertical bonds are established through compadrinazgo, the patron's economic resources, for example in southern Negros and eastern Samar, often are modest. The primary advantage of such patrons is their possible influence in seeking jobs, assistance with the local bureaucracy, etc. Vertical compadrinazgo relationships often are sought for a particular ritual occasion, for example, marriage sponsors in Manalad. In this instance the possible future benefits accrue mainly to the godchildren, not the compadres. Lastly, confirmation rarely is used to create patron-client relationships, since most Bisayans regard the ritual kinship bonds that this occasion generates as weak and transitory.

Caticugan and Lalawigan compadres usually can give each other little financial assistance during a serious crisis, for their own resources are small. Although they may be willing, most are ineffective patrons. As a Caticugan village official remarked, one may ask favors from a compadre with little reluctance, but because he is poor, "you should not expect too much." Yet this is not always true. Some Lalawignons are more apt to seek a small loan from a compadre than from a kinsman since the latter "can disappoint a relative but seldom a *padi.*" One man was said to have borrowed money from a local money lender to help his compadre; he felt it his responsibility to lend his *padi* the money because he had borrowed frequently from him in the past.

Filipino ritual kinsmen are helpful in many small yet comforting ways; they also provide some "insurance against unexpected risks and calamities" (Eisenstadt 1956: 93). One feels freer to borrow daily necessities or equipment from compadres than from mere friends or acquaintances. Lalawigan residents, for example, when visiting compadres in barrios some distances from Borongan, may be asked to stop in the poblacion to make a few personal purchases for a compadre. One woman lent her Lalawigan comadre a *carabao* to secure bamboo for a new house; she also sent a son to work (for a wage) for her comadre. In repayment, whenever the Lalawigan woman had extra fish (seasonally more scarce in Dolores than in Lalawigan), she sent some to her comadre.

Compadres can be useful in numerous ways. A temporary labor shortage annually occurs in parts of eastern Samar during the rice transplanting and harvest seasons. Ritual kin are more obliged and willing than noncompadres to help one another during these important agricultural periods. With volunteers to harvest Siaton corn and rice the problem is not a labor shortage but a surplus. The field owner may be more apt to favor a volunteer who is a compadre; for the same work the compadre usually gets a little larger share of the harvested grain than someone who is not a ritual kinsman.

Baptismal Godparents and Godchildren

The financial obligations of baptismal sponsors in the Philippines are similar to those elsewhere in Catholic countries. Most Caticugan and Lalawigan sponsors pay the baptismal fee (3.50 pesos in Caticugan, but only 3.00 pesos in Siaton poblacion "since it is less trouble for the priest," and 5.00 pesos in Lalawigan, 1972). The elite may have their children baptized *before* the high mass on Sunday or on Saturday afternoon; for these special christenings the church fee is Siaton is five pesos.

The sponsor also furnishes the christening dress (Ceb. *delantal*, Sam. *delantar*, apron). Some parents may agree to share or pay all of the fees to obtain a sponsor. Occasionally the dress may be borrowed or rented by the sponsor. A Caticugan mother furnished baptismal dresses for the christening of four of her ten children "to help the sponsor." The determining factor in who assumes these expenses is the person's eagerness to become a sponsor or the parent's desire to secure a reluctant person.

There is no formal reciprocal gifting of new godparents following the baptism and its usual meal in Caticugan or Lalawigan, although in parts of the Philippines (for example, Parañque, Rizal Province), ten days after the baptism parents present each new compadre with a gift equivalent in value to what he gave the godchild (Malay and Malay 1955: 34).

Ideally, Ilokan godparents should give gifts of food, clothing, money, or candy to their new baptismal godchildren (Nydegger and Nydegger 1966: 68). Tagalogs often give a suitable gift called *pakúmkin* (or *pakimkim*) to the new godchild (Hollnsteiner 1967: 207; Cruz 1958: 214; Cortez 1965: 21; Eggan 1956 2: 649). Supposedly this gift should be proportionate to the "splendor of the *handaan* [baptismal feast] provided by the parents on this occasion" (Tengco 1962). Sometimes co-sponsors vie in giving presents to their godchild (Cruz 1958: 214). The former Caticugan custom of giving the godchild a gift (Ceb. *pakumkon* or *kumkon*, from *kumò*, clenched hand) immediately after the baptism has largely been abandoned. Few gifts are given Manalad godchildren by their baptismal godparents (Sibley 1958: 64).

In Suba some parents carefully record the gifts (usually money) that baptismal sponsors give a godchild. If they later sponsor children of these compadres, they return the identical sum to these godchildren (Scheans 1963: 227). In Caticugan there is a similar attitude toward reciprocal gifts among compadres. For example, a godchild who asked her godmother for a Christmas gift was given a chicken. Shortly before the Caticugan fiesta, the godchild's mother, who lived in another barrio, sent her comadre five *gantas* (about 19 pounds) of unhusked rice. This informant commented cheerfully: "So I got back my chicken."

Although godchildren normally do not receive many presents from their godparents, gift-giving is traditional on Christmas day in parts of the Philippines. The following statement is typical mainly of the middle and upper classes in towns and large cities.

> The whole day of Christmas itself is traditionally reserved for making calls. First on the list are grandparents with whom Christmas lunch is shared. Next in priority are godparents—for it has been said that in the Philippines there is no Santa Claus, there are only godparents. Called *ninong* and *ninang*, godparents are ready each Christmas Day with presents—packets of money at the very least, packages of chosen gifts if they have the grace and concern. Many children have two sets of godparents, one for christening and another for confirmation, but traditionally it·is only the christening sponsors who are called upon at Christmas (Archipelago 1974: 48).

In Caticugan and Lalawigan some godchildren may visit their nearby godparents on Christmas day to kiss their hands and to receive gifts— perhaps a few centavos or some candy. As this holiday season approaches in Boroñgan poblacion, some godparents who have many godchildren begin to collect bright new coins for gifts. Supposedly, some godparents who have numerous godchildren and cannot give them money purposely visit relatives or friends in another town until after Christmas.

In Canaman godparents may give their godchildren new clothing for the town fiestas or birthday gifts, and even assist with their education if they are financially able and the parents are poor (Arce 1973: 53).

Confirmation Godparents and Godchildren

Detailed data are limited and incomplete on the responsibilities and privileges of ritual kinsmen through confirmation, perhaps because most folk Catholics usually consider confirmation a less important sacrament than baptism and the ritual kinship bonds created by its sponsorship less demanding.

The major expense associated with confirmation sponsorship in the Philippines is paying the church fee. In 1972, the fee was 1.20 pesos in Caticugan and 1.00 peso in Lalawigan. The Siaton priest explained that the fee for confirmation was less than the fee for baptism because "the ceremony is not so long." If a Filipino parent must seek a reluctant sponsor before the ceremony, parent and sponsor usually agree about whether the confirmation fee is to be shared or one is to pay all. One aged Siaton informant said that if he paid the confirmation fee he felt he had no ritual relationship with the child or its parents and would not call the latter compadre.

Confirmation in Caticugan and Lalawigan is never an occasion to give gifts to the godchild. Elsewhere in the Philippines, however, confirmation sponsors may give their new godchild a small sum of money (Cortez 1965: 21; Eggan 1956 2: 651–52). In the two Bisayan villages studies, the parents rarely served a meal to the sponsor after the ceremony.

For the most part, few advantages are given or gained by becoming a confirmation sponsor in the rural Philippines. Perhaps this is why shortly before the confirmation (but not the christening) ceremony in Siaton "parents scramble to find anyone to sponsor their child." Since sponsors secured this way often are strangers, a lasting relationship rarely unites them with the parents and their godchild. The adults may address one another as compadres, but rarely do sponsor and godchild or sponsor and parents expect significant mutual assistance.

Marriage Godparents and Godchildren

Only limited comparative data exist on the role of marriage sponsors in the Philippines. At one time marriage godparents in Hulo hired a brass band for the wedding and paid for the pew decorations and the ringing of the church bell (Malay 1957: 78). Traditionally, Tagalog sponsors gave the bride her wedding gown (Eggan 1956 2: 655). When a landlord sponsors a tenant's wedding in Canaman he pays the church fee and the cost of the wedding photographs and furnishes or pays for the rental of the bridal car, and perhaps for a band to play later at the wedding feast (Lynch 1959: 54). Similar costs are assumed by marriage sponsors in other parts of the Philippines (Cortez 1965: 21; Jocano 1972: 68).

In Manalad baptismal godparents of the groom may contribute a

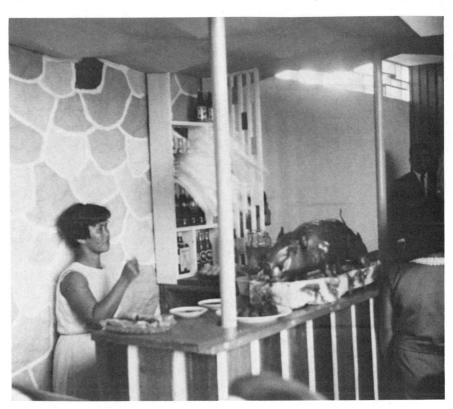

Wedding reception at bride's parents' residence in Siaton that included roast pig (lechon).

small gift toward the cost of their godson's wedding (Sibley 1958: 74–75). In Malitbog, the baptismal godparents may be consulted when the godson wishes to marry (or to mortgage family properties). They also furnish the wedding clothes of the bride and groom and help with part of the ceremony (Jocano 1968a: 28). In rural Cebu the parents of the bride and the groom begin to address one another as compadres at the feast served by the boy's group the evening before the wedding (Quisumbing 1956: 62–63). In Caticugan, but not in Lalawigan, the bride and groom's parents also refer to each other as compadre or comadre.

Baptismal (and less commonly confirmation) godparents *if asked* may play a role in the marriage negotiations of a godchild in Caticugan. Frequently, however, they are not involved in these discussions. When Caticugan godparents are asked to participate in the marriage negotiations of a godchild, the invitation is extended out of respect, and not because their participation is obligatory. Whether they help in these often lengthy negotiations depends upon the intimacy of their relationships with the couple's parents and whether they reside in the vicinity.

In Caticugan, though less so in Lalawigan, the dower the boy's group gives the girl's group prior to the ceremony covers the basic cost of the wedding. The dower usually includes the wedding gown and money (spent on food and drink), a pig, rice, and corn that the girl's parents also serve to their guests after the wedding. The involvement of godparents in marriage negotiations and their contributions to the wedding costs are greater for a godson than for a goddaughter.

In Caticugan marriage sponsors rarely contribute to the expenses of the bride's wedding since "she is receiving [the dower], not giving." If a contribution is made, it is usually a small gift of food or money. But the tradition of helping, as with a godson's wedding, is less obligatory. If the godson is marrying, the sponsor may pay the church fee, furnish some *tubâ*, or provide the musicians for the dance or the trip home from the church. Once, but no longer, the baptismal godmother usually gave her goddaughter the wedding dress. One Filipina, born in Siaton poblacion but living in Canada, was mailed a costly bridal gown by her baptismal godmother. When asked if this were common, the informant said no, adding: "But my godmother is unmarried and she has a good job."

A Siaton municipal official estimated that three to four civil marriages occur monthly in the poblacion. Civil marriages are for couples who are eloping, when the bride is pregnant, or for those who wish a "cheap" wedding. Sponsors are selected for the brief ceremony (often they are municipal officials who are easily available in the *municipio*), and regular ritual relationships are created among the participants.

For many Lalawignons and Caticugancrs sponsorship builds ritual kinship ties and mutual assistance obligations of varying importance. Sponsorship of a marriage is less important than that of baptism, but more important than sponsorship of a confirmation. As one Lalawigan informant explained:

> A compadre through baptism is considered more important [than through marriage] because he is the second parent of the child. He is responsible for the Christian training of the child from infancy. This kind of compadre helps his godchild become a good Christian. Thus the ties are closer and stronger than with a compadre through marriage whose duties begin only in the marriage of the person.

Funeral Responsibilities

The reported funeral duties of godparents and compadres in the Philippines are similar to those described for most of Latin America. In Luzon (Bulacan Province) Tagalog godparents once furnished an unmarried godchild's burial clothes and the cloth liner for the coffin, rented the hand-pulled hearse, and hired a brass band for the funeral procession. They did not have these duties toward a married godchild. On the death of a godchild with only one godparent, the latter's friends shared the funeral costs (Malay 1957: 84–85). Elsewhere in the Philippines, godparents have similar duties on the death of a godchild (Malay and Malay 1955: 28).

In Caticugan the baptismal godparents of minor godchildren have well-defined but limited funeral responsibilities. For such a gochild they furnish the paper wings and shroud (Ceb. *bestida sa angel*, Sp. *vestido de angel*, angel's clothes) placed on the body in the coffin, help dig the grave, and prepare the necessary meals for the guests. For the funeral of a compadre in Caticugan, Lalawigan, and Manalad, ritual kinsmen make whatever contribution is personally possible in money, food, or labor, but sometimes they may be unable to offer anything (Sibley 1958: 81).

Funeral responsibilities of Lalawignon baptismal godparents are much like those described for Caticuganers. How much assistance they give depends somewhat upon the needs of their deceased godchild's family and their own resources. They usually contribute to the food served on the day of the funeral. During the nine-day novena for the deceased that follows burial, the baptismal godparents should furnish the food served the participants on one evening.

At one time Lalawigan godparents furnished the *Virginia*, a white dress with a blue sash and a crown of artificial flowers, as their goddaughter's shroud. In the past, the sponsor supplied a godson's shroud, the costume of San Miguel (St. Michael the Archangel). Today, the people bury small children in a white dress or white pants and shirt, which may or may not be furnished by their godparents.

Adoption

According to Canon law, the responsibility of baptismal godparents includes not only the spiritual education of the godchild but also his care if he is orphaned or if the parents need assistance because of poverty or an unusually large family. Kinsmen generally take care of Filipino orphans, so that whether godparents are able or willing to assume this duty rarely is an important selection criterion (Tengco 1962). No Caticugan godparents were rearing or had adopted a godchild, but one instance of adoption (*de facto*) occurred in Lalawigan. Since such Filipino cases appear rare, it is worth looking at this one in some detail.

During the 1941 fiesta of an interior barrio of Dolores, a mother, who was a friend of a man in Lalawigan, requested that the latter's wife, Engracia, sponsor her child's baptism. As time passed the godmother became unusually fond of her goddaughter. Finally she decided to adopt the girl. "All of my children," Engracia explained, "are sons except one daughter who died when an infant."

The godchild's parents, poor tenant farmers, agreed to the adoption but asked Engracia to wait until their daughter could walk. During the interim Engracia and her husband often sent the parents gifts of food, soap, and clothing. The child was brought to Lalawigan when she was about fifteen months old. As a child the godchild was never told she had been adopted. Engracia was confident (in 1956) her sons would see that she inherited a fair share of their properties, although no will was made to guarantee an equitable division. In 1956 Engracia was still sending occasional gifts to her adopted goddaughter's parents, who had never visited their daughter since she began living in Lalawigan (Hart 1965b: 55–70). Later the girl married a man from Bulacan province (Luzon) where she now resides. She did not receive any of her adopted family's real property as part of her dowry, but her foster father said she could always live with them "as a real daughter."

Political Uses of Compadrinazgo

Politically active Filipinos recognize the relative ease with which a network of ritual bonds can be developed. They understand the potential value of ritual kinship ties to either a patron desiring numerous clients or an office-seeker looking for votes. The "political use" of the godparenthood complex by Filipino public officials, at all levels, is habitual and locally well-known (Landé 1973: 228). A former president of the Philippines utilized this technique to expand his political influence:

Want to be a "compadre" or "comadre" of President and Mrs. Dios-
dado Macapagal? Then take your baby to the Presidential Guards' chapel
between 10 a.m. and 12 noon on "Common Man's Day," which is held
every Friday—if the President is not busy stumping in the province.
Baptisms there are held free. Eighty-six babies became [have become?]
godchildren of the President and the First Lady. In five of the nine mass
baptisms held since last year, only Mrs. Macapagal was present as sponsor,
but the President nevertheless became "ninong" of the children and
"compadre" of their parents (Paguio 1965: 44).

The families of two former Filipinos presidents were ritually linked:
Sergio Osmeña was the godfather of one of Manuel Quezon's children,
creating a relationship that "is the closest possible among otherwise
unrelated people in the Philippines" (Pacis 1971 2: 205–6).

Although no detailed study exists of the association of Filipino
godparenthood with politics, scattered references are numerous. In
Matalom municipality (southern Leyte) locally prominent persons seek
compadres in the barrios to enhance their influence with government
officials by increasing the number of votes they can deliver to a political
candidate (Pal 1956a: 422). Pal classified leaders as municipal (vs. local)
and partisan (vs. nonpartisan). One type of municipal partisan leader is
the "influential compadre" who is "either an aspirant for an elective
office, or who desires influence over others. He acquires a following by
establishing ceremonial kinship ties with families in the barrio" (Pal
1956b: 189, 191). On the whole, most Filipino politicians "create a great
many compadre ties with those to whom they are allied or wish to be
allied politically" (Landé 1965: 21, 135).

The use of compadrinazgo for political purposes by candidates or
incumbents in Hulo often is noted briefly (Hollnsteiner 1962: 167–71).
Among upper-class Filipino and Spanish mestizo families in Cebu City
compadrinazgo is an important factor in assisting these individuals "to
adapt quickly and flexibly to volatile political conditions" (Liu, Rubel,
and Yu 1969: 397). In eastern Samar, several months before the
election, one candidate for a municipal office purposely came to the
Boroñgan church each Sunday to offer his services as a baptismal sponsor.

One brief glimpse into the secular use of compadrinazgo is provided by a recent study of the Chinese elite in the Philippines. "None
of the leaders in business was without a Congressional ally. In my
interviews, I regularly viewed a gallery of politicians—autographed
pictures of Presidents, Congressional leaders, Supreme Court Justices—
on the walls or desks of the offices of the elite" (McBeath 1972: 19). The

religious affiliations of the groups were: no religion (thirty people, or 37.5 percent of the group); Buddhist (nineteen, or 23.8 percent); Catholic (eighteen, or 22.5 percent); and Protestant (thirteen, or 16.2 percent). Yet seventy Chinese (or 87.5 percent) in this group of eighty had compadres. Obviously, Chinese who stated they were Buddhists or belonged to no religious organization must have had compadres for other than religious reasons (McBeath 1972: 16).

Although this aspect of Filipino compadrinazgo has not been extensively investigated, there probably are practical limits to the utility of multiplying compadre relationships to where their future validation may be difficult if not impossible (Davis 1970: 40). For example, the mayor in Siaton had so many ritual kinsmen he had forgotten many of their names. It is dubious if he would have been supportive of such individuals even if they were bold enough to ask for assistance.

Because Filipino compadrinazgo bonds usually do not imply automatic support, they must be validated by the participants. As one Filipino commented: "An important man as 'compadre,' or as a personal guest during a political campaign ... leaves only ephemeral ties" (Samson 1965: 418). If claims for favors his compadres make on a politician are not fulfilled, their relationship may lapse or become hostile. Hence the creation of numerous ritual bonds often constitutes a severe drain on a Filipino politician's resources. For these reasons many politicians supposedly economize compadre ties by restricting their relationships to persons controlling blocks of votes.

Our limited data on the responsibilities and privileges of Filipino ritual kinsmen often contain fundamentally contradictory statements. This makes it precarious to generalize extensively about the quality of Filipino compadrinazgo relationships. For example, "The compadre is a social insurance, a sort of patron-saint-on-earth who more than anything satisfies the inner need for security" (Samson 1965: 518), but "to most Manilans to be a sponsor is simply a social obligation—if not a big bother—and after baptism, one does not have to worry anymore except during Christmas when the godchild shows up to kiss the sponsor's hand and to accept a gift, either in cash or in goods" (Malay and Malay 1955: 27).

Philippine godparenthood apparently may either join friends ceremonially or reinforce existing kinship ties, or both. In contrast, some baptism or confirmation sponsors, such as those secured at the church by the child's escort, may never see their godchild again or even meet their new compadres. This form of ritual kinship may bridge social

Funeral of a well-known Chinese merchant in Boroñgan whose bier is accompanied to the church by a priest.

classes or unite intraclass friends "like siblings." Lastly, the ideal degree of intimacy and associated privileges and responsibilities depends on whether one is a compadre through baptism, confirmation, or marriage.

Godparenthood in Alcalá ideally creates an "irrevocable tie of mutual trust, stronger than that of kinship because it owes its existence to the free consent of both parties" (Pitt-Rivers 1961: 108). This attitude is not shared by most ritual kinsmen in Caticugan and Lalawigan, and perhaps the rest of rural Philippines. In the most serious crises, the performance of one's personal kindred is more succoring than that of the most intimate compadre. When their assistance is offered, the contribution of compadres is never expected to be as liberal or extensive as that of one's close kinsmen.

Every adult Christian Filipino has some intimate compadres, often but not always including those who are also consanguines and affines. These compadres have standing somewhere between the family and the least close of one's kindred. Other ritual kinsmen, affectively speaking, may be compared to "distant cousins," positioned slightly beyond the edge of one's personal kindred. They are persons one rarely sees, for they often reside in distant communities. A reasonable request for minor assistance or an unannounced visit may not be encouraged or especially welcomed by them, but it is difficult for them to deny the obligation to respond. Finally, one has compadres he has never met. If there was a meeting, the occasion was limited to the associated ritual. Their names often are forgotten, and they are slightly less than strangers.

Chapter Seven

Social Dimensions
of Ritual Kinship

This chapter focuses on similarities and differences between the functions of real and ritual kinship in the rural Philippines. Although ritual kinship bonds often are compared to those linking actual relatives, usually they lack the latter's intensity and permanency; however, like real relatives, ritual kinsmen frequently do not marry, since the Church or folk Catholicism proclaims such unions incestuous. Compadrinazgo is used both to create new ritual kinsmen and to reinvigorate inactive or lapsed kinship relationships: these are its "intensification" and "extension" functions. Finally, this chapter discusses compadrinazgo's role in minimizing social conflict among Filipino ritual kinsmen.

Real and Ritual Kinship Bonds

Since compadrinazgo creates ritual kinship bonds, often the concomitant privileges and duties are said to be those associated with specific kinship roles. Various sources state that ritual kinship roles are similar to those associated with consanguines and affines—and they are sometimes more demanding. More specifically, the compadre-comadre roles have been compared by some writers to those typical of younger and elder siblings. (Edmonson suggests that these ritual relationships involve aspects of brotherhood "but with more than a hint of husband-wife relations as well": 1957: 33.) The godparent-godchildren roles reportedly are similar to the roles typical of uncle/aunt and nephew/niece or parent and child.

Filipino compadres often describe their relationship as similar to that of siblings, while godchildren often address their godparents with parental terms. For example, Caticuganers claim, as did an informant, that "one can take problems to compadres for discussion, for they are like siblings." Yet in practice ritual kinsmen usually are treated as more than kith but less than close kin. Few if any of the barriofolk of Lalawigan and Caticugan consider compadres or godparents as members of their personal kindred unless actual kinship and past association has established their membership.

Some Filipinos permit marriages of compadres and godsiblings, although such unions between natural siblings would be incestuous. Similarly, the godparent's responsibility to care for an orphaned godchild is seldom observed, but the informal adoption of the orphaned child by a sibling is common practice. Although some compadres may play a sibling or in-law type of role, it is not unusual to find many ritual kinsmen treated as "remote cousins" (or even simply as persons lacking significant social or emotional ties vis-a-vis each other).

The interaction of most Filipino ritual kinsmen is characterized by the mutual respect and reserve described for Latin America and Europe. Although the residents of Lalawigan and Caticugan rarely have sponsors from the elite groups in Boroñgan and Siaton poblacion, intraclass compadre bonds require respect of young for older partners, within the framework of generational respect that "involves deference to the opinions of all individuals, regardless of sex, older than one's self" (Eggan 1956 1: 421).

Grandmother and mother in Caticugan sit beside the dead infant shortly before funeral. The infant is dressed like an angel.

On the whole, relationships between nonkin compadres who are contemporaries appear more informal and intimate in Caticugan and Lalawigan than in much of Hispanic America. As one barrio informant explained: "*Pare* [or *mare*] is a more intimate way to address persons than by nickname." And nicknames are more familiar terms of address than personal names. In Canaman "the use of the full first name (*nga-ran*) when addressing a fellow townsman is considered a sign of distance" (Lynch 1959: 66).

Caticugan and Lalawigan compadres and comadres can and do drink together. Indeed, it would be rude to let a compadre pass a *tubâ* stall without at least offering him a drink. Sexual topics do not have to be avoided by Caticugan and Lalawigan compadres. One local joke about compadres in Caticugan offers insight into associated attitudes. A pregnant wife refused intercourse and advised her husband to seek another woman. The husband chose his comadre to whom he paid five pesos. On returning home, he told his wife what had happened, hoping to annoy her. She became angry, shouting: "You fool! Why did you pay her five pesos? When your compadre visits me, I don't charge him a centavo!" An inference from this joke could be that its humor derives from the tabu on sexual relationships between compadres and comadres.

In Hulo ritual ties enable a person to dispense "with the need for extreme care in dealing with that individual, allowing a more relaxed attitude in his presence [such] as one would have with a socially close relative" (Hollnsteiner 1967: 205). In contrast, the relationship of ritual kinsmen in Manalad is subject to greater strain than with actual kinsmen. As a result, most compadre contacts are more circumspect in Manalad (Sibley 1958: 64) than in Caticugan and Lalawigan. Possibly the more reserved relationships of most compadres in Manalad result from the fact that interclass sponsors are more common in this village.

Compadrinazgo and Folk Beliefs About Incest

Catholic doctrine does not prohibit the marriage of baptismal or confirmation sponsors and co-sponsors and parents of the child. No incest tabu separates similar participants for marriage since the sponsors are merely "witnesses." While a baptized child and his godparents may not marry, this Church restriction is not extended to spiritual parenthood through confirmation (Gudeman 1972: 53). However, folk sanctions in Spain, Italy, Greece, and Latin America with a few exceptions prohibit the marriage of ritual kinsmen. In this aspect ritual and real kinsmen are alike.

Available comparative data on folk beliefs regarding the marriage of ritual kinsmen wherever compadrinazgo occurs often are vague and incomplete. Violations of the tabu sometimes are implied but rarely documented. Information usually is available for only some of the ritual kinsmen. On the whole, the traditional restrictions against the marriage of ritual kinsmen are more comprehensive than those the Catholic church requires. These folk prohibitions against the marriage of ritual kinsmen appear in the Philippines. Although comparative data for various Filipino cultural-linguistic groups are limited and incomplete, existing data indicate that prohibitions greatly outnumber permissions. The marriage of Filipino ritual kinsmen through confirmation and marriage are as strongly tabued as the union of those through baptism (see Table 11). These restrictions often are "ideal," however, since the rule of exogamy may be disregarded.

TABLE 11

Filipino Folk Attitudes Toward the Marriages of Ritual Kinsmen

Village (Linguistic group)	Marriage of			
	Godparents-Godchildren	Compadre-Comadre	Godsiblings	Co-Sponsors
Cabetican (Pampangan)	Prohibited	Prohibited	Prohibited	Prohibited
Caticugan (Cebuan)	Prohibited	Prohibited	Prohibited	Prohibited
Lalawigan (Samaran)	Prohibited	Prohibited	Prohibited	Prohibited
Manalad (Panayan)	Prohibited	?	Permissible	?
Suba (Ilokan)	Prohibited	?	Prohibited?	Permissible

The following account summarizes further scattered data on the subject. A pre-war account of life in Barrio San Pedro (Laguna) states that godparents and godchildren could not marry, nor could compadres-comadres (Parsons 1940: 441). The *damas* associated with baptism and marriage in Cabetican never marry each other (Santico 1973: 38). Possibly the reason godsiblings may marry among some Tagalogs (Eggan 1956 1: 428; Jocano 1972: 69) is that Filipino ritual kinsmen sometimes are ranked by degree of closeness; the most remote ritual kinship relationship is godsiblings (Lynch and Himes 1967: 22–23; Himes 1967: 132). In Suba, no normative incest rule regarding godsibling marriage could be elicited from informants. Though they were uncertain that such marriages were improper, they were sure they knew of no godsiblings who had wedded. Co-sponsor marriage was permissible in Suba, but only one instance had occurred.

In both Caticugan and Lalawigan, marriage of ritual kinsmen is regarded as incestuous since they are "like parents and children or brothers and sisters." But in both Borongan and Caticugan (but not Lalawigan) some marriages of compadres were known. In Borongan, a young man and woman taught in the same school. They both sponsored the son of the man's first cousin. Later the couple married. The husband explained, however, "We never addressed each other as *padi* and *madi,* so the people did not know of this relationship when we decided to get married. Often when people hear of this type of marriage, they make fun of the couple and tell dirty jokes about them."

Only one violation of the tabu against compadre marriage was known in Caticugan. A woman married a widower whose child she had sponsored at baptism. Her father, a former barrio official, explained that if this impediment had been mentioned during the marriage negotiations, he would have prohibited the wedding. Barrio informants privately scoffed at what they considered a lame excuse. Possibly the barriofolk considered it a mitigation that the man was widower with several young children. The couple, now residing in the poblacion, where the husband is employed, suffers no public ostracism. (The United Church of Christ in Siaton permits the marriage of compadres.)

Not only must godsiblings in Caticugan and Lalawigan not marry, but in the former village the marriage of godchildren of the same sponsor is regarded as incestuous. The identical tabu is also reported for rural Greece and for the Negroes of northern Brazil, although its force is weakening in Brazilian cities (Eduardo 1948: 38, 42).

Marriage restrictions associated with compadrinazgo in Caticugan do not end with the previously described prohibitions. In this village, ritual kinship ties are diffused to a wider circle of persons; however, this extension of ritual kinship ties creates none of the traditional obligations or privileges associated with the godparenthood complex; it regulates only marriages.

Ideally, Caticugan kinship norms forbid marriage between a person and anyone on this list: lineal or collateral grandparents, uncles and aunts, siblings, nieces and nephews, grandchildren, and cousins to the third degree. Furthermore, a "fictive" ritual relationship is created between two kin groups when a person who is a member of one serves as a sponsor to a member of the other. When two such persons wish to wed, this ritual linkage generates bonds similar to those of natural relationships. Three cases illustrate the nature and force of this secondary, diffused, ritual relationship in determining spouse selection in Caticugan.

One Caticugan marriage negotiation ran into difficulties when it was found that the baptismal sponsor of the suitor's father was the girl's paternal grandfather. Some regarded them "like nephew and niece" since the boy's father was a godsibling of the girl's father. However, the wedding finally was approved since the "boy was not the one sponsored." In another instance, the young man's baptismal godfather was his sweetheart's maternal grandfather. Since the suitor was "like an uncle" to the girl, the marriage was undesirable. When parental permission for the betrothal was denied, the couple eloped. Later they returned to Siaton, were remarried in the church, and now live in Caticugan.

Another proposed marriage that met opposition in Caticugan was between a man whose confirmation godfather was his girl's maternal uncle. This ritual kinship linkage made the couple "like first cousins." (Since the godson was "like a son" to his sponsor, he was considered ritually in the same category as a child of the girl's mother's brother.) When their marriage negotiations failed, mainly because of the disapproval of the orphaned girl's kin, the couple eloped. They too later returned to reside in Caticugan.

Some Caticugan informants believed that this last couple should have received sibling permission to wed since the ritual relationship was through confirmation, not baptism, and the marriage of ritual first cousins is less improper than the union of a ritual "uncle" and "niece." They also explained that the young girl was dominated by her deceased mother's siblings, who disliked her suitor. The ritual kinship tie between the young couple probably was only one reason to disapprove the marriage since "they thought their niece could marry better."

The precise dimensions of this extended yet limited ritual kinship bond and its regulation of marriage are not clear to all Caticuganers, as is illustrated by the girl who was asked to be a baptismal sponsor by a relative of her fiancé. She was apprehensive that acceptance of the request might create a secondary ritual kinship relationship between them that would complicate, and perhaps prevent, their future marriage. Consequently, she sought counsel from friends, but their advice was so ambiguous that she decided not to take a chance and declined to be a sponsor. If such a massive extension of ritual kinship bonds occurs in other Philippine communities—they do not in Lalawigan—Filipinos will have added a notable variant to a major function of the godparenthood complex, the regulation of marriage.

Burial of deceased, after a service in the Siaton church, in the municipal cemetery.

Intensification and Extension

Philippine ritual kinship complements or reinforces but never opposes the indigenous kinship system. The godparenthood complex either makes ritual kinsmen of nonrelatives or reinforces existing consanguineal and affinal bonds. These two contrasting motives have been identified respectively as intensification and extension (Paul 1942: 57). Intensification occurs when the sponsors are kinsmen, and extension when the sponsors are nonrelatives.

Philippine data are either too restricted regionally or statistically too shallow, or both, to permit a statement that either the intensification or extension function dominates. Hypothetically, Filipinos might be expected to emphasize the extension function since they are more concerned "with the lateral expansion and size of the family and kin group ... than with the lineal depth of relationship" (Eggan 1956 1: 423). Yet the "blanketing-in" process of compadrinazgo is interpreted in Malitbog as in "consonance with the bilateral kinship structure" that emphasizes the generational-extensional aspects of kinship bonds (Jocano 1969: 93).

Among Tagalogs, kinsmen often become baptismal godparents, particularly in well-to-do families. When they do, confirmation sponsors usually are not relatives (Eggan 1956 1: 428, 2: 664). In Hulo, especially among the upper class, consanguines often are chosen as baptismal sponsors, although another source for the same communities comments that this social class (in 1936) usually did not select relatives as baptismal godparents (Hollnsteiner 1967: 203, 205; Cruz 1958: 214). Jocano merely notes that both kinsmen and nonkinsmen are sponsors in Malitbog (Jocano 1969: 93). Data on compadrinazgo for Guinhangdan omit this topic (Nurge 1965).

Approximately 90 percent of baptismal sponsors in the Pampangan village of Cabetican are kinsmen (Santico 1973: 25). Santico states that about 40 percent of these individuals are classificatory kinsmen, indicating that distant kin are selected almost as frequently as close relatives, e.g., the parents' siblings. It is most important to select christening sponsors (especially the primary sponsor) carefully, since Cabeticaños believe that aspects of their personalities may be inherited by the godchild. This belief favors the selection of kinsmen, since the parents would be more knowledgeable about their personal and family lives. On the other hand, confirmation sponsors are more apt to be friends, although distant relatives are also chosen. The personal character of confirmation sponsors is not believed to be inherited by the godchild (Santico 1973: 28).

Ilokan peasants often choose their landlord or a member of his family as baptismal sponsor to enhance their patron-client relationships. In the town, however, Ilokans are more apt to seek sponsors who are friends or relatives (Eggan 1956 4: 1717). The most detailed, if limited, information on the extension-intensification motives among Ilokans is for Tempuyon, a Suba sitio (see Table 12). Eight households (representing about twelve percent of the population of Suba) were interviewed. The households were chosen to represent each of the family names in Tempuyog and the local range of wealth. As Table 12 indicates, in choosing baptismal sponsors Tempuyog barriofolk appear to prefer an even balance between kin (46 percent) and nonkin (54 percent). Within this balance, they favor male kin and female nonkin sponsors.

In Canaman sponsors usually are nonkinsmen; in fact, residents in this southern Luzon town claimed godparents often were selected because they were close friends, sometimes neighbors (Arce 1973: 64, 66). A detailed investigation of extension-intensification motives of Philippine compadrinazgo, yet to be published in full, was made in two Bisayan villages, Camangahan and Manalad (Sibley 1958; 1965a; 1965b). In Camangahan, composed mainly of subsistence farmers, close kinsmen

TABLE 12

Sex and Kinship Relation of Baptismal Sponsors to Their
Godchildren in Sitio Tempuyog, Barrio Suba: 1958[1]

Family Number	Sex of Godchild	Kin Godparents		Non-Kin Godparents		Totals
		Male	Female	Male	Female	
1	F	1	—	—	2	3
	M	1	1	1	2	5
2	F	1	—	—	1	2
	M	1	—	—	1	2
3	M	2	2	2	1	7
4	F	—	—	—	1	1
	M	—	—	1	1	2
5	F	4	1	—	4	9
	M	1	—	—	—	1
6	F	—	—	—	1	1
	M	1	—	—	—	1
7	M	—	1	1	—	2
8	F	—	—	2	1	3
	M	1	1	—	—	2
Totals	N 14	13	6	7	15	41

[1]The birth dates for the godchildren in Table 12 range from the early 1920s to the late 1940s.

predominate as sponsors. In Manalad, however, where most residents work in the surrounding sugar cane fields, relatives usually are not sponsors.

This difference in emphasis on the intensification-extension motives in these two Bisayan villages is explained by the decreasing dependence of the populace of Manalad on village-based kin groups. This change is mainly a result of their greater wage orientation.

In Camangahan, residents appear to be using compadre-comadre choices as a means for deepening reciprocal relationships among a functionally important group of persons for a community universe in which virtually everyone is already a kinsman ... [In Manalad] the extension of ritual kinship may enhance the chooser's chances for future employment or other needed assistance by widening the network of potential allies in times of difficulty (Sibley 1965b: 6–7).

For Esperanza, Pal estimates (through personal communication) that one-third of the sponsors are kinsmen. Many of these kinsman sponsors are either elderly and single or married but childless. The elderliness of these unmarried sponsors often minimizes their hope of future marriage, while the married couples have been unable to have children. In Estancia, Panay, Filipinos apparently favor nonkin sponsors. Sponsors usually are those with whom the parents already have informal relationships—". . . friends, neighbors, and political or business associates—persons whose willingness to serve is already predictable" (Szanton 1972: 111).

The extension-intensification motives for godparenthood were investigated in Lalawigan and Caticugan. Lalawignons correctly claimed that an overwhelming emphasis was placed on the extension motive of compadrinazgo. In a survey of Lalawigan baptismal sponsors, only six percent of their godchildren were also relatives. Informants explained that one seldom sponsored a kin godchild since the purpose of compadrinazgo is "to acquire more relatives."

Nearly all kinsmen-sponsors in Lalawigan were their godchildrens' real or classificatory aunts, i.e., were siblings or first or second cousins to the godchild's parents. The high frequency of female relatives as baptismal sponsors stems from the past escort system. Since the person to be baptized was an infant, female escorts were preferred to care for the new baby at the church. The escort usually was a relative of the parents; she agreed that if no other sponsor could be found, she would serve. In this way many Lalawignons obtained female kinsmen as baptismal sponsors, but more by failure of the ideal system than by purposeful choice of the parents.

Research was done in Caticugan to determine the role of the extension-intensification motives in shaping preferences for godparenthood sponsors. Table 13 indicates for the sample how many sponsors were kin and nonkin to their godchildren. This table demonstrates that 42 percent of all these sponsors were related to their godchildren. A higher proportion of confirmation godparents (48 percent) were kinsmen of their godchildren than of baptismal sponsors (39 percent).

Table 14 lists the various relationships of kinsmen-sponsors (see Table 13) to their godchildren. Excluding "distant" kinsmen (godparents for whom the informant was unsure of the exact genealogical relationship), aunts and uncles accounted for 44 percent of all sponsors. They are either the parents' siblings or classificatory kinsmen. Aunts, both real and classificatory, are more commonly sponsors than uncles.

TABLE 13

Relationship of Sponsors to Godchildren: Caticugan: 1965

Relationship of Sponsor	Godchildren		
	Baptism	Confirmation	*Totals*
Kinsmen	149	76	225
Nonkinsmen	232	84	316
Totals	381	160	541

In one way these sponsors are ideal compadres, for they are of the same generation as the godchild's parents.

Table 14 also indicates that one out of every three kinsmen-sponsors in Caticugan is a relative whose relationship is so distant the informants could not state the actual kinship linkage. It might be argued that such remote relatives were chosen to intensify diffused kinship bonds. If so, the effort did not promote more intimate relationships, for the godparents still were unable to describe their precise genealogical ties. Finally, 58 percent of Caticuganers' baptismal and confirmation godchildren were not relatives. There was no statistically significant difference in the ratio of nonkinsmen to total sponsors for baptism (92 percent) and marriage (89 percent).

Baptismal godchildren of the Siaton elite were more frequently nonkinsmen (92 percent) than those of Caticuganers (61 percent) (see Table 15). One probable reason for this pronounced difference for nonkin sponsors is that the elite are more often sought by persons wanting high-status sponsors. It is less necessary for kinsmen of the elite to create ritual kinship bonds to secure favors from the latter. Moreover, when the elite volunteer as sponsors, often for political purposes, they are more apt to seek individuals not already their kin. Yet the frequency of godchildren who were "distant" kinsmen (one out of every four) of their elite godparents indicates that some sought to intensify a remote kinship relationship.

Graph 3 charts the percentages of kin versus nonkin sponsors for eight Filipino communities. These percentages always include baptism, and sometimes confirmation and marriage sponsors. For Canaman the percentage of kinsman-sponsors in the observed groups differed from the percentage of kinsmen in the "expected" group that was based on

TABLE 14

Kinship Relations of Godparents to Godchildren: Caticugan: 1965

Kinship Relation of Godparents	Godchildren		Totals
	Baptism	Confirmation	
Stepfather	—	1	1
Aunt	7	11	18
Classificatory[1] aunt	33	9	42
Uncle	6	2	8
Classificatory[1] uncle	21	9	30
Grandmother	—	2	2
Classificatory[2] grandmother	11	3	14
Classificatory[2] grandfather	5	3	8
First cousin	6	4	10
Second cousin	10	6	16
Third cousin	4	1	5
"Distant kinsmen"	46	25	71
Totals	149	76	225

[1]Children of ego's grandparents' siblings' children.
[2]Ego's nonlineal grandparents.

a random sample of the entire population (Arce 1973: 66–67). Graph 3 illustrates the great variation in the relative importance of the extension and intensification motives as exemplified by Christian Filipino communities. Which motive, if any, dominates in the population as a whole is unknown.

If the Lalawigan and Caticugan data can be generalized beyond the environs of the villages, intensification is the result of factors other than the desire to strengthen kinship relations. Ideally, most of the barriofolk preferred nonrelative sponsors, but they gave many reasons for the volunteering or selection of kinsmen-sponsors, e.g., they are less

TABLE 15

Siaton Elite Sponsors' Relationships to Their Godchildren: 1972

Relationship of Sponsor	Godchildren		Totals
	Baptism	Marriage	
Kinsmen	10	10	20
Nonkinsmen	123	81	204
Totals	133	91	224

apt to refuse, they more frequently volunteer, and one can offer them a simple baptismal party or even dispense with it. Kinsman-sponsors reportedly feel a greater moral responsibility to facilitate a young relative's christening "for it cleans the soul of the original sin."

No informant expressed the idea that kinsman-sponsors were purposely sought to minimize the number of one's ritual kinsmen. Since folk tradition in Caticugan decrees that sponsors cannot be permanent members of one's household, compadrinazgo in this barrio cannot be utilized to promote harmony among the members of one's family or larger household. Hence, kinsman-sponsors are not chosen for this purpose. Since the barriofolk comprise a single social class, kinsman-sponsors rarely are selected to enhance interclass cohesion, as sometimes is the practice in Latin America.

One could hypothesize that if the crucial importance of an elaborate baptismal feast were reduced (or continues to decline) or if the meager resources of Caticuganers expanded, the frequency with which they seek nonkin sponsors would increase significantly. Undoubtedly, other economic variables are involved in the determination of the relative emphasis given to the extension and intensification motives, e.g., a wage versus a subsistence economy and market versus non-market oriented economics, social class, etc.

Social Classes and Compadrinazgo

Social-class relationships within compadrinazgo have attracted the attention of some researchers in Latin America, although this topic was never the sole focus of their investigations. The scarcity of detailed data

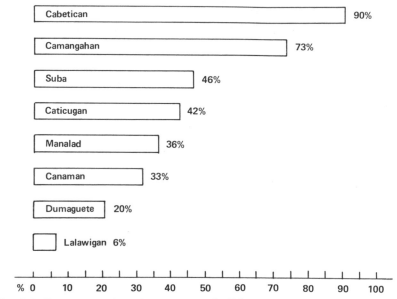

Graph 3: *Percentages of Kin Sponsors in Eight Filipino Communities.*[1]

[1]For Manalad, Graph 3 omits figures on kin and nonkin sponsors of the ten- to nineteen-year-old group. Their godparents predominantly are nonkinsmen, as a result of the population dispersal during the Second World War. This period's "general confusion led to a temporary withdrawal of extension of ritual kin ties to non-kinsmen" (Sibley 1965b: 6). Most likely these factors were at work elsewhere in the Philippines; however, most residents of Caticugan (including Siaton) and Lalawigan did not evacuate their communities during the Japanese occupation (Hart 1956).

on this subject for the Philippines makes most generalizations precarious. A major reason for the gap is that most studies of the godparenthood complex in both Latin America and the Philippines have centered on villages that normally are composed of a single social class. Hollnsteiner and Lynch and Arce have studied compadrinazgo in Philippine cities, but the relationships between social class and ritual kinship were only one of several topics examined. The one major exception is Potter's recent investigation of the godparenthood complex among the residents of Dumaguete, a middle-sized provincial city in Negros Oriental province.

In Canaman lower-class parents usually seek upper-class baptismal sponsors, while the town's elite select sponsors from their own class.

Arce interprets these choices as an attempt by the lower class to increase their security and by the upper class to preserve their status (1973: 64–65). The major criterion for the selection of sponsors in Canaman "is relative social standing where the rite is marriage" (Lynch 1959: 54, 121). As a result, Canaman elite usually seek still higher-status sponsors outside their communities—largely because the upper class in this town is so small.

In the Bisayas, Sibley found that slightly more than one-half of his sample of Camangahan baptism, confirmation, and marriage sponsors were of equal status. Informants judged most of the remaining sponsors to be of higher status than themselves, with only a few sponsors of lower status. In Manalad (originally settled by migrants from Camangahan), the percentage of higher status people serving as baptism and confirmation sponsors to those of equal status was only a little larger than in Camangahan.

A drastic difference between these two Bisayan barrios was the significantly larger percentage of higher status marriage sponsors in Manalad (Sibley 1965b: 19). In contrast to those in Camangahan, Manalad marriage sponsors "are seen as very important intermediaries with the outside world of employment and other opportunities" (Sibley 1965: 11).

In the Ilokan village of Tarong helpful ritual kinsmen are sought, but they appear to be persons of the parents' social class, often neighbors.

> Since the favor of those in power can be of considerable advantage, people of importance are sought as godparents and *sitio* and *barrio* leaders often are obligated in this way to a large number of families (Nydegger and Nydegger 1966: 68).

There are no elective government officials at the *sitio* level. The elective Barrio Council captain, in many Bisayan Filipino communities, is a person whose authority and prestige do not extend beyond his village.

Although this aspect of compadrinazgo in Siaton poblacion was not extensively investigated, the impression is that marriage sponsors of the elite often were yet higher-status persons from Dumaguete or other nearby cities. For example, when the daughter of a teacher in the poblacion elementary school married, one sponsor was a local Protestant congressman. The elite group usually has multiple sponsors for the marriage of their children, while in Caticugan there normally was only one sponsor each for the bride and for the groom.

In Caticugan and Lalawigan, compadrinazgo creates primarily intraclass bonds. When sponsors are sought who live outside these one-class communities, they too normally are equal-status persons. One repeated explanation given in Caticugan for not having elite patron sponsors is that it would be embarassing to ask them, for the barriofolk are "too poor" to provide the appropriately lavish feast. "But some are bold enough to ask the mayor. Then they will kill their last animal to have a big feast."

Social Control and Compadrinazgo

Outside the Philippines, compadrinazgo may be purposely exploited as a method of social control, to minimize or to prevent conflict (Eisenstadt 1956: 92). This is achieved, in large part, by the attitudes of extreme repect and reserve associated with the interaction of ritual kinsmen. Ideally, they must not fight, drink, or dance together. They should not swear at each other, and sexual relationships usually are prohibited (Gudeman 1972: 56). Some, however, have questioned the effectiveness of the godparenthood complex as an important means of social control (Sayres 1956).

Compadrinazgo does appear effective in minimizing conflict among most Filipino ritual kinsmen. When compadres do quarrel, their conflict is publicly and harshly criticized. If compadres rarely quarrel over property, it is because they rarely share common properties or inherit from the same person. Yet one common cause for sibling conflict in Lalawigan and Caticugan is disputes over the inheritance of one's parent's properties, especially land (Hart 1954a). In this aspect, the compadre relationship is not similar to the bonds uniting

Yet Filipino compadres do quarrel. In 1956 in Lalawigan two disputes involving ritual kinsmen occurred. In one instance a woman had borrowed some rice from her comadre. When she repaid the rice, the lender claimed she returned less than had been lent. This squabble eventually involved their husbands. The disagreement was settled, but "the two women never were friends again." Another dispute was between two compadres. One allegedly wounded the other's fighting cock in secret, with the idea of betting against the injured bird in a coming fight. When this act was discovered, the owner left the cockpit and went home to get his *bolo*. The police prevented an armed confrontation between the two compadres, but they remained enemies. Our informant for the latter incident remarked: "The people were surprised, for compadres rarely quarrel."

Lieban reports an interesting dispute between two compadres who live in Cebu.

> While Raymundo [a sorcerer] was visiting in another community, a *compare* of his approached him and asked him for an amulet . . . Raymundo declined, telling the man, "I know you are a *barangan* (sorcerer), and if I give you this you will be able to do it with impunity." Raymundo said his *compare* was hurt by this refusal, and after his *compare* left the house, Raymundo felt a pain in his chest, and he fell to the floor. He treated himself, and after 30 minutes the stinger of a ray [fish] came out of his chest. He then went to his *compare* and asked him what was the meaning of this. His *compare* told him that he should not be angry, that he (the *compare*) had just wanted to test him and he (Raymundo) had proved himself (1967: 37).

Quarrels occasionally occur among ritual kinsmen in Siaton municipality. In a barrio near Caticugan the wives of two compadres became involved in a bitter dispute because one claimed the other was having an affair with her husband. As a result of the wives' animosities the two husbands were "dragged into the quarrel." The two parties later amicably settled their dispute, but their "relations are not as good as before." In Siaton poblacion two compadres, arguing about the ownership of a piece of land, "almost shot it out." Their dispute was taken to the local court, but the accuser eventually dropped his charges. "Today the two compadres are again good friends."

One of our informants in Siaton sent a clipping from a (Cebu?) newspaper. The news story concerned a dispute over the age of a person running to be a delegate to the Constitutional Convention in Manila. It was the delegate's godfather who "charged his god-son in court with falsification of public documents."

One important study of compadrinazgo, based on research in two Colombian communities, asserts that the value of godparenthood as a social binder is "vastly overrated" (Sayres 1956: 351). It is a "social binder" only by diligently suppressing its negative effects. Such a conclusion does not apply generally to ritual kinship in the Bisayas. In Caticugan and Lalawigan most informants assert that compadres, especially, should not quarrel since they are older and are "like brothers and sister." What they forget is how often siblings quarrel, particularly over the inheritance of parental properties or their just division. But a quarrel among siblings is thought disgraceful; other kinsmen hasten to the threatened breach to prevent a public eruption. This same attitude is effective in minimizing conflict among compadres. Only after a diligent investigation was it possible to discover the disputes reported in this chapter. In each incident, the informants remarked that these disputes were extremely uncommon since compadres should "respect each other." Another reason for the relative rarity of quarrels involving ritual kin in Caticugan and Lalawigan is that most compadres live in different communities, so their daily interaction is restricted. While compadres do quarrel, compadrinazgo's positive role in maintaining social harmony is rather impressive.

Chapter Eight

Compadrinazgo: Comparative Structural and Functional Variations

This chapter compares and contrasts Filipino compadrinazgo primarily with that of Latin America, but includes secondarily that of Spain, France, and Italy. When available, information is also included for the variety of ritual kinship associated with the Eastern Church. This exposition is selective, since a comprehensive and detailed comparison is beyond the scope of this book. Sufficient data are presented, however, to indicate that the godparenthood complex in the Philippines, although closely related to Latin American compadrinazgo, is less varied in structure and function.

One prominent difference between compadrinazgo in the Philippines and Latin America is that Filipinos have relátively few occasions where sponsors are required or desirable. As indicated earlier, in the Philippines compadrinazgo occasions are, with a few exceptions, restricted to baptism, confirmation, and marriage. Among the Ilokans and Pampangans, sponsors are required, and ritual kinship bonds result, when a ceremony is held for a sick child. Curiously, where sponsorship occasions (often of a secular nature) proliferate in the Philippines, they are associated with an urban, often non-Catholic, minority (Potter 1973 and 1974). Perhaps as more data become available for the Philippines, additional sponsorship events will be discovered.

It is difficult to explain the relative paucity of occasions for ritual sponsorship in the Philippines in comparison with those of Latin America. As Chapter Two indicates, there is no convincing evidence that pre-Hispanic Latin Americans had more ceremonies that could be converted to or reinterpreted by the diffused godparenthood complex. As discussed earlier, compadrinazgo in Latin America and the Philippines is associated with various indigenous (and current) ceremonies related to sickness and its cure. It is attached in both realms to pre-Hispanic commercial activities and institutionalized friendship complexes. Blood brotherhood was a widespread institution that met the first Spaniards to the Philippines. This variety of ritual kinship was not as widespread in pre-Columbian South America.

Although the pre-Hispanic baptismal ceremonies of Latin Americans (e.g., the Aztecs and Mayans) possibly were more easily adapted to compadrinazgo, a similar if weaker association occurs in the Philippines—*buhos tubig.* The connection of the godparenthood complex with the activities of the Latin American midwife and shaman appear more prominent, but this affiliation is not absent among Filipinos. Most likely, compadrinazgo was more attractive to Latin Americans, whose social cohesion was threatened by the dissolution of their unilineal kinship units under Spanish domination. Bilaterally organized Filipinos did not suffer this change as a result of their colonization, although this factor does not fully explain the proliferation of occasions for ritual sponsorship in Latin America. Lastly, there are events of pre-Hispanic origin in contemporary Filipino rural society that could have been associated with compadrinazgo (as they are in Latin America) but are not. In Lalawigan and Caticugan house-warming ceremonies are connected with the occupation of a new dwelling, but sponsors are not (Hart 1959). In Lalawigan a common illness of young children is a sickness (*lanti*) similar to *susto* in Latin America; three different curing rites are prescribed but never ritual sponsorship (Hart 1975b).

No information could be located that the Church, based on earlier experiences in Latin America, purposely tried to limit the number of events in which Filipinos sought sponsors. Although the Church attempted to halt the economic and political "abuses" of ritual kinship associated with the Chinese participation in compadrinazgo, no similar edict was located that prohibited or discouraged the multiplication of sponsorship occasions. In fact, Catholicism in the Philippines was extensively "Filipinized" (Phelan 1959).

Significantly, however, urban Filipinos have added new occasions requiring sponsorship and often, but not always, resulting in ritual kinship ties among the participants. These occasions are associated not with rural but with city life. Potter's investigation found that in Dumaguete, among the more educated, often Protestant, Filipinos, sponsorship is associated with social "gangs" (*barkada*, also popular in the provinces), blessing of a new house, fraternities and sororities, release from prison, etc. In other words, the increase of sponsorship occasions beyond Church-prescribed rites and several additional described ceremonies widely and traditionally associated with folk Catholicism in the Philippines are associated at least in part with modernization and urbanization.

Folk Occasions for Sponsorship

Gudeman's proposed rules governing the variations of compadrinazgo were briefly summarized in Chapter One. This section illustrates these rules by listing the numerous events associated with folk compadrinazgo. Without doubt, this enumeration is incomplete; some sources for Latin America probably were overlooked, and, most certainly, future investigations of compadrinazgo will discover new ones. The variety and number of occasions appear almost endless.

The following occasions, all examples of the first variety of structure replication, represent extension of compadrinazgo from Church-prescribed rites in Europe, Latin America, the United States, and the Philippines: birth (*eschar de agua, bautismo de agua,* and *bautismo de campo*); emergency baptism, *evangélios* (a blessing and gospel-reading rite immediately following baptism); first hair-cut; first trimming of fingernails; ear-piercing; hanging scapulars on a child; presenting children to saints in an outdoor ceremony; *hetzmek*; first communion; initiating children into drinking mescal; graduation from sixth grade and high school; a girl's fifteenth birthday; engagement; placing a saint's crown on a child's head; seeking health or success from the Virgin; illness, often that of children suffering from fright (*susto*); donning of a *hábito* to avoid sickness; adoption; naturalization (Philippines); ordination into the priesthood; a priest's first mass; release from prison; seeking persons to help defray the cost of a funeral; and last communion (Anderson 1956: 40–46; Beals 1946: 102; Buechler and Buechler 1971: 48; Doughty 1968: 116; Edmonson 1957: 34; Fals-Borda 1962: 197; Foster 1953: 5; Gillin 1947: 105; Gudeman 1972: 61; Harris 1956: 152; Hollnsteiner 1963; Ingham 1970: 282–83; Jocano 1968a; Larson and Bergman 1969: 40; Lewis 1963: 351; Lomnitz 1973: 43; Madsen 1960b: 99; Manners 1966: 150; Middleton 1975: 461–75; Mintz and Wolf 1950: 354; Nuñez del Prado 1973: 21; Nurge 1965; Pal 1956a; Parsons 1936: 26–27, 55; Potter 1973: 203; Redfield and Villa Rojas 1962: 188–90; Reina 1966: 230; Rubel 1966: 83, 198–99; Sanders 1962: 169; Scheans

1962; Seda 1966: 295; Sibley 1965b; Spicer 1940: 95–101; Spielberg 1968: 208; Stein 1961: 131; Thompson 1971: 384; Van den Berghe and Van den Berghe 1966: 1237; Vincent 1966: 57; Whitten 1965: 111; Wolf 1966b: 209).

The second variety of structure replication occurs when in the ceremony objects are substituted for the godchild. All the following ceremonies, with two exception, are limited to Latin America: purchase or house-warming of a new residence; installation or removal of crosses on the residence for certain religious feasts; installation of a new residential altar; celebration for a household saint or saint's picture; ownership or protection of a new personal object; cross-raising ceremony for the dead; the cermonial opening of a new container of maize drink; buying a new tractor, a store, or a mule; opening a new saloon; the godmother's washing the sacred oils of christening from the godchild's baptismal bonnet (*comare de coppola*); the making of cookie-dough dolls; and the sale of cattle (Anderson 1956: 40–46; Beals 1946: 104; Doughty 1968: 116; Gillin 1947: 105; Grimes and Hinton 1969 8: 803; Gudeman 1972: 61; Harvey and Kelly 1969 8: 669; Ingham 1970: 282–83; Lewis 1963: 351; Lomnitz 1973: 43; Romanucci-Ross 1973: 79; Madsen 1960b: 102 and 1969: 625; Reina 1966: 231; Spielberg 1968: 208; Stein 1961: 131; Whitten 1965: 111).

The third variant of structure replication has substitutes replacing both the godchild and parent. An individual may "sponsor" an object for an institution, a group, or the community. An officiating priest may or may not be involved in these ceremonies. For these ceremonies, sponsors may be selected for a carnival, a party, a fraternity or sorority, a basketball or soccer game, a May Day celebration, or the visit of a bishop; sponsors may also be selected as donors of a new chapel or additions or improvements to a church, a new religious image or a new robe for the Virgin, a new bridge, or an object acquired by a school or club (Beals 1946: 104; Doughty 1968: 116; Gillin 1947: 105; Lewis 1963: 351; Madsen 1960b: 109–12, and 1969: 625; Parsons 1936: 249–50, 283–84; Potter 1973: 203; Pitt-Rivers 1961: 107, footnote 1; Service and Service 1954: 172; Wagley 1964: 153; Whitten 1965: 111).

It might be argued that an additional rule should be added to those Gudeman offers to explain the variations of compadrinazgo. This new variation is the creation of ritual kinship bonds without the sponsorship of a person or object. For example, *compadres de voluntad* in Puerto Rico may be friends or "buddies" who establish compadre relationships simply by shaking hands (Seda 1966: 294). This purely secular form of compadrazgo is also used by neighborhood toughs or bullies to establish nonaggression pacts with each other (Wolf 1966b: 209). Although most *compadres de voluntad* usually are considered less important than ritual kinsmen through baptism, and such sponsorship is uncommon, they address each other with the formal *usted*. Similar highly secular forms of compadrazgo have been discussed earlier; *compadres del dedo* in Martineztown; compadres through *pinalit nga relacion* in Samar; and *compadres de fogueira* in Brazil. In none of these examples is a person or object sponsored. In some a brief rite occurs, but for others there is no ceremony.

These pacts are meaningful only in relationship to sacred forms of sponsorship. In some instances the religious "mooring" is implicit. For example, the person initiating *pinalit nga relacion* compadrazgo must give the parents money equal to the baptismal fee. Moreover, they choose this form of sponsorship only when neither has a child to be christened. *Compadres de fogueira* often select St. John's Day for the occasion, an event six months prior to Christmas, a birth ceremony. More important, St. John baptized Christ. Although neither a person nor an object is sponsored, there is a logic of ideology concerning birth, rebirth, and baptism associated with St. John's Day. Possibly "jumping over the fire" may have a symbolic "cleansing" function.

These purely or largely secular occasions for ritual sponsorship are based explicitly or implicitly on an ultimately religious justification of the rites. The basic model proposed by Gudeman applies, although the purposes for creating ritual kinship bonds may be solely secular in nature. In a sense, there could be no "secular" compadres without the prior existence of a model for "sacred" compadres.

Position Replication

Position replication for compadrinazgo is accomplished by three procedures: repeat sponsorship; the "blanketing-in" process; and multiple sponsors. All three of these processes, resulting in "a proliferation of children or ceremonies for the same godparents" (Gudeman 1972: 63), occur in the Philippines. What follows is a comparison of these aspects of the Philippine godparenthood complex with compadrinazgo elsewhere in the world.

Repeat Sponsorship

Although Canon law prohibits repeat sponsorship (Gudeman 1972: 63), it is frequently associated with compadrinazgo in Europe and Latin America. Among Greek peasants it is the marriage godparent's "right and duty" to sponsor the baptism of the couple's children (Campbell 1964: 222; also Sanders 1962: 170, 177). If the godparent cannot attend the christening of his godchild's first-born, the child's father is permitted to select another sponsor.

Greek parents with many children rarely permit an unmarried sponsor to serve as the godparent of all their offspring (Sanders 1962: 177). For example, when a second son is born, the father may slyly ask his wedding sponsor "if he would mind surrendering his right on this occasion because X has asked him if he might have that honour" (Campbell 1964: 222). If the couple's first child is a daughter, the wedding sponsor serves as her baptismal sponsor and normally also for the first son when he is born. "However, if two or three girls are born in succession, he may be asked to waive his right before the birth of the next child in case he is bringing bad luck by having an 'unlucky hand' . . ." (Campbell 1964: 222–23).

If childlessness, still-birth, or infant mortality is considered the fault of the marriage godparent in rural Greece, repeat sponsorhip may be stopped. One informant's first child died almost immediately after birth; later she had a pseudo-pregnancy. The godparent was blamed. After she recovered from giving birth to a healthy daughter, the mother put the infant on the porch of the church dedicated to the Virgin. She then waited to see who would find the infant and, by this act, be designated its godparent.

> People standing around consider it lucky to be a godparent on such an occasion, and several may be inclined to volunteer. An especially eager person may throw a handkerchief ahead of a rival and thus stake out a claim. The mother watches from a distance. When the child has been taken into the church for the ceremony, she goes home to prepare sweets and other food for the baptismal feast (Sanders 1962: 177).

In the Balkans, if age prohibits repeat sponsorship, it may be continued by succession from father to son (Halpern 1958: 161; Hammel 1968).

Repeat sponsorship frequently is associated with compadrinazgo in Latin America. Although detailed data rarely are presented, a sufficiency of sources agree that godparents may sponsor, in addition to the godchild's baptism, either or both confirmation and marriage (Reina 1966: 229–30; Stein 1961: 133; Whitten 1965: 103; Madsen 1960b: 88; Osborn 1968: 599; Manrique 1969: 714; Laughlin 1969b 7: 306; Diaz 1966: 62). In at least one part of Latin America, as in the Balkans, if the original godparent is dead, one of his children may serve as the sponsor (Reina 1966: 229). One unique variation of repeat sponsorship occurs when a Kwaiker couple is given a chance to marry in the church. At that time they also bring their children for baptism. "They will then use the same sponsor(s) for the two ceremonies, which are performed at the same time" (Osborn 1968: 599).

Although the same godparents may sponsor all the children of a couple in Latin America (Lewis 1963: 350), sometimes a limit is placed on the number of children they may sponsor for a couple. The same godparents in Tzintzuntzan are rarely asked to sponsor two or more children of the same parents (Foster 1967: 83; 1969: 274). The Zinacanteco Mayas and the Mitleyenos believe that the same godparent should sponsor only three children of the same family (Vogt 1970: 64; Parsons 1936: 395). Mexican-Americans limit to three the number of repeat sponsorships in one family. "This multiple relationship is described as making the sign of the cross . . ." (Rubel 1966: 81).

Most sources for Latin America do not indicate the frequency of repeat sponsorship when this kind of position replication is necessary or permitted. An exception is that in Tlayacapan, repeat sponsorship occurred in 21 percent of all baptisms (Ingham 1970: 284).

A variety of reasons is given for repeat sponsorship in Latin America. In Santa Cruz Chinautla, one criterion in the selection of a baptismal godparent is the prospect that he will sponsor his godchild's later confirmation and marriage, and the christening of the latter's first-born (Reina 1966: 229–30). In one instance the failure to follow the local custom of repeat sponsorship is believed to be a sin (Villa Rojas 1945: 90, 142). This custom is also used to limit the burden of too many compadres (Lewis 1963: 350). Repeat sponsorship "satisfies the demands of religion and adds very little to the charges of compadrazgo ties . . ." (Foster 1969: 274). However, as in Greece, when repeat sponsorship is traditional or mandatory, exceptions usually occur.

As has already been indicated, repeat sponsorship appears, on the basis of limited data, to be only a minor aspect of Philippine compadrinazgo. Although it is permissible, repeat sponsorship rarely is obligatory. In fact, in southern Negros the people have a diffused feeling that it may be supernaturally harmful. It certainly is not extensively used as a way to limit the number of one's ritual kinsmen. However, a definitive statement on this aspect of Filipino compadrinazgo awaits future research.

"Blanketing-in" Process

A second variety of position replication is the extension of ritual kinship terms and relationships to kinsmen of the principals (Gudeman 1972: 62). This variety also has been called the "blanketing-in" process (Foster 1967). The extension of ritual kinship bonds also is associated with some non-Church-prescribed rites. Of course, such extension does not occur for these rites when the principals are not ceremonially related. Ritual kinship ties may be diffused beyond the principals automatically or by choice by participating in the *abrazo*. The extension normally but not always is reciprocal. For example, in Tobatí most sponsors extend compadre terminology to the godchild's grandparents, but the reverse usage is rare (Service and Service 1954: 177).

Usually, only compadre terms are extended, although sometimes the children of one's compadres' siblings or the godparent-godchild relationships may be included (Gudeman 1972: 62; Nelson 1971: 56). In San Cruz Chinautla one woman considered herself the godgrandmother of her son's godchild (Reina 1966: 233). In Tobatí the terms *pa'ino (ma'ina) guazú* may be used by the godchild to address the father or mother of his godparents. "These terms mean 'big godfather (mother)' in Guaraní. We never heard a similar extension in Spanish" (Service and Service 1954: 177). In parts of Brazil and Greece, as in Caticugan, ritual kinship bonds unite all the godchildren of one sponsor.

Although extension of ritual relationships often is limited to specific persons, in other cases it is truly "blanketing" (Reina 1966: 223). For example, in Yalálag (Mexico) "in addition to the baptismal relationship between parents, child, and godparents, all living ascending relatives of both groups are recognized as being in the compadrazgo unit" (Foster 1953: 8). A more elaborate system for the extension of ritual kinship terms is reported for Moche. In this community

> the *compadrazgo* terms generalize to blood relatives of the parents and of the godparents. Thus, brothers and sisters of the parents always stand in this relationship to the godparents and also to the latters' respective brothers and sisters. The relationship even extends to cousins of the same generation. Some informants say that it also extends to the grandparents of the child, but in testing this I have never heard a godfather spontaneously call his godchild's grandfather, *"compadre"* (Gillin 1947: 107).

However, in Huaylas baptismal godparents sometimes are regarded as compadres by the godchild's grandparents (Doughty 1968: 118).

The "blanketing-in" process is also part of Philippine compadrinazgo, although its occurrence varies among the various cultural-linguistic groups. In Lalawigan and Caticugan ritual kinship bonds rarely are extended beyond the principals; in Malitbog, on the other hand, the "blanketing-in" process is quite comprehensive. And whether these ceremonial ties are diffused beyond the primary sponsors often depends upon individual choice. In comparison with Latin Americans, Filipinos appear to have made less use of these two varieties of position replication. For Caticugan and Lalawigan, the rarity of repeat sponsorship suggests that these Filipinos do not seek purposely to limit the number of their ritual kinsmen. On the other hand, the infrequency of the "blanketing-in" process indicates a contrary attitude on the part of many rural Filipinos.

Caticugan informants admit that when such extension occurs, the ritual kinship bonds usually are not as intimate or demanding as the "real" ties linking actual participants in the ceremonies—an attitude shared by many Latin Americans (Foster 1953: 8). Both peoples seldom confuse the extension of compadrinazgo terms with the extension of ritual kinship relationships. "Because an individual stands in the category of *compadre* does not mean that all the concomitant rights and obligations of the bond are extended to him. The latter may depend upon such factors as proximity, social closeness and so forth" (Gudeman 1972: 63).

Multiple Sponsors

A third permutation of compadrinazgo results from position replication of the godparent/compadre role. "The number of godparents chosen for any occasion may vary; each godparent stands in place of the other" (Gudeman 1972: 62). The number of sponsors may not be fixed by local custom; it may instead reflect the social class or personal wishes of the principals. In one Hungarian village a child may have as many as twenty extra pairs of sponsors for his christening (Fel and Hofer 1969: 165, footnote 8).

It is not unusual for some Latin Americans, especially individuals of some social or political importance, each to accumulate during a lifetime hundreds of godchildren and compadres. A Cherán resident had 100 compadres of baptism alone (Beals 1946: 104). In Merida, one person claimed over 1,000 godchildren (Redfield 1941: 222). An informant in a small Colombian town, who claimed 200 godchildren, added: "One day in Buenos Aires, that small community in the mountains above San Pedro, I obtained twenty-five godchildren" (Richardson 1970: 84). One woman in Huaylas had 258 ritual kinsmen, a number possibly higher than the average but not unusual (Doughty 1968: 118). Multiple sponsorings bring other benefits beyond social, political, and economic advantages. One couple with 100 godchildren explained: "We are preparing a better heavenly reward through the favors we have done for all the people" (Reina 1966: 208).

Multiple sponsorship normally occurs most frequently for baptism and marriage. In one rural Spanish-American community in New Mexico the usual custom for a baptism is to have three sponsors; two are the same sex as the infant, and one is of the opposite sex (Edmonson 1957: 43). An example of the elaboration of the number and specialized functions of marriage sponsors is given for San Cristobal de las Casas.

> At marriage, there are often several sets of *primerios padrinos* or *padrinos de velación;* and, in addition, from four to six madrinas (*de laso, de anillo, de arras, de ramo, de rosario, de libro*) perform distinct functions during the church wedding (Van den Berghe and Van den Berghe 1966: 1237).

The number of sponsors chosen in Latin America is not always, however, a direct reflection of the importance of the ceremony (Romney and Romney 1966: 53).

For individuals who have hundreds of compadres and godchildren, many of the ritual bonds often are weak and uncertain. For example, a woman in Itá, whose social position probably was the highest of that of any resident in the community, kept a notebook listing the names of her godchildren. When a young man came to her, saying he was godchild, she first checked her notebook. If his name was omitted (the notebook was incomplete) she then asked him his age, the names of his parents, and when he was baptized. When she was convinced he was her godchild, she extended the appropriate home hospitality and credit at her store (Wagley 1964: 158).

Multiple sponsorship, like repeat sponsorship and the "blanketing-in" process, is part of Filipino compadrinazgo. Multiple sponsors are almost always limited to baptism and marriage. Moreover, the number of sponsors for these ceremonies is a direct reflection of the social prominence of the parents. For this reason, many Filipino peasants consider multiple sponsors inappropriate for their social class. In Caticugan and Lalawigan multiple sponsorship was rare and occurred only for those few prominent village residents.

Permanent or Transitory Ritual Kinship Bonds

In some instances, sponsorship of prescribed Church rites may not create permanent ritual kinship bonds. Ceremonial ties and associated duties may cease immediately after the event or at a later date. For example, obligations of marriage godparents in Italy and Tobatí end with the ceremonies (Anderson 1956: 14, 19; Service and Service 1954: 173). The same is true of confirmation sponsors in Castile (Kenny 1962: 73) and of Tarascan baptismal godparents when their godchildren wed (Beals 1969: 767). When a godchild dies the compadre relationship between the baptismal sponsor and the parents is dissolved. And in Aritama if a sponsor returns to the parents the baptismal fee he paid, their ritual kinship bonds are severed. Moreover, the parents can give the same money to another person who "automatically assumes the function of the former godparents" (Reichel-Dolmatoff 1961: 173). In this same community, co-sponsors are not ritually related unless one of them is the biological father of the child (Reichel-Dolmatoff 1961: 172). But in San Lorenzo, an Ecuadorian town of 2,221 people, the compadre relationship is important "even after the nominal responsibility for the child disappears, and *sometimes the bond is a lifelong one* [underscore added]" (Whitten 1965: 104–5).

Whether rites not prescribed by the Church result in ritual kinship relationships, and how permanent or transitory these ceremonial bonds are, varies throughout Latin America. In different communities the same or similar events may or may not create ritual kinship ties. In Huaylas, godparents are chosen to sponsor the inauguration of "something new that is acquired by some institution such as the school, a club. No interpersonal relationships [are] established" (Doughty 1968: 116). Yet in San Francisco Tecospa, a village of 800 Nahuatl Indians in Mexico, sponsors for the erection of a new bridge or the reconstruction of a church become compadres to the town's inhabitants (Madsen 1960b: 109–12). In Cherán, a town of about 5,000 people in Michoacán, Mexico, when a new church image is blessed, sponsors are invited, but they never call each other compadre (Beals 1946: 104); a similar sponsorship in Moche does create ritual kinship ties among the participants (Gillin 1947: 104).

In Tecospa a sponsor for a new scapulary (a cloth necklace with the image of the Virgin of Carmen) is secured in this impersonal way. A person usually asks any stranger he chances to meet on the street to serve as his sponsor. The two individuals go to the church for the brief rite. After the ceremony the owner of the scapulary may buy his new godparent some fruit. "Since the godfather has no further obligations he is known as a 'godparent of twenty-four hours' " (Madsen 1960b: 99). The same impersonal method of selecting sponsors occurs in Aritama; the ritual kinship ties appear equally transitory (Reichel-Dolmatoff 1961: 173).

The durability of ritual kinship bonds created by folk rites often depends upon the wishes of the participants. The ritual kinship relationship may be lightly accepted or be as intimate and demanding as ceremonial bonds resulting from baptism. For example, on St. John's and St. Peter's day in Brazil, persons may become *compadres de fogueira* (of the fire) by jumping "over the fire" (glowing embers) with clasped hands while reciting an oath of unison (Wagley 1964: 153). Although the ritual bonds resulting from this rite may be slight or fleeting, "co-fathership [co-fatherhood] by fire can be as intimate and stable as that formed by baptism" (Wagley 1964: 153–54). A unique aspect of this Brazilian ceremony is that sometimes individuals also " 'confirm' their kinship or their previously existing co-father relationship 'over the fire' " (Wagley 1964: 154, footnote 9). In Minas Velhas this ritual linkage, created by a similar rite during the fiesta of San Joao, is not as vital as compadreship through baptism (Harris 1956: 152).

If a ritual kinship relationship for a Kwaiker Indian in Colombia is unsatisfactory, he simply withdraws. He "will avoid his mestizo co-parent or godparent, however much the mestizo harasses and entreats him to continue the relationship" (Osborn 1968: 604). If a mestizo wishes to break the compadre bond, he ignores the Indian and his family. In one Mexican village in Morelos a compadre may disregard the ritual relationship, causing it to lapse (Romanucci-Ross 1973: 80).

In the Philippines ritual kinship bonds generated by sponsorship of Church-prescribed rites are permanent. Informants in Caticugan and Lalawigan (and the literature searched) reported no instances when compadrinazgo ties ceased to exist (with the death or marriage of a godchild, etc.). Folk rites requiring sponsorship (for example, those reported for Cabetican) create regular ritual kinship relationships. The one exception is that sponsorship for some secular rites in Dumaguete may not result in compadre bonds.

The functional vitality of ritual kinship bonds does, however, vary among rural Filipinos. For example, sponsors secured through the former escort system of Lalawignons or "picked up at the church" in Borongan and Siaton often have no functional value since the participants were strangers or rarely interacted with each other after the ceremony was finished. Social class and geographical mobility may diminish the practical value of compadres. In Estancia ritual kinship ties last "only as long as their utilitarian functions remain" (Szanton 1972: 113). It is presumed, however, that in this instance the ritual kinship bonds are not dissolved, but merely that they are not used. Perhaps the less permanent nature of some ritual kinship ties in Latin America, in comparison with the Philippines, is explained by the fact that Latin Americans have more opportunities to obtain ritual kinsmen than do Filipinos, so the permanency of the ties is less important. Additionally, the permanent nature of compadrinazgo relationships in the Philippines reflects the fewer folk occasions for sponsorship and the less "secularization" of ritual kinship among Filipinos.

Selectee and Volunteer Sponsors

Considerable information is available, mainly for Latin America, on the ways sponsors are selected, but the conditions under which sponsors volunteer and the relative frequency of selectee versus volunteer sponsors rarely are reported in the extensive literature examined.

Although kinship and friendship may be primary determinants in the selection of ritual sponsors, other criteria also are used.

> The selection of godparents appears to be simple, but actually it is a complicated process in which many rules are brought to bear and careful consideration is given to personality, blood and ethnic relationships, age, economic condition, political views, and any other factors which might prove a handicap to either co-parents, godchildren, or godparents (Reina 1969: 113).

In Martineztown parents may choose sponsors for desirable personality and physical traits supposedly transmitted to their godchildren (Vincent 1966: 34). In one Peruvian community sponsors should be selected whose home life is harmonious and tranquil, since these desirable qualities later are transferred to their godchildren when they establish a family (Nuñez del Prado 1973: 23). Among the Mixtec (Costa Rica), children sometimes are permitted to select their (confirmation?) godparents and thus have an opportunity to "learn about these significant relationships" (Ravicz and Romney 1969 7: 392).

Ceremonial sponsors, when selected, may be chosen by the parents, godparents, a friend, as dictated by tradition (for example, repeat sponsorship), or, for a marriage, by the bridal pair (Lewis 1963: 350, 361, 368; Lewis 1960: 67; Ingham 1970: 282; Paul and Paul 1952: 242, 245; Redfield 1941: 221–22; Gillin 1947: 107; Madsen 1969: 625; Ravicz and Romney 1969 7: 392; Gudeman 1972: 56; Stein 1961: 132; Redfield and Villa Rojas 1962: 98, 194; Ravicz 1967: 247; Kottak 1967: 434; Service and Service 1954: 173, 273; Foster 1967: 70; Vincent 1966: 52; Pitt-Rivers 1961: 107; Kenny 1962: 63).

Less information is available on volunteer sponsorship. Tepoztecans in Mexico City volunteer more frequently as sponsors than those who remain in Tepoztlán (Lewis 1965: 433). Some data on volunteer sponsorship are available from statements describing the difficulties of rejecting such a sponsor. In Cortina d'Aglio, parents must accept a person who makes known his wish to be a sponsor, even if they desire another to sponsor their child. Likewise, one cannot reject a volunteer sponsor since one cannot refuse San Giovanni, the patron of godparents (Moss and Cappannari 1960: 30–31). In Tepoztlán a spurned volunteer may regard his rejection as an insult. The net effect is to restrict parental control over the selection of godparents (Lewis 1965: 433).

It is somewhat easier, and apparently more common, for a person who is asked to be a sponsor to refuse the honor. In Cherán, individuals may refuse to be batismal sponsors, for if the parents die they have the responsibility of caring for a minor godchild (Beals 1946: 104, 171). Hualcan parents, with a gift of food, visit a potential baptismal sponsor. If the person refuses the gift, they look for another possible sponsor (Stein 1961: 132). Sponsorship refusal occurs in San Lorenzo, but almost never among peers (Whitten 1965: 105). In Manta (Ecuador) one rarely refuses when asked to be a godparent, although a few do (Middleton 1975: 465). In one Mexican village, refusal to be a sponsor is regarded as "humiliating the poor"; Romanucci-Ross knew of no one in this community who had rejected sponsorship (1973: 80). Among Puerto Ricans in Chicago, "asking to baptize a child is an accepted practice and being refused is regarded as an affront to one's character" (Press 1963: 476).

Latin Americans may avoid the selection of intimate friends as sponsors (Stein 1961: 203). For instance, the Mayans of Guatemala do not seek intimate friends as sponsors. One's "choice is restricted by the desire not to accept offers from very close friends, for this means that the friendship would be terminated because of the substitution of respect relationships" (Nash 1958: 66). A Peruvian informant in Huaylas expressed an identical opinion. He did not wish to become a close friend's compadre since it required replacing the informal address term *tú* with the formal *usted*. " 'For this reason,' the man remarked, 'I do not like the system because my relationships with my friends lose some of their warmth' " (Doughty 1968: 115).

Baptismal Meal and the *Abrazo*

The traditional meal following a christening in Latin America is the primary responsibility of the child's parents. In Mexico, if not for much of Latin America, this meal (or feast) is, for the parents, the most costly aspect of a baptism (Foster 1948: 262; 1953: 5; 1960: 122; 1967: 77; Gudeman 1972: 56; Redfield and Villa Rojas 1962: 184; Paul and Paul 1952: 182). Normally, the baptismal meal (called *convite* in Spanish) is served in the parents' house. In Middle America, if the child is first taken to the sponsor's dwelling, the meal later is held there (Ravicz 1967: 245). The godparents may later reciprocate with a food gift to their new compadres (Ravicz 1966: 281).

For most of Latin America, the ideal baptismal meal is a fancy one. In Moche, for example, the parents are "obligated to provide as elaborate a party at their house as their circumstances permit" (Gillin 1947: 108). In Hualcan, the baptismal fiesta following the christening may begin after the ceremony and can continue throughout the following day (Stein 1961: 279). One well-to-do Puerto Rican lawyer residing in Chicago rented a large hall for the baptism of his child and for three other children he sponsored. "Expenses for hall rental and food for nearly 300 guests ran to more than five hundred dollars" (Press 1963: 478).

The amount of money the parents can or are willing to spend for the baptismal fiesta has an important influence—often the determining one—on the selection of the baptismal sponsor(s). For example, in Cherán the main reason for the frequent selection of kinsman-sponsors "is a desire to save money, as between relatives there need be no ceremony or expense" (Beals 1946: 103).

In Latin America the baptismal meal often is conceived as more than merely an entertainment for the new godparents. In Moche the meal is regarded "as a public recognition of the newly established kinship relationship" (Gillin 1947: 108). In Tonalá compadrazgo bonds are not considered final until the parents serve a meal to their new compadres. In one instance in which the parents in this Mexican community were unable to give a christening party, the sponsors refused to address them as compadres (Diaz 1966: 131). In Tzintzuntzan the baptismal meal (and wedding feast) is equally essential since the new relationships are ritually formalized by the *abrazo* during this feast. "Only if the embrace, the *abrazo* is given, is the compadrazgo legitimized" (Foster 1967: 71, 77).

Either before or after the baptismal or the wedding meal, the new godparents in Tzintzuntzan kneel, embrace the parents of the sponsored person, and declare: " 'Formerly we were friends; now we're going to be compadres. Here, and in the presence of God, we will respect each other as God commands' " (Foster 1967: 71). The *abrazo* also extends valid ritual relationships with other eligible persons who desire them and are present at the celebration (Foster 1967: 84). A similar ceremony for the same purpose is also held by Tarascans (Beals 1969 8: 767). Not only are ritual kinsmen secured by Zinacantecos through the traditional Catholic sacramental rites but "dozens of *compadres* are added, by extension, in the ritual meals at home which follow the rites of baptism and confirmation, and more especially in the 'house entering' and 'wedding ceremonies' " (Vogt 1970: 64).

The *abrazo* is of crucial importance in determining the extension of ritual kinship ties in Cherán. There are two categories of matrimonial compadres in this small town. First, there are the marriage sponsors of the bride and groom and, second, the couple's relatives, including the parents of the bridal pair and "all of their [parent's] brothers, sisters, and first cousins, in short, all the people the bride and groom may call aunt and uncle." For this second group the ritual embrace is also required to formalize the compadre ties. The bride's and groom's parents, kneeling on a mat, are embraced by all who wish to be compadres, proclaiming: " 'In the future, you will be my *compadre* (*comadre*) of Heaven and I pray God that we never offend one another.' . . . When this act is completed all have the right to call each other *compadres* in the future" (Beals 1946: 103). Unlike in Tzintzuntzan, in Cherán the ritual embrace is not required of the principal marriage sponsors and is not performed for baptism. Also, the compadrinazgo relationship in Moche is extended, without a ritual embrace, to cousins, and some informants claimed to be the grandparents of the godchild (Gillin 1947: 107).

The following statement has been made concerning the function of the ritual embrace.

> This is true [that the choice of ritual kinsmen often depends on the existence of appropriate sentiments] even in the extension of the *compa-drazgo* to the parents of *compadres;* the relationship is established only when they exchange the ritual embrace, and it is always therefore possible to avoid (Pitt-Rivers 1968: 412).

The ritual embrace occurs neither in Caticugan nor in Lalawigan, nor is it reported in the literature on Philippine compadrinazgo. In this regard Latin Americans again have greater choice than Filipinos in deciding whether or not they wish to be ritually related to persons other than the principal participants in the ceremony.

Baptism

A child in Latin America (less commonly so in the Philippines) may have two different sets of baptismal godparents. For example, in Puerto Rico newly-born infants usually are baptized in the home shortly after birth. Such baptism (*echar de agua,* to throw water, *bautismo de agua,* or *bautismo de campo,* field baptism) is not recognized by the Church (unless the child is dangerously ill), nor does it remove the stigma of original sin. While it may be an emergency baptism, most Puerto Ricans use this occasion to postpone temporarily the necessity for a church baptism. Sponsors usually are family members or grandparents. The same sponsors may be selected later for the church christening (Manners 1966: 150; Wolf 1966b: 209; Mintz 1966: 388).

As indicated earlier, emergency baptism for a dying or sick infant occurs in the Philippines. Sometimes the same sponsors may be selected for the church baptism, if the child lives. Filipinos, however, never use this variety of baptism unless the infant's health indicates that it may not survive long enough for a church baptism. Filipinos usually delay the formal christening if they are financially incapable of paying their share of the cost of a church baptism. Baptism may also be delayed in more remote villages until the priest visits the community during the annual fiesta. On this occasion mass baptisms are held in the village chapel.

An unbaptized child in rural Spain and in parts of Latin America is called a *Moro*, or Moor, that is, one not of the true faith (Kenny 1962: 73; Manners 1966: 150; Whitten 1965: 103; Reichel-Dolmatoff 1961: 171; Foster 1960: 120). Muslim Filipinos are also known as *Moros*, but this generally pejorative term is never applied to unbaptized children in Caticugan and Lalawigan. In one Panayan village the popular nickname for an unbaptized child is *muritu* or "not yet human" (Jocano 1969: 15).

Godparents usually are obliged to pay the cost of the christening, including the church fee and baptismal dress for the godchild (and sometimes other infant clothing). Less frequently, the godparent may contribute food and drink for the christening feast, pay a photographer for pictures of the event, and give the godchild a gift. On occasion, the new godparents may entertain their godchild's parents at a later date (Kenny 1962: 72; Tax and Hinshaw 1969 7: 87; Osborn 1968: 599; Parsons 1936: 80; Romanucci-Ross 1973: 80; Nuñez del Prado 1973: 21; Madsen 1969 8: 264; Lewis 1960: 67; Wellin 1949: 19; Redfield and Villa Rojas 1962: 245; Ravicz 1967: 245; Harris 1956: 154; Gudeman 1972: 56; Middleton 1975: 466; Ingham 1970: 283; Rubel 1966: 83; Seda 1966: 295; Vincent 1966: 62; Mintz 1966: 388).

About one year after the christening meal, parents in Chan Kom invite their compadres to their dwelling and formally acknowledge gratitude. During this event (*tzicil*), the parents wash their compadres' hands. Rum and cigarettes are served, and a turkey, other food, and candles are given the godparents when they depart (Redfield and Villa Rojas 1962: 187–88).

The ceremonial responsibilities of baptismal godparents in Latin America may extend beyond the christening. In Tepoztlán, "about forty days after the baptism, the godparents present their godchild with a tray on which they have placed his baptismal clothes for the *sacamisa* or the first mass attended by the mother and new baby" (Lewis 1960: 67, 72; Lewis 1963: 351; Redfield 1930: 138). After the mass, the godchild's parents may visit the godparents with food and drink. Later in the day the godparents go to their compadres' house with some musicians and friends. "This celebration involves considerable expense, and most families are able to fulfill only a minimum of the obligations" (Lewis 1963: 369). (For example, gifts for the godchild may be omitted: Lewis 1963: 351.) In fact, many Tepoztlán godchildren "actually never receive anything from their *padrinos*" (Lewis 1960: 67).

In many areas in Middle America parents are required to honor their child's godparents in a costly ceremony called "washing the hands." In one Mixtec village this rite usually is held when the godchild is "between four and eleven years of age" (Ravicz 1966: 282). The godparents are invited to the residence of their godchild's parents where their hands are ritually washed ". . . to remove from the *padrino* [and *madrina*] the parental sins transferred through the baptism of the child" (Ravicz 1966: 285). This rite, like the *abrazo*, formalizes the ritual kinship ties created by baptismal sponsorship. (This ceremony does not occur in Caticugan and Lalawigan.

Of all ritual kinship relationships, those created by baptism usually are considered the most important and demanding. There are, however, some exceptions. In San Lorenzo only middle-class sponsors pay the christening fee. The sponsors neither furnish the baptismal clothing, give gifts to their godchild after the ceremony, nor entertain their new compadres. Although the godparent-godchild dyad is stressed in Arembepe, gift-giving is rare in this Brazilian fishing village of 730 persons located in Bahia. The relationship between the godparent and godchild is mainly ceremonial; the godparent's first obligations are to their kinsmen (Kottak 1967: 442). And in Puerto Rico godparents often have no permanent obligations to their godchildren other than the exchange of ritual greetings (Seda 1966: 295).

The magical elements that adhere in the minds of the peasants to baptism were mentioned earlier for the Philippines. This associated folk concept of baptism also occurs in Europe and Latin America. Christening is one technique for protecting the infant from harm from both Christian and pagan supernatural entities. This folk preternatural function of baptism is also associated with sponsors. In Greece, Latin America, and the Philippines some sponsors are "lucky" godparents; their godchildren are healthy and survive. Their "luck" may be transferred to their godchildren. In Greece, a sponsor may stand as godparent to several children in one family. However, if his compadre has unusual difficulties during pregnancy, a stillbirth occurs, or an infant godchild dies, another sponsor is selected. For some Latin Americans a "lucky" godparent can transfer this desirable quality to his godchildren (Reina 1966 7: 113). One municipal official in Siaton was popular as a baptismal sponsor since none of his more than a dozen godchildren had died. Early Spanish priests in the Philippines encouraged the Filipinos' belief that baptism had certain curative powers.

Postponement of Baptism

The folk attitude toward christening does not appear sufficiently robust in either Latin America or the Philippines to eliminate the postponement of a christening when it is convenient for the parents to do so. For example, in Huaylas baptism may be delayed until a child is ten years old, if the child is healthy and postponement is desirable for all concerned (Doughty 1968: 221). Baptisms in Latin America, as in the Philippines, are delayed for months to coordinate them with a fiesta. In such instances, the primary reason for delay probably is economic. Moreover, in parts of Latin America some children are never baptized (Wagley 1949: 25). Although belief of peasants in the magical qualities of baptism appears to be widespread in Latin America and the Philippines, apparently social and economic factors may, on numerous occasions, be of greater importance. (In one French village infants once were christened within a week of birth because of the high mortality rate. Since this danger is rare today, the ceremony often is postponed until the mother has recovered and may attend the baptism: Wylie 1966: 287.)

Confirmation

Most folk Catholics consider confirmation the least important of the three traditional sacraments; as a result the ritual kinship bonds are weaker and less demanding (Whitten 1965: 103). Since not all Latin Americans are confirmed, they may lack sponsors for this rite (Reichel-Dolmatoff 1961: 171). Sometimes no ceremonial relationship arises between the principals. In Castile, the duties of a sponsor (often a religious or lay teacher) are limited to the confirmation ceremony, and no lasting spiritual ties are created. In Spain, such religious organizations as Catholic Action may furnish confirmation sponsors to the poor. These personally unconcerned sponsors only pay the fee, and sponsorship rarely develops any ritual kinship bonds (Kenny 1962: 73; Pitt-Rivers 1961: 108–9). Among the Negroes of northern Brazil, a godchild mourns one year for a parent or baptismal godparent but only three to six months for a confirmation sponsor (Eduardo 1948: 42).

The sponsorship of confirmation is less costly than that of baptism or marriage. Its cost usually is limited to paying all or part of the church fee. A feast may or may not be held after the christening (Foster 1967:

78–79; Gillin 1947: 110; Ingham 1970: 283; Madsen 1960b: 95; Gudeman 1972: 56). In Mitla, a few days after confirmation the new godparents are invited for a meal at their godchild's residence or a gift of food is sent to them (Parsons 1936: 90).

This summary for Latin America and Europe reflects the same general patterns associated with baptism and confirmation as in the Philippines. Filipino sponsors normally are expected to bear the same costs—paying the church fee, furnishing baptismal clothing, etc. It is the responsibility of the godchild's parents to serve the christening meal, although sometimes Filipino sponsors may make a modest contribution. In both Latin America and the Philippines the ritual linkage through baptism is considered the most important. Filipino sponsors for baptism and confirmation are obtained in basically the same ways as in Latin America. However, many Latin American post-baptismal ceremonies are not held in the Philippines. While impersonal means for securing sponsors are reported for Greece and Latin America, they appear less common than in the Bisayas.

Marriage

In Latin America, godparents often take an active part in the marriage negotiations of a godchild (Redfield and Villa Rojas 1962: 99; Nelson 1971: 57; Beals 1969 8: 767; Madsen 1960b: 99–100; Stein 1961: 281; Foster 1948: 244; Foster 1967: 78). In Tepoztlán, if the godson is an orphan his godparents may serve as parental substitutes in requesting the girl's hand in marriage (Lewis 1960: 81). The boy's group in Tonalá may include a compadre of the girl's father, to assure a friendly reception when the two groups meet for marriage discussions (Diaz 1966: 53). In the past (but not today) the boy's baptismal godfather in Martineztown formally requested the girl's hand from her parents. At present, he merely accompanies the boy's parents when they visit the girl's residence to arrange the wedding (Vincent 1966: 66).

In Spain, Europe, Latin America, and the United States marriage sponsors sometimes pay a large part of the wedding expenses: they may furnish the *arras* and the bridal gown, pay the wedding fee, offer wedding gifts, buy candles for the ceremony, arrange for a dance band at the wedding reception, etc. (Kenny 1962: 72; Halpern 1958: 162; Ravicz 1967: 246; Ingham 1970: 282; Madsen 1960b: 99; Tax and Hinshaw 1969: 87; Foster 1967: 67, 70–71; Foster 1969: 132–33; Campbell 1964: 220; Friedl 1962: 58; Sanders 1962: 173; Diaz 1966: 62; Harvey and Kelly 1969 8: 678; Parsons 1936: 68; Reina 1966: 208, 215; Paul and Paul 1952: 189; Rubel 1966: 83; Vincent 1966: 56). As one might expect, there are some exceptions to these statements. In San Pedro, Chan Kom, and Moche marriage sponsors do not pay any of the cost of the wedding (Richardson 1970: 83; Redfield and Villa Rojas 1962: 194; Gillin 1947: 111). In Aritama the sponsors have few, if any, obligations to their godchildren beyond giving them a wedding gift (Reichel-Dolmatoff 1961: 171).

A bride in Tepoztlán may stay at her godparents' house the evening before the wedding and be given marital advice (Lewis 1960: 82). Among some Middle Americans the godmother traditionally is responsible for arranging the bride's hair (Parsons 1936: 102; Madsen 1969 8: 634). "On the night before the wedding the *peinadura* (a ritual in which the godmother combs the hair of the bride) is carried out [among the Ichatec] in the padrino's home . . ." (Hoppe and Weitlaner 1969 7: 505).

The newly wedded couple in Latin America usually returns to the home of one of their sponsors for a festive breakfast immediately after the wedding (Foster 1967: 70; Foster 1960: 132–33; Nelson 1971: 57; Lewis 1970: 82). When the bride and groom return to their respective residences, godparents and parents may accompany them or greet them on their arrival. Their sponsors may also, along with the parents, offer advice on the duties of their new status or give the couple a benediction (Nelson 1971: 60). In one instance the wedding feast is started when the marriage sponsors ceremonially feed the bride and groom (Ravicz 1967: 246).

Church weddings are infrequent in many parts of Latin America, so wedding sponsors for a religious marriage may not be required. Sponsors also may not be selected when a church wedding is held. In San Lorenzo, Whitten knew of "no Costeño who has had an honorary padrino or madrina as a wedding attendant" (1965: 103). In the Ica valley, Peru, peasants often are unable to secure a marriage sponsor since the expenses involved are considerable. "They often select the Virgin and St. Anthony as their *padrinos*" (Hammel 1969: 90). Sponsors usually are selected for a civil marriage (Wagley 1965: 132).

The Philippine pattern of responsibilities and activities associated with the sponsorship of marriage differs in numerous ways from that outlined earlier in this subsection. First, godparents are less active in the marriage negotiations of their godchildren, an obligation of close kinsmen of the engaged pair. Second, although Filipinos sponsors pay some of the cost of the wedding, their financial obligations are considerably less than those of sponsors in Latin America. The expenses of the wedding and the subsequent feast are covered entirely or largely by the dower the boy and his group give the girl's parents before the wedding. Third, postnuptial advice is given the newly wedded couple by the parents or close relatives. The occasions are at the feast held at the girl's residence, and later that afternoon, at the second banquet served at the boy's house. Fourth, nearly all Filipinos are married in the church; when an elopement occurs, the couple usually remarries in the church. For either ceremony (civil or religious) sponsors are selected.

Funeral Assistance

One type of aid typically associated with compadrinazgo is the godparents' assistance on the death of a godchild. Even when compadrinazgo is not stressed, this obligation is widespread and often obligatory except in Italy, Greece, and Serbia, where ritual kinsmen apparently lack any traditional responsibilities for the burial of their godchildren or compadres. For example, in Italy assistance usually is offered one's ritual kinsmen during illness, death, or disaster "only to the extent that godparents and parents are already consanguineally or affinally related and depends a good deal on the pre-existing affection between all parties concerned" (Anderson 1956: 12, 18–19).

In Latin America (and Spain) godparents commonly have well-defined funeral responsibilities for a godchild. Assistance often is extended only for godchildren under a certain age (varying from ten to fourteen years). The death of a married godchild imposes fewer demands, probably reflecting the attitude that the sponsors' responsibilities are shared by the deceased's spouse and children. On occasion, godchildren may help to bury a godparent. Funeral assistance is less frequently extended to compadres. It appears to be rare or nonexistent for the death of secondary ritual kinsmen.

The aid given during the death of a godchild typically includes sharing in the cost of the funeral, buying or making the coffin, furnishing the shroud or burial clothes, dressing the deceased, carrying the coffin to the church and cemetery, and helping to dig the grave and to prepare the meal that usually is served to mourners (Gudeman 1972: 66; Beals 1946: 207–8; Stein 1961: 116–17, 286–87; Madsen 1969 8: 624; Parsons 1936: 68, 148; Spicer 1940: 103; Pitt-Rivers 1958: 425; Lewis

1960: 67 and 1963: 352; Ingham 1970: 283; Richardson 1970: 84; Holmes 1952: 101; Ravicz 1967: 245; Gillin 1947: 108, 149; Diaz 1966: 131; Foster 1960: 122 and 1948: 246, 269; Wagley 1949: 47–48; Whitten 1965: 104; Spielberg 1968: 209; Nuñez del Prado 1973: 21; Reichel-Dolmatoff 1961: 173; Middleton 1975: 466).

In the Yaqui village of Potam (Sonora), one major duty of a godparent is managing the funeral of a godchild.

> The considerable amount of handling of the body necessary in the funeral ritual is regarded as something which would sadden parents or other relatives greatly, and therefore there must be other persons to take over these necessary duties ... They [godparents] prepare the burial clothes, dress the dead body, and in general carry out the activities at funerals which require close contact with the body (Spicer 1945: 60).

Since funerals for adults are sorrowful occasions for the deceased's immediate kinsmen, the Yaqui believe it best not to have compadres who are also consanguines.

As expected when generalizing about compadrinazgo, exceptions occur. Contrary to the funeral activities of Yaqui ritual kinsmen is the near exclusion in Los Boquerones of such kinsmen from the preparations for the bural of godchildren and compadres. These Panamanians believe one should attend the funeral of his compadres and offer some aid, but compadres, like other close members of the deceased's family, are prohibited from dressing the corpse, carrying the coffin to the cemetery, or helping to dig the grave (Gudeman 1972: 56, 66).

Political Uses of Compadrinazgo

Politically active persons have recognized the relative ease with which a network of ritual bonds can be developed. They have understood the potential value of ritual kinship ties to either a patron desiring numerous clients or an office seeker looking for votes. Individuals who aspire to a position of leadership in Latin America often must have many compadres (Lewis 1963: 350; Richardson 1970: 84; Whitten 1965: 187, 193; Larson and Bergman 1969: 280). Kwaiker Indians vote for a particular political party at the "suggestion" of their mestizo compadres (Osborn 1968: 598). Mitla government officials often were charged with favoritism when their compadres were involved (Parsons 1936: 160, 164).

An individual who has the political protection of an important politician in Brazil is called an *afilhado politico* or "political godchild" (Wagley 1964: 152).

A much more durable political maneuver than "kissing babies" is to stand as godparent for children at baptism. An old and practiced politican in the Amazon region, for example, kept a notebook in which he entered the addresses and birthdays of his three to four hundred godchildren. They were strategically scattered over the entire state, and both his god-children and his co-fathers were certain voters and excellent political campaigners for him (Wagley 1964: 152).

Sources on this aspect of compadrinazgo, for both Latin America and the Philippines, are scattered, lacking in detail, and often specula-tive. A comprehensive investigation is needed of the *effective* relation-ship between ritual kinship and political activities.

Adoption

According to Canon law, the responsibility of baptismal godparents includes not only the spiritual education of the godchild but also his care if he is orphaned or if the parents need assistance because of poverty or an unusually large family. Yet in Latin America, adoption of godchil-dren by godparents is extremely uncommon, either *de facto* or legally (Nelson 1971: 81; Lomnitz 1973: 44; Manners 1966: 150; Mintz 1966: 388; Middleton 1975: 466; Reichel-Dolmatoff 1961: 176–77; Reina 1966: 233). This survey of the literature on compadrinazgo located only two specific instances of godchildren who had been adopted by their godparents (Gudeman 1972: 60; Kottak 1967: 434). Another possible exception is in Saució, where "if a padrino adopts a godchild, he treats it as one of his own children, and these likewise accept the newcomer as a brother or sister" (Fals-Borda 1962: 197). But the author reports no actual adoptions.

Godparents may temporarily care for an orphaned godchild until a permanent arrangement is made with his relatives (Lewis 1963: 369; Ingham 1970: 283). Among the Pokomames and Chorti of Guatemala, "the padrino system is effective in case of the parents' death. They [godparents] receive the portion of land belonging to the child in pay-ment of expenses and at the age of eighteen the young person receives the land again" (Reina 1969: 127).

Adoption of godchildren is also rare in the Philippines. In both Caticugan and Lalawigan a special effort was made to investigate this aspect of compadrinazgo; only one instance of *de facto* adoption was discovered in these two villages. It appears most likely that adoption is uncommon among ritual kinsmen because compadrinazgo complements but does not displace normal responsibilities of consanguines and affines. Moreover, formal adoption would disturb the traditional channels of the inheritance of property.

Inheritance

For Latin America, Mintz and Wolf "are convinced that the rare usages of compadrazgo in inheritance indicate the lack of utility of this mechanism in dynamically affecting prevailing patterns of ownership" (1950: 355). In the two Latin American cases where compadrinazgo was associated with land inheritance, they found that the heirs received only the right of usufruct. With two possible and one actual exceptions no more recent information on Latin American compadrinazgo was found that qualifies this statement.

In the Peruvian community of Kuyo Chico, when an Indian sponsors the first cutting of the hair of another Indian, the ritual kinship relationships have greater significance than between Indian and mestizo. "In this case the godfather (*padrino*) is obligated to make a considerable gift, often equivalent to constituting the godchild as his sole heir, if he has no children of his own. For this reason, it is with great difficulty that the typical Indian accepts being godfather for the cutting of the first hair" (Nuñez del Prado 1973: 21). Although this source states that such sponsorship is uncommon, it does not indicate if this obligation is always or only rarely honored in fact. In one Colombian mestizo village godparents are expected to leave a substantial part of their properties to their godchildren; however, since ritual kinship ties are "of little functional importance," apparently such inheritance rarely, if ever, occurs (Reichel-Dolmatoff 1961: 170–71).

In Martineztown five different godchildren inherited from their godparents, although none was legally adopted. Some were ritual children of godparents who lacked immediate heirs. When the godparents had children, the godchildren received a smaller share of the properties. Vincent speculates that since her sample was small, more cases of godchildren inheriting from their godparents may have occurred (1966: 103–4).

Filipino ritual kinsmen rarely, if ever, inherit each other's properties. This pattern is repeated among Filipinos residing in Songsong, Mariana Islands. (These islands were occupied by Spain in 1668; Spanish traditions remain strong among the people, many of whom have Spanish, Mexican, and Filipino ancestors.) In a personal communication, J. Jerome Smith reported that for nearly 500 parcels of agricultural land subject to title determination, not one instance of direct transfer of land from Filipino godparent to godchild occurred. One informant suggested that godchildren might inherit from godparents they cared for during their old age.

Mutual Assistance Among Ritual Kinsmen

In the preceding pages the traditional, and often specific, exchange of goods and services among ritual kinsmen associated with baptism, confirmation, and marriage was described. This subsection focuses on the more general patterns of mutual assistance typical of ritual kinsmen. Some obligations are almost universally associated with compadrinazgo, for example, the aid given when one's godchild dies. Other types of assistance vary from lending one another small sums of money to giving credit and discounts, exchanging inexpensive gifts, house moving, sharing food and labor, helping with the education of godchildren, etc. (Ingham 1970: 263; Doughty 1968: 122, 191; Middleton 1975: 471; Wagley 1964: 155; Mintz 1966: 390; Hammel 1969: 69–70). In fact, the various favors extended to ritual kinsmen are too varied to list. In many instances, as Mintz reports for Puerto Rico, the assistance received is primarily "gifts of labor" (1966: 389). In one Colombian community the major function of the godparent-godchild relationship is for the latter to supply free labor for the former (Reichel-Dolmatoff 1961: 173).

Numerous factors decide the nature and extent of mutual assistance among ritual kinsmen. Among some of the more important factors are age, residence, real kinship relationships, geographic mobility, personal inclination, strength and degree of intimacy, the manner in which sponsors were secured, social class distinctions, sponsorship of Church-prescribed or folk rites, the rite involved (e.g., baptism or marriage), mutual resources available for sharing, permanent or transitory ritual bonds, etc. (Harris 1956: 154; Anderson 1956: 18–19; Manners 1966: 164; Wagley 1964: 154).

Foster has described the importance of compadrinazgo in establishing patron-client relationships (1963: 1284). Probably economic support is the most frequent and valued aid—emergency loans, help in finding employment, financing the education of godchildren, etc. The following material clearly demonstrates that the extent of this type of assistance varies from none to some to much.

In Eleodoro Gomez, a village 180 miles southwest of Buenos Aires, compadres (an address term the author heard only once during his residence) offer each other but little assistance that is based solely on their ritual kinship (Strickon 1965: 33). Compadrinazgo among the Maya of Guatemala does "not lead to much increased interaction, to the borrowing or lending of money, or to the exchange of work in the field" (Nash 1958: 66). In one Latin American community the sole economic obligation of godparents is to help with the medical expenses of an ill godchild whose family requires financial assistance (Whitten 1965: 104).

The peasants of Los Boquerones explain the lack of economic obligations among ritual kinsmen by stating that "loans and favours often lead to ill will between the parties; since the bond between *compadres* must be one of respect it is best not to permit other entangling relations to enter. At the most, they save *compadres* for cases of extreme emergency, for it is true that a *compadre* ultimately would be obliged to offer financial aid no matter how strained this would make the bond" (Gudeman 1972: 57). The attitude of the peasants of Los Boquerones toward lending to compadres is shared by the Ticuleños. Loans to ritual kinsmen are regarded as the most "onerous" obligatory feature of compadrinazgo. Lending often results in hostile feelings on the part of the lender, among the Ticuleños and Puerto Ricans, particularly when he gives but rarely is repaid (Thompson 1971: 385; Mintz 1966: 390).

The reluctance or absence of an obligation to give economic assistance to one's ritual kinsmen is not unique to Latin America. In one Greek community few patron sponsors "give away anything for nothing" (Campbell 1964: 224). In Serbia the chief function of a godparent is to select the godchild's name; no economic considerations adhere to the ritual relationship (Halpern 1958: 61). Mutual assistance among Italian ritual kinsmen, based solely on this ceremonial linkage, is largely insignificant (Anderson 1956: 18–19). The major reward Italian informants associate with *comparaggio* is psychological—affection, intimacy, and security (Anderson 1956: 19).

Yet in one Italian village the godfather takes a genuine interest in his godchildren, and his assistance is mainly monetary (Maraspini 1968:

200). In the village of Cortina d'Aglio "the godparent is morally reponsible for the education and welfare of the child if its parents should die" (Moss and Cappannari 1960: 31). Whether this responsibility is usually or rarely fulfilled is not stated.

Many ritual kinsmen in Latin America would agree with this opinion of a Mexican informant: " 'For a man is truly poor when he does not have compadres' " (Nelson 1971: 85). In Potam "it is to one's ritual kin that one goes first to borry money . . . Borrowing among Yaquis to a very large extend follows the lines of the ritual kinship structures. To have few ritual kin is to be indeed a poor man, and consequently everyone seeks to have many" (Spicer 1945: 62).

Among the Zinacanteco Mayas of Mexico "a compadre can be called upon to loan money, help build a house, become an assistant in a ceremony, or assist in political crises" (Vogt 1970: 65). In Tzintzuntzan compadres feel obliged to lend and would have no respect for a man who refused to repay a *compadre* (Foster 1948: 264). Compadrinazgo has been described for one Mexican community as "a mutually contingent exchange system [for] it also involves sentiments that emphasize the moral propriety of repayment—the idea of contract. Repayment is not interpreted as a matter of exchanging equivalent items, but the feeling of a sense of moral obligation to another individual" (Nelson 1971: 78).

Another economic aspect of compadrinazgo is that it may serve as a means of graduated taxation. In Huaylas *padrinos protectores* (the most wealthy members of the community) are sponsors of a new acquisition of the church, school, or government. In recognition of the honor bestowed by their selection, they are expected to make a contribution or gift to the institution. "Such a ceremony accompanies virtually every new public acquisition and is thus a principal source of income for institutions" (Doughty 1968: 118–19).

In summary, although mutual assistance of various types, especially of an economic nature, is associated with ritual kinship relationships, significant economic aid may be absent. Numerous variables determine what ideal assistance is required and, more important, is actually given. For these reasons the generalization that "on the economic level, compadrazgo system forms a kind of social insurance" (Mintz and Wolf 1950: 356) requires qualification. In regard to its structure and functions, compadrinazgo in the Philippines, with the exceptions previously noted, matches the general pattern of this variety of ritual kinship, and especially fits that for Latin America.

Social Control

Compadrinazgo may be purposely exploited as a technique of social control, to minimize or prevent conflict. Such control is achieved, in part, by the attitudes of extreme respect and reserve associated with the interaction of ritual kinsmen. Public opinion is unusually condemnatory of quarrels involving ritual kinsmen. Compadres should avoid social occasions, such as drinking parties, that might result in disputes. Sayres argues, however, that the role of compadrinazgo in promoting harmonious relationships in Latin America has been greatly exaggerated (1956). Given the chameleon-like qualities of the godparenthood complex, both Eisenstadt and Sayres appear to be correct for different sets of circumstances.

Undoubtedly, compadrinazgo often is an effective means of social control. In Puerto Rico neighborhood groups of toughs may minimize conflict between their members by becoming *compadres de voluntad* (Wolf 1966b: 209; also see Mintz and Wolf 1950: 357). Deshon found that household quarrels were avoided or lessened by making members ritual kinsmen (1963). In Huaylas disputes often were settled or arbitrated by godparents or compadres, preventing the official involvement of government officials (Doughty 1968: 124, 126). An instance was reported of two compadres who had become "bitter enemies" yet addressed each other with the proper terms and refrained "from outright conflict" (Hammel 1969: 90).

Informants in Cerrada del Condor state that sometimes they selected sponsors so they could "live in peace with them" or end a quarrel (Lomnitz 1973: 44). Compadrinazgo is used to prevent sexual aggression (Rubel 1966: 80), as when a husband asks his wife's unsuccessful suitor to sponsor their first child (Manners 1966: 150).

> Occasionally a man asks to be a godparent to a child to demonstrate to his own spouse that he has not had sexual relations with the child's mother. Also, a woman with a child but no husband may curb the sexual advances of another man by asking him to be her child's godparent (Whitten 1965: 104).

Yet compadrinazgo in Latin America, as the literature attests, includes instances where it is specifically not used for social control and also numerous incidents of conflict among ritual kinsmen. Contrary to

Deshon's findings, household members in Tzintzuntzan rarely are selected as compadres since these ritual kinsmen should not be involved in household disputes. Compadre relationships in this community may sour; sometimes two compadres stop speaking to each other (Foster 1969: 80). In Guatemala City two compadres became political enemies (Roberts 1973: 174).

Crowded conditions in the slumlike housing settlements of Mexico City often make it difficult to maintain the traditional formal, mutual respect expected of compadres. Arguments among their children may lead to quarrels between compadres (Lewis 1970: 436). In one Mexican village "no relationship [including compadrinazgo] is proof against conflict" (Romanucci-Ross 1973: 89). In a dispute described, some of the antagonists included the man's compadres. Ritual kinship ties minimize friction resulting from the geographical crowding of Kwaiker families "only where there is an existing kin tie" (Osborn 1968: 602).

Lastly, that compadrinazgo is severely limited as a means of social control is illustrated by its ineffectual operation in one village of Colombian mestizos.

> Enmities, or sexual relations among coparents, or between coparents and godchildren are quite common, and although public opinion sometimes denounce and condemn such behavior, there are no effective means to control it (Reichel-Dolmatoff 1961: 173).

One partial exception to this statement is that ritual kinship ties in this community reinforce and support traditional behavioral patterns between godparents and godchildren.

In summary, Latin American compadrinazgo may or may not be an effective technique for promoting social control. It may even encourage discord, especially when compadres do not fulfill their traditional obligations. Ritual kinsmen are not always required to interact with extreme respect and reserve. Moreover, the use of the formal *usted* can imply social distance as well as respect, and the informal *tú* either closeness or lack of respect (Nelson 1971: 78–79). It appears, however, that where compadrinazgo is not a significant means of social control, the institution often has lost much of its original vigor. On the other hand, in the Philippines ritual kinship bonds often are an effective "social damper" of potential conflict. This quality may reflect less "secularization" of compadrinazgo in the Philippines, in contrast with most of Latin America. Possibly the "sacred sanctions" of the godparenthood complex have greater force in the rural Philippines.

Incest Tabus and Ritual Kinsmen

In a thorough study of incest tabus associated with ritual kinship, Eramus noted there were no reported exceptions to such rules, although the presence or absence of marriage restrictions for ritual kinsmen was not always indicated in the sources consulted (1950: 43). Since this investigation, a number of instances have been reported of the permissible marriage of ritual kinsmen.

A study of compadrinazgo for Italy stated that there were "no taboos to prohibit the marriage of compadres with anything approaching the forcefulness of the compadrazgo regulations in Latin America" (Anderson 1956: 17). In one Italian village, bad luck supposedly dogged ritual kinsmen who married within a year of the baptism involved. This mild folk sanction "is as close as any informant comes to a stand on the prohibition of marriage between persons linked by the bond of *comparaggio*" (Anderson 1956: 18).

A recent study of Italian compadrinazgo offers some new data on marriage prohibitions. In Calimera, a peasant community of 5,805 in southern Italy, the marriage of a baptismal godfather and his goddaughter or her mother is incestuous (Maraspini 1968: 160). No instances were known of the marriage of godsiblings, although some informants believed such unions permissible.

In rural Greece, the marriage of godparent-godchild and compadre-comadre is incestuous (Campbell 1964: 221; Sanders 1962: 178). In the Greek village of Vasilika this incest tabu is extended from the original sponsor to his wife and also to his siblings and children and their spouses (Friedl 1962: 72). Finally, in most of rural Greece godchildren sharing the same godparent are considered "spiritual brethren" and cannot wed (Sanders 1962: 169).

Marriage sponsors in Spain do not become compadres of the bridal pair's parents, so no impediment to their marriage is created (Pitt-Rivers 1958: 426; 1968: 411). In rural Castile marriage sponsors are "usually close kin," often the couple's parents. In Madrid wedding sponsors frequently are the bride and groom's aunts and uncles (Kenny 1962: 183). Hence "the question of spiritual kinship and consequent impediments to marriage hardly ever arises" (Kenny 1962: 72, 183). However, the marriage of ritual kinsmen through baptism is classified as incestuous in some Spanish communities (Kenny 1962: 71; Pitt-Rivers 1961: 107).

In Martineztown, compadres can marry with a dispensation. Marriage of co-sponsors of the same godchild is licit if there is not a natural kinship barrier to their union. In fact, some residents consider such marriages desirable. But most informants believe that the marriage of baptismal and confirmation godparents and their godchildren is incestuous (Vincent 1966: 86–87). In a rural Spanish-American community in New Mexico Edmonson found "no explicit extension of the incest tabu to *compadres* . . ." (1957: 33).

Incest prohibitions do not prevent the marriage of ritual kinsmen among the Kwaiker Indians and mestizos of the Andean foothills of Colombia (Osborn 1968: 607, footnote 10). Since marriage sponsorship in Tzintzuntzan, a Mexican village of 1,877 people (1960) in Michoacán, is not *de grado,* it does not "establish impediments to marriage between the people's immediately involved, and their children as well" (Foster 1967: 76).

In Latin America incest tabus, with the exceptions noted, almost always prohibit the marriage of ritual kinsmen. Marriage restrictions may be extended from the principals to co-sponsors, godsiblings, and the sponsors' siblings—and sometimes to the children of these siblings. In some instances marriage between any members of the two families is interdicted. The tabu on sexual contact and marriage of compadres in Middle America is "stronger than between affinal and consanguineal relatives" (Ravicz 1967: 240–41). Marriage of ritual kinsmen is described as "worse than murder," a sin bringing certainty of hell fire, or as reprehensible as brother-sister intercourse (Manrique 1969 8: 714; Whitten 1965: 103–4, 120; Villa Rojas 1969: 7, 267; Ravicz 1967: 240–41; Harvey and Kelly 1969 8: 667; Grimes and Hinton 1969 8: 803; Nelson 1971: 56–57; Gudeman 1972: 56; Wagley 1964: 155; Lewis 1963: 67; Reina 1966: 199, 233; Vincent 1966: 86–87).

The frequent intensity of incest tabus, and the punishment of those who violate them, are reflected in folklore. A Yucatan myth ranks incest in the following order of decreasing seriousness: compadre-comadre, father-daughter, and mother-son (Redfield 1941: 212). "To have sexual relations with one's comadre, even to think of her sexually, is considered a sin, and the Chimaltecos tell stories of men who were punished by the Guardian of the Mountain for having sexual relations with their *comadres*" (Wagley 1949: 19). A Mitla folktale explains that a compadre and comadre had sexual relations. As punishment, the Sun changed them into two large stones still seen in the locality and known as *piedra compadre* and *piedra comadre* (Parsons 1936: 94).

In San Cristobal de las Casas class differences influence the incest beliefs associated with ritual kinsmen. The working class in this Mexican town believe that the union of ritual kinsmen is a mortal sin; sexual relations between godparents and godchildren are regarded as a "somewhat attenuated form of father-daughter or mother-son incest. . . . Many upper- and middle-class informants seem vaguely aware that such a taboo exists, but do not appear to find relations between ritual kinsmen morally reprehensible and offer no clear rationalization for the prohibition" (Van den Berghe and Van den Berghe 1966: 1241). (In addition to the regulation of marriage, incest tabus may be used as a means to minimize or prevent conflict. See the section on Social Control.)

The pattern of incest tabus associated with Philippine compadrinazgo is similar to that reported for Latin America, although it is somewhat more restrictive. Marriage among all ritual kinsmen in Caticugan and Lalawigan is prohibited. Only two violations of this tabu could be discovered. In some communities informants were not sure if a tabu existed for some ritual kinsmen, but their uncertainty seemed as effective in preventing such marriages as a recognized tabu. Lastly, compadrinazgo in Caticugan, as described earlier, results in a more comprehensive restriction on mate selection than reported elsewhere in the general literature on ritual kinship.

Comparison of Ritual and Real Kinship Bonds

In the Greek village of Vasilika people bound by ritual ties are said to behave toward one another as affines. Like affines, ritual kinsmen are selected. Moreover, both affines and ritual kinsmen are covered by the incest tabu that prohibits marriage between any of the relatives of the two families involved. Although the villagers rarely have kinsmen-sponsors, when they do, their network of associations is expanded, as also is true with relatives through marriage (Friedl 1962: 72–73).

In Latin America compadres should treat one another like younger and older (godparent) siblings (Beals 1969 8: 767); in fact, the "relationship may be more fraternal than between real siblings" (Wellin 1949: 7). (The fact that compadre ties often are described as fraternal is not surprising, since sponsors frequently are siblings.)

Nash states that compadre bonds are a "weaker" version of those associated with a biological uncle (1958: 66). The godparent-godchild dyad most commonly is compared to the parent-child relationship (Kluckhohn and Strodtbeck 1961: 182; Wagley 1964: 155; Ravicz 1967: 240). Ritual bonds in Moche and Tepoztlán often have greater strength than consanguineal and affinal ties (Lewis 1963: 350; Gillin 1947: 104).

Respect, formality, and mutual helpfulness typically and ideally characterize ritual kinship relationships. In Chan Kom parents treat their children's godparents with greater respect than they, in turn, receive (Redfield and Villa Rojas 1962: 8). More trust is placed in compadres than in remote kin since ritual kinsmen must fulfill their obligations (Nelson 1971: 85).

> [In Tepoztlán] compadres address each other with the respectful *Usted* [to avoid] . . . intimacy or undue familiarity. The latter includes joking and discussing sex or any other subjects of a personal nature (Lewis 1960: 67).

Compadres should not fight or dance together (Gudeman 1972: 56; Pierson 1951: 142). They should not drink alcoholic beverages together lest a dispute or quarrel arise when they are intoxicated (Lewis 1963: 287). In Manta godparents and godchildren should not drink together for fear that overindulgence might result in a quarrel; however, compadres occasionally drink with each other (Middleton 1975: 466).

Yet ritual kinship relationships (especially for compadres) in Europe and Latin America are not always so circumspect. A mildly joking relationship is reported for compadres in an Italian village (Maraspini 1968: 160). Although compadres in Alcalá respect each other, they converse with considerable ease (Pitt-Rivers 1961: 108–9).

Compadres in Latin America may and should drink together (Whitten 1965: 104–5; Ravicz 1967: 341). Among the Indians of Vicos (Peru), compadres, including godparents and godchildren, participate in boisterous drinking bouts; drunkenness rarely creates serious social strains (Mangin 1957: 61). In Moche, a joking relationship with sexual overtones exists between co-sponsors, based on the fact that they can "almost" consider themselves married (Gillin 1947: 108–9).

In Tobatí compadres who are equals interact with considerable familiarity "even to the point of privileged 'disrespectful joking' " (Service and Service 1954: 177–78). In one instance a man chided a local priest (who was also his godfather, relative, and compadre) about such topics as illegitimate children and sexual prowess. Also in Puerto Rico the compadre relationships may be the topic of jokes (Manners 1966: 163); humorous stories about alleged illicit sexual relations between compadres and comadres are told by Puerto Ricans (Seda 1966: 295).

Given the versatility and flexibility of the godparenthood complex, it is difficult to present, with accuracy, any one pattern of roles and behavior typical of most ritual kinsmen. The dilemma appears to have this character: Many patterns have been reported, but the relative frequency and vitality of each pattern is not well-documented. It is believed that future investigations will uncover additional exceptions to present generalizations regarding compadrinazgo. Hence, what is typical is not known. It may be that what is typical is that no typology exists.

The comparisons of ritual kinsmen in Europe, Latin America, and the Philippines to a wide variety of actual relatives reflect a basic dichotomy in the nature of the former relationships. On one level of conceptualization, ritual kinsmen parallel affines, for they are chosen rather than inherited. Another similarity is that the connective bond may be severed, while the ties that bind consanguines are permanent. As this chapter indicates, ritual kinship bonds may lapse after a certain period or purposely be avoided by the participants. But this comparison is weakened, since tradition often decrees their selection where repeat sponsorship is practiced or where the choice of sponsors is prescribed.

On the other hand, compadrinazgo terminology is that borrowed from the vocabulary associated with consanguines ("godparent" and "godchild," and the equating of compadres with siblings). The generational position of these ritual kinsmen favors this comparison since one's compadres normally are of the same generation, while godparents and godchildren usually are separated by one generation. Actually, the identification of these persons with affines and consanguines is more appropriately applied to fictive than ritual kinsmen, as argued effectively by Pitt-Rivers. In many ways these comparisons obfuscate as much as they clarify compadrinazgo relationships.

Although ritual kinsmen often are treated with the respect and deference associated with many actual relatives, an impressive number of exceptions occur. Sexual joking among and drinking bouts ending in the drunkenness of ritual kinsmen are permissible. In Latin America and the Philippines ritual kinsmen also may interact with the same ease and intimacy as real kinsmen. The failure of compadrinazgo to prevent conflict (Eisenstadt 1956: 92) indicates that this typical relationship of respect and mutual consideration often is absent. The respect and formality of the compadrinazgo bond varies according to the social class affiliations of ritual kinsmen (Ingham 1970: 282). Finally, some Latin Americans and Filipinos have ritual kinsmen who were strangers before the ceremony and may not be seen again.

Filipino ritual kinship roles and behavior fit this spectrum of variations. Future research may discover, for Filipinos as a whole, that their compadrinazgo relationships are more relaxed and intimate than those of most ritual kinsmen in Latin America. Moreover, the respect and formality often associated with Filipino ritual kinsmen probably are as much the result of their traditional deference to age and social superiors as they are to compadrinazgo bonds. Generally speaking, however, the similarity of these aspects of Latin American and Philippine compadrinazgo is striking.

Chapter Nine

Selected Issues and Compadrinazgo

Previous studies that dealt with compadrinazgo, especially for Latin America, often focused on associated issues and problems. This concluding chapter selects for comparative discussion four major theoretical issues related to the godparenthood complex: 1) the varying importance of kinsmen or nonkinsmen as preferred sponsors; 2) the reticulative efficacy of compadrinazgo vis-a-vis social classes; 3) the centrifugal and centripetal integrative functions of ritual kinsmen; and 4) the response of compadrinazgo to urban environments.

Kinsman or Nonkinsman Sponsors

In some parts of the world preferred compadrinazgo sponsors are relatives, while in other parts the preference is for nonrelatives. In most of Spain and Italy sponsors usually are kinsmen. In Hispanic America sponsors supposedly are predominately nonrelatives. Data for France are too limited to determine whether the intensification or extension motive is stressed. Available information for the Philippines indicates that only future research can document if either of these motives is primary.

Most sources do not furnish detailed data on the exact relationships to the godchild of relatives who are chosen (or volunteer) as sponsors. The sources that give detail indicate, however, that usually these sponsors are siblings or in-laws of the godchild's parents, although when uncles and aunts are listed as sponsors, it is not known if they are real or classificatory kinsmen of the godchild. For example, in Caticugan sponsors often are of the latter category. Grandparents as sponsors are a less common choice, although they are preferred godparents among elite Puerto Ricans (Scheele 1966: 445). Cousins are rarely mentioned as sponsors. Although Canon law does not prohibit choosing sponsors from the godchild's generation, the ideal responsibilities of godparent-hood favor older persons. Moreover, the selection usually is made by the parents (marriage sponsors are an occasional exception), who prefer persons of their age group, especially if the primacy of compadre bonds is stressed.

In Spain, "relatives rather than friends are usually selected as god-parents, so that, rather than extending kinlike relationships, the system folds back upon itself, re-emphasizing existing ties rather than establishing new ones" (Foster 1960: 122). For example, in Alcalá, preferred godparents often are grandparents or parental siblings, for they "feel for the child the same kind of indulgence proper to a godparent" (Pitt-Rivers 1958: 430; also see Foster 1953: 4).

Marriage sponsors in Spain (allowing for regional variations) frequently are the baptismal godparents of the bride and groom, one godparent of each, or parents of the couple "in the formula 'groom's mother and bride's father,' or vice versa" (Foster 1960: 133). A conventional choice of marriage sponsors in Alcalá is the groom's elder brother and that brother's wife (Pitt-Rivers 1961: 107). Influential nonkin patron sponsors may be sought by poorer peasants in Alcalá. Yet the frequent selection of relatives as sponsors in this Spanish community normally results in the ritual reinforcement of the parent-in-law or sibling-in-law relationship (Pitt-Rivers 1961: 108). In summary, for most of Spain, "new relationships outside the family are sought through godparenthood in a minority of cases," (Foster 1953: 6). For French compadrinazgo the data are based on one village study. In Peyrane baptismal sponsors of the first child, "are usually a close relative of the father and a close relative of the mother. For successive children, an attempt may be made to choose godparents who may be of some practical help to the child in later life—a childless, well-to-do friend, for instance. In Peyrane, people say such attempts are rarely successful" (Wylie 1961: 41).

Kinsmen usually are baptismal sponsors in most Italian villages where Anderson's informants lived. The relatives normally selected as godparents are prescribed. The first child is sponsored by the husband's brother or the wife's sister, the second child by the husband's mother or the wife's father, etc. (Anderson 1956: 8–9 and 1957: 35).

In Hispanic America, in contrast to Spain and Italy, the pattern usually is for "relatives to be bypassed in favor of friends or sponsors of superior status who are willing to serve" (Foster 1953: 8). For example, nonkinsmen usually are preferred sponsors in Cherán, Moche, Tepoztlán, Tzintzuntzan, Tonalá, San Miguel Milpas Altas, Pascua, and other

Latin American communities (Beals 1946: 103; Gillin 1947: 108; Lewis 1963: 350 and 1965: 432; Diaz 1966: 132; Spielberg 1968: 208; Foster 1967: 30; Middleton 1975: 466; Zantwijk 1967: 79–80; Miller 1973: 80; Romanucci-Ross 1973: 82; Reina 1966: 231; Spicer 1940: 95–96, 116). In all of these communities, of course, some sponsors are kinsmen. Only a few sources state the percentage of compadres who are friends when nonrelatives are preferred sponsors. Baptismal records (1958–1967) for Tzintzuntzan showed that 67 percent of the sponsors were nonkinsmen (Foster 1969: 269). In the Los Llanos region of Mexico a household survey indicated that 83 percent of the compadres were identified as friends (Miller 1973: 80). In another Mexican community "less than 20 percent of our married adults have chosen kin for their most important compadres" (Romanucci-Ross 1973: 82). In Manta 90 percent of the baptismal sponsors were relatives (Middleton 1975: 466).

Two decades have passed since Foster's summary statement of 1953. Evidence that has accumulated since indicates that while many Latin Americans do not prefer kinsmen-sponsors, the weight of the present evidence no longer sustains the dominance of the extension motive. Kinsmen usually are sponsors in Yucatan (in Chan Kom, Tusik, etc.) Puerto Rico, San Lorenzo, Tobatí, Coroico, Hualcon, and other Latin American communities (Redfield and Villa Rojas 1962: 99; Wellin 1949: 8, 16; Grimes and Hinton 1969 8: 803; Deshon 1963: 577; Mintz and Wolf 1950: 359; Whitten 1965: 120; Lomnitz 1973: 42–43; Service and Service 1954: 175; Kottak 1967: 434; Riley 1969 8: 826; Heath 1971: 181–82; Vogt 1970: 64; Stein 1961: 132).

In this aspect, instances exist of places where Latin American ritual kinship resembles its Spanish antecedents. For example, in Eleodoro Gomez, an Argentinian community 180 miles southwest of Buenos Aires, compadrinazgo "seems closer to the institution as found in Spain than to that characteristic of much of the rest of Latin America" (Strickon 1965: 330). Between 1931 and 1969, 61 percent of compadres in Eleodoro Gomez were relatives to one or both of the parents, to each other, or both.

Lastly, in some clustered communities a balance appears to occur regarding preferred sponsors. In the villages surrounding Minas Velhas sponsors normally are kinsmen (Harris 1956: 152–53). In Minas Velhas itself, however, about half the sponsors for the lower and middle classes are not relatives, although members of the upper class usually select kinsmen (Harris 1956: 153).

Numerous reasons are given for Latin Americans preferring non-

relatives as sponsors. Parents may be seeking patrons. In Moche kinsmen "usually are passed over," since a major function of compadrinazgo
is to broaden and increase the future resources of the child. This is best
done normally by obtaining higher-status nonkinsmen as sponsors (Gillin 1947: 108).

Van den Berghe and Van den Berghe hypothesize that in San
Cristobal "intensification is preferred by people whose position,
whether high or low, is relatively secure and independent, while those
in a precarious or dependent position extend their compadrazgo ties
thinly over greater numbers of more distantly related persons" (1966:
1240). Yet in Manta, Middleton found that the motives of extension and
intensification were stressed by both secure and insecure families
(1975: 472).

In Tepoztlán kinsmen rarely are sponsors, "for it conflicts with the
basic notion of respect and social distance that should exist between
compadres" (Lewis 1965: 432). Impersonal means of securing sponsors
(e.g., the "godfather for twenty-four hours") often explain the selection
of strangers. Mexican-Americans in one community in Texas never select members of their family as baptismal sponsors, since these will not
"look after one" in heaven (Rubel 1966: 82). (Contrary to this belief, in
Chan Kom "the old people say that only if one is compadre with one's
father and mother will one meet with them in heaven [Gloria]": Redfield and Villa Rojas 1962: 99.)

In Manta nonkinsmen are overwhelmingly selected as baptism
sponsors to avoid conflict with relatives. The Mantenses explain that
family members or close relatives often have many problems that ritual
kinsmen should avoid. Kinsmen also are not trustworthy, often are ill-
mannered, and lack mutual respect (Middleton 1975: 466). Moreover,
friends who live nearby, within the same block or the same neighborhood, usually are less desirable sponsors than friends who live in more
distant parts of the city. The Mantenses believe that "many friendships
are based on propinquity, but these are mercurial and untrustworthy
relationships which generally should not be formalized through compadrazgo . . ." (Middleton 1975: 473).

Two hyotheses have been proposed to explain why kinsmen are
preferred baptismal sponsors in some communities but not in others.
Deshon argues that, in one Yucatan plantation, kinsmen usually are
initially selected as baptismal sponsors to insure continued internal
harmony within the joint household. During the early part of their
married life, a young couple usually is involved in conflict situations

with other adult members of the joint household. Such household tensions are avoided or minimized by the restraining influence of the compadre bond. Additionally, these ritual ties establish roles that are similar to the ideal kinship patterns linking generations (1963. 580). Later, when the couple establishes an independent nuclear family, unrelated sponsors are favored for social and economic purposes.

Yet in Tzintzuntzan "where the same development cycle of the domestic group is the rule, the pattern is just the opposite" (Foster 1969: 276). In this Mexican community, it is believed that since serious friction within the joint household cannot be avoided, the compadre relationship's sanctity is best maintained "by selecting unrelated outsiders not subject to the stresses of shoulder-to-shoulder domestic living" (Foster 1969: 277). When the couple sets up an independent household, some years after marriage and with several children, kinsmen sponsors may be sought both to reduce baptismal costs and to escape the burden of an excessive number of compadres (Foster 1969: 273). In summary, in one Yucatan hacienda, the solidarity of the family is promoted by selecting sponsors from within this group, while in Tzintzuntzan compadrinazgo is strengthened by choosing nonfamily members among whom the chances of disputes and quarrels are fewer.

Among the Ticuleños compadrinazgo primarily is an instrument for integrating into the broader kinship system those who do not follow the traditional rules prescribing patrilocal residence after marriage. The baptismal sponsors of couples who reside patrilocally normally are evenly divided between kinsmen and nonkinsmen. However, when a couple resides neolocally or matrilocally, there is a pronounced preference for kinsmen as sponsors. Moreover, those who live patrilocally select patrilateral relatives as sponsors, while the deviant group prefers matrilateral kinsman-sponsors (Thompson 1971: 386–88).

Thompson argues that those in the patrilocal group have fulfilled the basic kinship obligations relative to residence. They are freer, therefore, to extend formal interpersonal bonds beyond kinship. Those Ticuleños who do not reside patrilocally have placed themselves in an anomalous position vis-a-vis the traditional kinship network. They utilize compadrinazgo to redefine their position in the kinship system. Alliances for the structural requirement of kinship assume priority for this group. The value to them of this type of ritual kinship system in creating formal nonkinship networks is secondary (Thompson 1971: 388–89).

Kinsmen-sponsors may be selected for reasons already given. Economic factors may be crucial in the choosing of relatives as sponsors; the cost, for example, associated with the baptismal feast may be minimized by the parents if those they entertain are their siblings or other kinsmen. As Foster indicates, kinsmen-sponsors provide one way to lessen the burden of too many ritual kinsmen.

Middleton has commented that in Hispanic America compadrinazgo is "characteristically found in mestizo communities featuring bilateral kinship systems" (1975: 461). In this regard Stein argues that the preference for kinsmen-sponsors in Hualco is not surprising since the kindred is the most important society unity in this bilaterally structured community (1961: 132). However, since all Filipino cultural-linguistic groups share a bilateral kinship system, and there is great variation among them about whether kinsmen or friends are preferred sponsors, other selective factors must be operative in the Philippines.

Possibly nonrelatives will be sought more frequently among people who find their kinship system inadequate for present-day needs. Compadrinazgo is used to replace elements lost through Hispanization or to bolster the indigenous social structure in the face of rapidly changing conditions. This "replacement" value of the godparenthood complex has been argued as a major reason for its almost universal popularity in Latin America. Despite the disappearance of the multiple functions of the clan, including mutual assistance and the regulation of marriage, similar bonds could be created through compadrinazgo.

However, in the Philippines, where the indigenous social structure was relatively undisturbed by the Spaniards, the "replacement value" of compadrinazgo is an inadequate explanation for its popularity. One is tempted to believe that the Filipinos' eager adoption of compadrinazgo reflects, in part, their desire to model all enduring social relations on the basis of family roles (Scheans 1962). This urge may explain the widespread occurrence of blood brotherhood in pre-Hispanic Philippines. With the arrival of the Catholic Spaniards, Filipinos were presented with another, more prestigeful means for achieving this goal. Yet this reasoning would be more impressive if there were a predominate preference for nonkinsmen sponsors—which is not the case in the Philippines.

There is some evidence to suggest that when padrinazgo is favored, establishing vertical, intergenerational relationships, sponsors usually are kinsmen. In Italy and Spain (with exceptions for Galicia and Andalusia) greater emphasis is placed on padrinazgo than on compadrazgo (Kenny 1962: 73; Anderson 1956: 7, 18). In both countries kinsmen are preferred sponsors. Where padrinazgo occurs in Latin America, sponsors usually are kinsmen (Strickon 1965; Madsen 1960b: 94–95; Richardson 1970: 84; Vogt 1970: 64). Although information on the Filipinos' preference for either kinsmen or nonkinsmen sponsors is limited, no overwhelming emphasis for either category appears at this date. It is believed, however, that as data on Filipino compadrinazgo accumulate, the extension motive, as in Latin America, will be found to predominate. Furthermore, future research will also confirm the present Filipino stress on compadrazgo, another similarity shared with Latin America.

Social Class and Compadrinazgo

Most investigations of compadrinazgo in Latin America discuss, sometimes only briefly and often incompletely, its relationship to social classes. As a result, the data on this topic are scattered in numerous sources, and no recent synthesis has been made. Several decades ago Mintz and Wolf wrote that when a community with a class-structured society is a "self-contained class, or tribally homogeneous, *compadrazgo* is prevailingly horizontal (intraclass) in character" (Mintz and Wolf 1950: 364). These ritual relationships normally create or strengthen horizontal contacts among people having similar status and economic resources. In communities composed of several classes, compadrinazgo relationships tend to be vertical (interclass). How prevalent horizontal and vertical bonds are in a community depends "on the amount of socio-cultural and economic mobility, *real* and *apparent*, available to an individual in a given situation" (Mintz and Wolf 1950: 358).

A recent illustration of this proposition is that those Mayos Indians who cherish the traditional and basic values of their society, and are frequent participants in its ceremonial life, seek Mayos, not Ladino compadres. However, those Mayos who find the dominant values of their society less attractive frequently seek Ladino compadres (Crumrine and Crumrine 1969: 52). In this multi-class society, Mayos subjected to the greater amount of cultural change seek vertical (Ladino) ritual kinsmen. Although compadrinazgo provides the social context for the integration of individual Indians and Ladinos, it contributes little to the overall social integration of the society (53, 56).

Decreased economic mobility of the people of San Luis Jilotepeque, a community of about 1,100 Ladinos and 2,400 Pokoman-speaking Indians ninety miles east of Guatemala City, resulted in increased interclass ritual kinship bonds. The Indian loss of land ownership in this community both disrupted their traditional culture and created considerable insecurity. As a result, the Indians added a new function to the godparenthood complex, "that of exacting from one's Ladino godparental relatives a sense of obligation to provide privileged rights of rental of milpa land" (Tumin 1952: 126). Such is not always the impact of a changing cultural scene. In Tlayacapan, it was found that while economic mobility may generate more extensive compadrinazgo ties, vertical ritual relationships do not necessarily result (Ingham 1970: 287).

Yet Thompson found that economically mobile persons tend to select multiple higher status sponsors (1973: 261). He decided that, contrary to Ingham's statement for Tlayacapan, economic mobility in the context of change does not necessarily result in the elimination of asymmetrical ritual kinship bonds (1973: 263). Middleton concludes from his study that each hypothesis is a partial explanation for the selection of sponsors in Manta and suggests that "there is no reason why both explanations of the dynamics between upper and equal status choices cannot coexist under the same conceptual umbrella" (1975: 471).

In parts of Puerto Rico where the modernization process made the worker's job security more dependent upon his skills and experience than upon personal ties with the employer, ritual kinship relationships with the managers of sugar cane plantations lost much of their value and declined in importance (Mintz 1966: 389). As a result, compadrinazgo's main function was to unite members of the working class, in part to reduce job competition among themselves (Steward 1966: 475). This situation is contrary to what one would expect from the Mintz and Wolf proposition.

Compadrinazgo may be a major force in developing interclass contacts in some Latin American communities. In one Peruvian community the integrative function of compadrinazgo is such that it "cuts across caste lines, and it is one of the mechanisms which enable us to speak of San Carlos as one community, even though it has two cultures" (Gillin 1947: 150). In San Luis Jilotepeque, compadrinazgo also reduces caste social distance more effectively than any other "formally defined situation of relationship between Indians and Ladinos" (Tumin 1952: 127). Finally, in one Mexican town, "compadrinazgo more than any other single institution, makes for important and often fairly intimate relationships between Indians and Ladinos and between Ladinos and different classes" (Van den Berghe and Van den Berghe 1966: 1238).

But compadrinazgo does not always promote interclass socio-cultural integration.

No amount of compadrazgo will make a Kwaiker socially acceptable in the mestizo group; the Kwaiker remain, in the eyes of the mestizos, clients and/or peóns. Likewise, from the Kwaiker point of view, however skillfully a mestizo may manipulate the patron-compadrazgo relationship, he will not become socially acceptable or admitted into the Kwaiker society (Osborn 1968: 605).

In parts of Argentina, Ecuador, Brazil, Puerto Rico, Mexico, and Panama ritual kinship functions mainly to strengthen intraclass relationships, since sponsors primarily are socioeconomic equals (Strickon 1965: 329–30; Kottak 1967: 434; Wagley 1964: 159; Gudeman 1972: 56; Seda 1966: 295; Mintz 1966: 389; Steward 1966: 475; Middleton 1975: 468; Foster 1969: 266).

The godparenthood complex may encourage increased social interaction and integration between members of two (but not all) social classes. In Huaylas every social class seeks sponsors only from its own or a higher class. As a result some upper-class people must find prestigious outsiders as sponsors (Doughty 1968: 79). In Tobatí compadrinzago does not promote social integration of the middle class with either socioeconomic superiors or inferiors. In this Paraguayan city members of the middle class usually seek ritual bonds within their own class. The peasants, however, try to obtain upper-class patron sponsors. Although upper-class townspeople often sponsor lower-class godchildren, their own children's sponsors rarely come from the middle or lower classes (Service and Service 1965: 76).

In some instances members of a social class must have a unique quality before they are selected as sponsors. Ritual kinship in San Lorenzo generally formalizes an existing patron-client relationship between members of the middle and lower classes (Whitten 1965: 105). Middle-class residents also seek upper-class patron sponsors both to enhance their social status and to obtain economic or political favors. However, members of the upper class only establish compadrinazgo bonds, largely exploitative of them, with "community-oriented" middle-class persons. In this sense, compadrinazgo interconnects all those persons Whitten calls "community-oriented," that is, individuals who regard community approval of their behavior as essential to the maintenance of their "status image" (1965: 112, 96).

It has been extensively documented that compadrinazgo in Latin America often stresses paternalism and dependency on a patron sponsor (Van den Berghe and Van den Berghe 1966: 1239). In Peru and elsewhere in Hispanic America such dependency reinforces the traditional class structure and makes the Indian walk small in his relationship with the elite. The godparenthood complex thus becomes a social mechanism to keep changeless the social structure and its relationships (Larson and Bergman 1969: 43–44; Doughty 1968: 119; Tumin 1952: 130–31; Nuñez del Prado 1973: 21–22). In Puerto Rico compadrinazgo may actually hinder socioeconomic mobility. For example, one's compadres rarely, if ever, lend money to a ritual kinsman (unless an affine or consanguine) who wishes to migrate (Mintz 1966: 391).

In Tepoztlán, poor persons look for patron sponsors among prosperous families. They also seek compadres in Mexico City who can help their godchildren settle and find work in the capital. Transitional groups in Peru, striving to achieve upward social mobility, seek patron-client ritual ties with the elite, who can help them reach their goals (Larson and Bergman 1969: 178). In Peguche, "white compadres are an asset for anyone who has business in Otovalo or Quito" (Parsons 1945: 45).

Yet compadrinazgo and patron-client relationships are not inevitably linked. In Dzitas, Yucatan, the poor often hesitate to ask a well-to-do person to be a sponsor. " 'You are pretty smart to pick a rich compadre. As for me, I wouldn't dare because I am poor' " (Redfield 1941: 222). In the Mexico City "shanty-town" of Cerrada del Condor, sponsors should be poor " 'so no one can say that you picked them out of self-interest' " (Lomnitz 1973: 42). Peasants who seek patron-sponsors may be rejected (Scheele 1966: 445). If a middle-class patron in San Lorenzo thinks he is being approached for purely economic reasons, he may refuse to be a sponsor (Whitten 1965: 106). In Guatemala City social superiors were rarely selected as sponsors by the residents of the two urban neighborhoods studied in this city (Roberts 1973: 173–74).

Some Indians may not consider Ladinos as potential sponsors since they are not members of their community as compadres should be (Wagley 1969: 58). Moreover, Ladinos frequently do not treat their Indian compadres with the same intimacy and equality they show their Ladino compadres (De la Fuente 1952: 87; Nuñez del Prado 1973: 21–22; Tumin 1952: 132; Gillin 1951: 61). In San Cruz Chinautla, however, Indian and Ladino compadres may address each other as equals (Reina 1966: 232).

A peasant incurs disadvantages in selecting a patron-sponsor. His new compadre must be given excessive deference, and the christening fiesta should be more elaborate (Ingham 1970: 285). On the other hand, Indians in San Cruz Chinautla prefer Ladino baptismal sponsors because the gift they must give to the new godparent can be cheaper than if an Indian were the sponsor (Reina 1966: 230).

Patron sponsors often recognize the social and economic liabilities of the position. In Ica "having compadres among the peasants was more trouble than it was worth, for they always try to worm extra favors on the basis of the relationship" (Hammel 1969: 84). When wealthier Puerto Ricans living in Chicago sponsor lower-class children, the ritual kinship relationship "presents exploitation on the part of both and is reciprocal in value rather than in kind. Such a bond is impersonal and instrumental to a great degree and derives its viability from the utility of each participant for the other" (Press 1963: 480). Vertical ritual kinship bonds usually exploit the patrons economically, yet many serve as sponsors both because it is difficult to refuse a request to be a godparent and because so often having many godchildren is a prestige symbol (Van den Berghe and Van den Berghe 1966: 1239; Tumin 1952: 130–31; Tax 1953: 178; Heath 1971: 181; Osborn 1968: 593; De la Fuente 1967: 443).

Finally, ritual kinship bonds linking persons of the same class or status may be asymmetrical. Choices may not be reciprocated. While in Manta reciprocal choices were common (Middleton 1975: 470), they were rare in Tlayacapan (Ingham 1970: 284). Hammel found, however, that reciprocity was a vital element in creating group alliances in the Balkans that persisted for decades (1968). Moreover, godparents normally are given greater deference, although they share the same class or status as their compadres.

Data on the association of ritual kinship and Filipino social classes (or statuses) add nothing unique to the varied patterns already described, but most investigations of compadrinazgo in the Philippines have been limited to villages where class distinctions are of minor importance. Although patron sponsors are sought, in Caticugan and Lalawigan ritual kinsmen usually are members of the same class or status. Filipinos follow the trend reported for many parts of Latin America in that when interclass sponsors are chosen, it is usually for the marriage rite, (for example, in Manalad, Canaman, Siaton, etc.). A common explanation is that marriage sponsors are potential patrons for the newly wedded couple in their effort to establish economic independence.

Upper-class sponsors, as in Latin America, may be forced to select appropriately prestigious sponsors outside their own community, e.g., in Siaton, Canaman, and Dumaguete. Although upwardly mobile people in Dumaguete desire vertical ritual kinship linkages, nevertheless compadrinazgo bonds in this city consist mainly of horizontal relationships. On the whole, compadrinazgo appears to maintain the status quo in Dumaguete from generation to generation as it does in Caticugan and Lalawigan.

Equal class or status ritual kinship bonds in Caticugan, Siaton, Lalawigan, and Boroñgan normally are asymmetrical. Reciprocal choices are rare. In fact, no such reciprocity of choice was discovered in the two villages. The ideal and real responsibilities and privileges of equal status godparents are more extensive; they receive even greater deference from their godchildren than from their compadres. Since baptismal and confirmation godparents usually are of the godchild's parent's generation, the deference they merit is augmented by the respect and obedience their older age commands. These two elements of the relationships reinforce each other.

Centrifugal-Centripetal Aspects of Compadrinazgo

Ideally, compadrinazgo creates a social network that "acts as a cohesive and integrative force within the community [and] channelizes reciprocal behavior . . . so that the individual achieves a maximum degree of social, economic, and spiritual security" (Foster 1953: 10). For this reason ritual kinsmen often are members of the same community; when not, the preference is for them to live nearby (Vogt 1970: 64; Gudeman 1972: 56). In 1925–1928, only three percent of Tzintzuntzeños' godparents lived outside the town, and all of these resided within a ten-mile radius. In 1958–1967 "nearby outsiders continue to outnumber those living farther away, but the gap is closing" (Foster 1969: 267). For this latter period, 13 percent resided beyond the ten-mile radius.

Of course, there are advantages when one's ritual kinsmen live in different and not necessarily adjacent communities. In the Guatemalan Indio village of San Miguel Milpas Altas, nonresidential compadres are actively sought by nearly all San Migueleños (Spielberg 1968: 209).

In San Miguel there is an almost total absence of *compadre* bonds between fellow villagers. This is certainly a different picture from what we would expect if compadrazgo were an integrating force. In a survey of twenty heads of households, only two reported having *compadres* in the village; reliable informants said that these were the only two cases in the entire village (Spielberg 1968: 208).

Two factors explain why San Migueleños preferred their compadres to be outsiders. First, "addressing a fellow villager as *compadre* would violate the norm that one should treat all villagers alike" (Spielberg 1968: 209). Second, most informants believed that residents of San Miguel could not be trusted—"a man would be a fool to let others know too much about his affairs or to let others get too close to him" (206). If compadres lived in the same village they "would decrease the safe and appropriate social distance that should be maintained among villagers" (209).

The strong preference of San Migueleños for ritual kinsmen who live beyond their village is not unique to them. As already mentioned, Mantenses believe it is unwise to select sponsors who live in their own block (or neighborhood)—and for the same reasons they are usually avoided by San Migueleños. Tepoztecans often seek nonkin sponsors outside their town, for similar reasons (Lewis 1963: 350).

Another reason peasants often have sponsors from other communities is that patron godparents are sought (Campbell 1964: 223). In one Greek village, where most sponsors are outsiders, the most important criterion in the selection of sponsors is to secure persons "whose wealth and position will be a source of potential help for themselves and their children" (Friedl 1962: 72). Patron sponsors usually live in the town or city and not the village. In the predominantly rural Philippines, with the typical one-class structure of most Filipino villages, patron sponsors normally must be sought in the municipal capital or provincial towns. Upper-class families often can only find prestigeful sponsors in other communities; they may also choose ritual kinsmen from other towns to avoid undesired compadre ties with lower status residents (Hammel 1969: 84).

In Aritama the permanent residence of sponsors in the community often is of little importance. A temporary visitor or a traveler passing through the community may be requested to be a sponsor. Whether or not such sponsors return is not considered important. Such an attitude reflects the minor functional significance of ritual kinship in this community (Reichel-Dolmatoff 1961: 173).

Throughout the countries under consideration, improved transportation facilities and traditional patterns of economic and socio-religious interaction among the members of different communities are additional reasons for having ritual kinsmen from outside one's community. The first factor explains why today more sponsors of Tzintzuntzeños live farther from their community than in the past. The annual voluntary agricultural work groups and the popularity of the patron saint fiestas of Siaton, Zamboanguita, and Dauin municipalities largely explain the numerous ritual kinsmen shared by these Filipinos.

As mentioned earlier, Bisayan Filipinos in general (and Lalawignons in particular) often secure sponsors in more impersonal ways than most Latin Americans. The nature of the former escort system of obtaining sponsors at the Boroñgan church was an important reason Lalawignons had many ritual kinsmen (often strangers to the parents) who resided outside of, and often at some distance from, their village. This trend probably has been reversed because a priest now lives in the village, and the sacramental rites are held in the community chapel.

In summary, sponsors may be sought purposely in one's own community to increase one's economic and social security and to create more intimate and succoring relationships with both kinsmen and friends. However, nonlocal sponsors may be favored precisely to avoid these traditional affective bonds of compadrinazgo. Local or regional conditions in both Latin America and the Philippines (e.g., Siaton and Lalawigan) may be determining factors in whether sponsors usually are insiders or outsiders—and these conditions may change quickly. In Caticugan and Lalawigan, if not in the rest of the Bisayas, compadrinazgo is a minor factor in integrating Filipinos on a provincial basis. Significantly, this condition is also typical of compadrinazgo in Dumaguete City. Individuals in both Latin America and the Philippines weigh the advantages and disadvantages of local versus nonlocal, intra- or interclass, and kinsmen or nonrelative compadres. The decisions they make are those deemed most personally beneficial.

Urbanization and Compadrinazgo

The available (and limited) data on the current status of compadrinazgo in cities, as compared to its role in villages and rural regions, concentrate primarily on the differential importance of horizontal or vertical ritual kinship bonds, the intensity of associated and traditional obligations and privileges of godparents and compadres, the relative emphasis on kinsmen versus nonkinsmen as sponsors, and the number of occasions for sponsorship. This subsection focuses on these four topics.

Mintz and Wolf (1950) and Pitt-Rivers (1968) claim that compadrinazgo is unable to thrive in an urban environment where impersonal, nonkin relationships are stressed and socioeconomic mobility is extensive. More recent information on the godparenthood complex—as it functions in cities in Latin America—confirms their belief that an urban environment is not congenial to ritual kinship. However, additional evidence also suggests that in some Latin American cities the flexibility of compadrinazgo has enabled it to adjust successfully to city life. In these cities it remains a vital aspect of urban social relations—beyond the boundaries of the crowded residential clusters of recent peasant migrants.

The deterioration of compadrinazgo in Merida (Redfield 1941: 222) and elsewhere in urban Latin America (Holmes 1952: 112) has been explained as a response to increased socioeconomic mobility and a cash economy. These two factors were also crucial in sapping the vigor of compadrinazgo in industrial Europe (Mintz and Wolf 1950: 352).

Maraspini writes that both directly and indirectly compadrinazgo is less important in Italian cities than in the villages. Members of the professional group in one southern Italian community rarely mention their godparents, who frequently are close friends of the family residing in another town. He adds, as an explanatory comment, that the standards of the professional group "are, to a great extent, urban ones" and that they look "to the city, and not to the village for guidance" (Maraspini 1968: 205).

Redfield used the relative importance and vigor of compadrinazgo in Latin America as an index of urbanization (1941: 338). In the "cityward progression" of Yucatan peasants, social control through ritual kinship was diluted (Redfield 1965: 25). Compadre bonds in rural Yucatan were intraclass, paralleling and supporting parental and parent-in-law relationships. The ceremony of handwashing (whereby parents in rural areas acknowledged their obligation to their compadres) disappeared in Merida (Redfield 1965: 26). The emphasis on interclass compadrinazgo bonds in the capital weakened the reciprocal nature of these ritual linkages. Godchildren were less respectful of godparents. These, in turn, showed decreasing interest in the proper behavior of godchildren. Seeking a sponsor in Merida was less a religious activity than a perfunctory, customary gesture.

Echoing Redfield, Harris reports that in Minas Velhas "the fact that such godfathers [with over 100 godchildren and several hundred *compadres*] are separated from their *compadres* and godchildren by class barriers is sufficient to rob the relationship of the kind of intensity which characterizes it in a homogeneous rural community" (1956: 153). As a result, compadrinazgo shows signs of weakness and disorganization, and the "institution is comparatively superficial and prone to becoming a mere formality" (Harris 1956: 153–54).

In San Pedro, "a small town in a developing society," changes—population mobility (particularly in-migration), the decreasing fear of God, and "creeping modernism"—have largely destroyed the traditional nature of compadrinazgo (Richardson 1970: 85). Hammel also found that compadrinazgo was less viable in the urban and industrial areas of the Balkans (1968).

Ingham asserts that the importance of patron-client linkages may diminish among city dwellers as prestige becomes associated with consumption rather than giving. As a result, the significance of compadrinazgo declines, and horizontal intraclass sponsorship increases (1970: 287). Similar changes have occurred on Puerto Rico sugar plantations (Mintz 1966: 389–90; Seda 1966: 295) and in Tobatí (Service and Service 1954: 174). In urban centers, compadrinazgo often consolidates status groups; the rich, for example, act as one another's compadres (Nelson 1971: 86; Wagley 1964: 151; Press 1963: 478).

Compadrinazgo was found to be an insignificant institution in two urban neighborhoods of Guatemala City which at the time of the investigation had over 600,000 residents (Roberts 1973: 27, 43). When godparents did see their godchildren, such meetings were seen only as part of the normal relationships among friends. Compadres rarely were a source of financial assistance during a crisis and the names of many ritual kinsmen had been forgotten. "I found little evidence that *compadrazgo* relationships served as a basis for continuing interaction of any kind within the urban milieu" (Roberts 1973: 173). This situation was explained as the result of the instability of city life. Ritual kinsmen moved, losing contact with each other. A ritual linkage originally established for economic advantages ceased to be useful when a person took another job (174). Basically, compadrinazgo in Guatemala City was found to be "too inflexible a relationship to be useful in their secular ambitions. . . ." (174). Interestingly, this is one of the rare cases where the inflexibility of compadrinazgo is stressed.

The mobility and changing nature of an urban population is also a reason for the lack of vitality of compadrinazgo in another Latin American town.

Only 54 percent of the present household heads were born in San Pedro or in nearby Buga or Tulua. Thus, nearly half of the town's population has lacked behavioral experience in being godchild and godparent to their present neighbors (Richardson 1970: 91).

In this instance, contrary to Pitt-River's earlier statement, the migration of peasants to cities has not preserved the typical functions of compadrinazgo in rural areas.

Yet conpadrinazgo, in both Europe and Latin America (and in one Philippine city), can "withstand the onslaught of modern market and secular conditions, its form signaling the absence of other systems to satisfy needs created by such conditions, as well as mirroring the nature of the needs" (Ravicz 1967: 251). Change may, in the long run, lead to reorganization of compadrinazgo to meet new requirements or needs of life in the city. Reorganization is the other face of disorganization often associated with ritual kinship in cities.

Not all the information for southern Europe indicates that compadrinazgo is a fading institution in its cities. Patron-client relationships can remain an essential aspect of urban existence. In Madrid, for example, the godparenthood system is "one of the most important links in the chain of patronage" (Kenny 1962: 183–84). The selection of sponsors by most urbanites in Spain (and Italy) is determined largely by efforts to maximize the potential socioeconomic benefits associated with the high-status sponsors (Kenny 1960: 18). Although Anderson's informants reported that the vitality of compadrinazgo in Italian cities had declined, the institution continues to persist (1957: 52).

Patron-client relationships continue to be sought by urban residents in Latin America. In Cuidada Industrial, a new and modern industrial center created by the Mexican government, ritual kinship remains an influential force among the workers. A compadre in the factories is "a reliable source" about job openings and working conditions and can "lobby in the interest of the job-seeker" (Miller 1973: 109). In fact, real or ritual kinship ties are almost requisite to secure a job in the factories. In San Salvador, the capital city of El Salvadore, godparents often are former villagers who have achieved success in an urban setting. These patron sponsors offer more immediate and tangible benefits to the godchildren than would the other, more distant and aloof city dwellers (Kottak 1967: 434).

Compadrinazgo performs many useful functions for the residents of Manta. In this Ecuadorian city "compadres serve as important sources of information and points of contact with other networks of individuals and must therefore be conceptualized as a significant mode of social support, both from an affective and instrumental perspective" (Middleton 1975: 465). Higher-status sponsors (small storeowners and market vendors) may be sought throughout the city for the discounts, credits, and small gifts this ritual linkage promotes. Compadrinazgo enables Mantenses to transform "interpersonal relationships in the wider society into predictable social ones, through which various exchanges of respect, information, and economic tokens take place" (Middleton 1975: 472).

The one detailed investigation of compadrinazgo in Mexico City found that it had adapted to urban conditions. "With one or two exceptions the changes that compadrazgo have undergone represent an adaptation to urban life rather than a breakdown or even a weakening of the system" (Lewis 1965: 432). One innovation was the shift from a preference for nonkinsman-sponsors in Tepoztlán to kinsman-sponsors in Mexico City. Relatively friendless in the big city, Tepoztecans turn to kinsmen for their sponsors, resulting in the reinforcement of family ties (Lewis 1965: 433). The compadre relationship in Mexico City is transformed from the formal and ceremonial one of Tepoztlán to the more informal and personal. Other changes are that in Mexico City godparents of baptism are not consulted in the selection of confirmation sponsors and that the children of Tepoztecan parents are baptized much later in life. (Children in urban La Laja also are not baptized until three years of age: Peattie 1968: 41.)

An identical shift in the choice of godparents also occurs among urban Zapotecans. In the city, Zapotecans select godparents from among family members. In traditional Zapotec villages, however, baptism and marriage sponsors usually are chosen from outside the family (Nader 1969a 7: 349).

A feature of most Third World cities that appears almost universal and permanent is their "squatter settlements" or "shanty-towns." The adaptive value of compadrinazgo in an urban setting has been described for rural immigrants to the *barriada* of Lima, Peru. Compadrinazgo helps provide security for these people, often recent peasant migrants. Compadres often are selected from the various *barriada* clubs. The regional associations in Lima may represent a functional extension or alternative to some godparenthood functions (Mangin 1965: 315). Although interclass compadrinazgo occurs in the provinces, the regional associations provide the setting for *barriada* residents to secure interclass patron sponsors who would otherwise be impossible to obtain. (A similar association between compadrinazgo and social clubs occurs in San Lorenzo: Whitten 1965: 107.) In general, compadrinazgo in Lima is of utmost importance in getting things done at all levels in every governmental ministry (Mangin 1965: 315) and in reducing much of the impersonality of city life (Holmes 1952: 112).

Occasionally, brief statements are made about the vitality of compadrinazgo among peasants residing in these migrant communities of Latin American cities. For example, in the *favelas* of Rio de Janeiro nonkin godparents have been given virtual status as kin-group members (Pearse 1961: 199). In La Laja "relations based on kinship or *assimilated to kinship* [underscore added] are dominant in the social network" (Peattie 1968: 40). In one low-cost housing settlement (*vecindad*) in Mexico City, all the families are related by ritual kinship bonds (Lewis 1970: 436).

Some comparative data are available for compadrinazgo among Puerto Ricans in Chicago (Press 1963) and residents of San Cristobal de las Casas, a Mexican town of about thirty thousand people. Among the lower class in both these cities, compadrinazgo is active and ritual kinship bonds are strong. In San Cristobal "compadre ties tend to take precedence over bonds of kinship and friendship . . ." (Van den Berghe and Van den Berghe 1966: 1240). However, for middle- and upper-class Puerto Ricans and residents of San Cristobal, ritual kinship ties are of slight socioeconomic importance, and the godparent role is considered more of an imposition than an honor. Middle-class Puerto Ricans favor kinsman-sponsors; if they need economic assistance, it often is sought from close relatives or public agencies, not from compadres. Members of the upper class in both cities usually seek sponsors among their social equals. In San Cristobal, for example, the growing national orientation of the elite discourages them from seeking local vertical ritual kinship linkages (Van den Berghe and Van den Berghe 1966: 1241; also Press 1963: 478).

One difference occurs in the attitude of Puerto Rican and San Cristobal elite or "progressives" toward compadrinazgo. Wealthy Puerto Ricans in Chicago consciously and proudly preserve compadrinazgo and its associated activities as an "old country custom" (Press 1963: 478). Some "progressives" in San Cristobal, however, consider the folk beliefs and practices of compadrinazgo "an unnecessary folk custom; the secular functions of ritual kinship, they argue, would be better performed by the state, and its religious side could be reduced to the minimum Church-sanctioned form" (Van den Berghe and Van den

Berghe 1966: 1241). This contrasting attitude of some Puerto Ricans probably is explained by the fact that they are recent migrants to the United States.

Among Italian-Americans, compadrinazgo is increasingly conforming to the American Catholic pattern that stresses the importance of padrinazgo, not compadrazgo (Ianni 1972: 123). Several decades ago, Foster (1953) suggested that secularization of compadrinazgo in the city and among the middle and upper classes might reduce it to the Church-sanctioned minimum form, thus reverting to the original model of Spain.

One unique innovation is reported for compadrinazgo among Italian-American families involved in organized crime in the United States. Although American Catholics and Italians in southern Italy usually have contemporaries as their children's godparents, the sponsors for these families normally are from the generation preceding the parents', hence linking different generations. Members of the most powerful family (Lupollo) were the ones other families usually asked to be sponsors, reflecting their prestige and authority within this tightly-knit group in this country (Ianni 1972: 123).

Mintz and Wolf believed that in the face of "rapid social change, *compadre* mechanisms may multiply to meet the accelerated rate of change" (1950: 364). In more advanced Middle American societies, or those with greater external contacts, occasions for ritual kinship were found to be more plentiful than in isolated communities. Recent information on this aspect of compadrinazgo is inconclusive. The number of occasions creating ritual kinship bonds decreased among workers on a Yucatan hacienda (who have been subjected to extensive social change), for Tepoztecans living in Mexico City (a focal point of innovation for Mexico), and among the inhabitants of Martineztown (Deshon 1963: 574; Lewis 1965: 432; Vincent 1966: 157). In San Cristobal and Dumaguete, however, occasions for developing compadre bonds have increased (Van den Berghe and Van den Berghe 1966: 1237; Potter 1973). Contrarily, in rural Italy, where change is far less extensive than in most cities, the occasions for ritual sponsorship have proliferated (Anderson 1957).

As the preceding survey indicates, most generalizations proclaiming the desuetude of compadrinazgo in Latin American urban society appear premature. First, detailed evidence on the structure and functions of ritual kinship in Latin American cities is extremely restricted. Second, conditions often cited as indicating the decreased importance of ritual kinship bonds—an excessive number of godchildren and compadres or neglect of the traditional duties associated with sponsorship (De la Fuente 1967 6: 44)—are common in rural areas where there is no question that compadrinazgo flourishes. Third, impersonal or instrumental ritual kinship bonds are not limited to urban compadrinazgo. In fact, Lewis claimed that impersonal institutions and behavior are not unique to the city and demonstrated his claim for rural Mexico (1951). Tax has commented on the impersonal character of all social relations, both within the community and between people of different communities in Guatemala (1941: 33). Whether urbanization and social change will increase or decrease the number of occasions for ritual sponsorship depends on many variables whose interactions are not simple and whose effects are not easy to predict.

The adaptability of compadrinazgo is reflected in its dominant local rural motive (whether extension or intensification) often being reversed when peasants move to the city. While the elite in one city cherishes the traditional customs associated with the godparenthood complex, another elite deprecates them. In cities with interacting social classes, compadrinazgo does not always emphasize vertical ritual bonds (Mintz and Wolf 1950: 364). Latecomers to the city may before long shift to padrinazgo the traditional emphasis on compadrazgo in their natal village.

The continued importance of compadrinazgo among peasants living in the *favelas, barriadas,* and slums of Latin American cities cannot be discounted, for these communities are an increasingly important, and possibly permanent, aspect of Third World urban life. Hollnsteiner (1967: 24) and Ravicz (1967: 251) question if life in these slum communities is "truly urban." The Tondo slum of Manila has been described as a "haven of primary, highly personalized relationships, a folksy milieu not unlike the barrio" (Hollnsteiner 1967: 13–14). Jacobson argues, however, based on research in Cebu City, that such continuities between rural and urban life as kinship and family possibly reflect adaptations to a new environment (1969: 16).

Philippine Urbanization and Compadrinazgo

Most data concerning the godparenthood complex in the Philippines have come from investigations of peasant communities. As a result, knowledge of contemporary compadrinazgo practices in Philippine cities, and especially among the urban elite, often is speculative in addition to being fragmentary.

Of course, rigid adherence to the obligations of compadrazgo may be undergoing change today, particularly in the metropolitan Manila area and other urban centers. Although politicians make wide use of the system, businessmen interested in running an efficient factory or office may be increasingly reluctant to take on a compadre relationship which appears primarily exploitative. Executives can hardly dispense unlimited favors to a large set of employees-compadres. In doing so they can endanger the position of the company by promoting inefficiency and jealousies possibly culminating in a strike by the labor unions (Hollnsteiner 1963: 71).

Among residents of a modern low-cost urban housing development outside Manila, however, compadrinazgo "is very strong" (Mendez and Jocano 1974: 310). In one Manila community 23 percent of the nonrelatives in extended households were ritual kinsmen (Eslao 1966: 206). In a slum of Cebu City, the second largest Philippine city, "the extended family which includes consanguineal relatives and compadres, is not altered in the least" (Dischoso 1965: 62).

A recent research study (1970–71) of compadrinazgo in Dumaguete City has been made by Potter (1973). It is not our purpose to cite in detail the findings of Potter's four-hundred-page dissertation. It is enough, at this point, to note that he found compadrinazgo in this middle-sized Philippine city "alive and well."

Data for Potter's study were obtained through various techniques. First, both ritual occasions establishing compadrinazgo relationships and subsequent forms of post-ritual celebrations were observed as a participant observer. Second, interviews were conducted with key informants who occupied various positions in the urban, economic, political, and bureaucratic institutions. Third, parish baptismal and civil registry marriage records were analyzed to determine numerical indices of participation in compadrinazgo by initiates and sponsors. A fourth source of data was a questionnaire administered to 500 residents.

The questionnaire sample was based on geographical quotas to guarantee a spatial measure of urbanization. Within Dumaguete municipality, composed of a central urban core (poblacion) and twenty-two barrios, four sample areas were chosen on the basis of their distances from the poblacion. The urban core and three barrios, at varying distances from the poblacion, were studied. The barrio nearest to the poblacion had a significant white-collar population, while the farthest barrio was settled predominantly by farmers.

Compadrinazgo in Dumaguete normally is restricted to baptism, confirmation, and marriage. For Protestants (United Church of Christ), ritual kinship bonds are established only through baptism and marriage. A small group of Dumagueteños establish ritual relationships through a variety of nonprescribed rites previously mentioned. Those who assert that participation on these other occasions results in ritual bonds are a hightly educated, sophisticated minority. A disproportionately large number are Protestants.

In recent years the selection of multiple sponsors for a single rite has increased, particularly among Dumaguete poblacion residents. For example, in 1949 the number of baptisms and marriages with multiple sponsors was less than one per one hundred rites. By 1969 this proportion had increased to nearly one in every six rites (Potter 1975: 5). This increase is explained by Potter by the fact that it was usually middle-class residents who sought multiple sponsors as a means either of exhibiting or of augmenting their community status.

The attitude of these middle-class members seemed to be that if one created a sufficient number of ritual relationships some would be profitable for patronage purposes. However, they also used multi-sponsor rites as a strategy to demonstrate their status at the ceremony, even if the parents realized that few compadres would become their patrons. In these instances the focus of compadrinazgo was on the rite rather than on future patronage or other forms of return.

The most desirable sponsors (those chosen most frequently in Potter's sample), when compared with the typical sponsors, were relatively older and better educated and lived in the poblacion; a disproportionate number were Protestants serving mostly for Catholic rites. (The popularity of Protestant sponsors reflects seventy years of influence of Silliman University.) It may be suspected (although the sample did not gather this information) that most members of this group were also nonkinsmen since, on the whole, Dumagueteños normally do not select relatives as sponsors. Finally, among the recurrent sponsors (based on a separate survey of parish and civil registry records) appears a group of people who were not of the upper class but were active in the civic and professional life of the city (Potter 1975: 8). They share social features similar to the "community-oriented" group of San Lorenzo described by Whitten (1965).

Dumaguete respondents clearly prefer local residents as ritual kinsmen. Many of the ties a minority have with nonresidents were formed before moving to Dumaguete. Patterns of sponsor residence within Dumaguete illustrate the effects of proximity on ritual kinship. Parents most frequently choose barriomates or, if they live in the urban center, poblacion residents. A large number of barrio parents also select poblacion residents, emphasizing this area's role as a central prestige place in the community.

Dumagueteños usually do not select kinsmen as sponsors. Only about one-fifth of all ritual relationships is with relatives. When kinsmen are chosen, parents demonstrate a strong preference for ones of their own age group. Particularly frequent choices include aunts and uncles (real or classificatory) of the child. This pattern tends to intensify the solidarity of the sibling group that is fundamental to Filipino social organization.

Interaction between ritual kinsmen does not always take place, particularly where contacts between godparents and godchildren are intermittent. In these circumstances ritual kin often rely upon "structural closeness" when making appeals, trusting to others' commitment to the ideals of the formal bond. Although this anticipation of assistance is buttressed by traditional Filipino values stressing reciprocity within groups as well as sacred values associated with compadrinazgo, support is not always forthcoming.

Realistically, compadre interactions are marked by reciprocal exchanges, sociability, and special concessions. That these forms of behavior take place depends greatly upon the persistence of contacts between compadres. These contacts facilitate social interaction and help the individual cultivate reciprocity within a local political and economic system that is personalistic and elitist. Compadrinazgo provides a competitive advantage over those who must depend upon impersonal, less functional qualifications.

Institutionally, compadrinazgo in Dumaguete is related to status identification and status seeking in the religious, economic, social, and political domain. The Catholic church has recognized the secular functions of compadrinazgo and has accommodated some of its practices to conform to these concerns. Protestant (or non-Catholic) churches have borrowed some Catholic ceremonial practices. Their memberships' patterns of ritual choice and the timing of rites are recently similar to those of the Catholic majority.

Economic functions of ritual kinship include gifts and other reciprocal exchanges with symbolic or real redistributions. Compadrinazgo influences the labor market through its supplementary impact on hiring, promotion, and transfer decisions. The extent of this assistance to ritual kinsmen depends upon the patron's and recipient's resources and the structure of the bond (vertical or horizontal).

Townsmen often accuse of abuses politicians who actively participate as sponsors in compadrinazgo. Residents expect office-holders to redistribute resources, especially to those who have personal claims on the leaders. The political assistance incumbents render is limited by scarce patronage opportunities and competing demands of various kinds of allies. Tactical considerations help to determine patronage distribution and support by followers. These calculations seem to differ among urban and nonurban residents whom compadrinazgo links to politicians; the former have lower expectations of aid and consequently utilize other criteria in choosing whom to support.

Some argue that secularization of compadrinazgo can be measured by a reduction in ritual occasions. However, for Dumagueteños ritual occasions are a function of normal participation in required Church functions. Moreover, the number of nonsacramental occasions for sponsorship has increased. Urban parents perform the ritual obligations more faithfully than do nonurban residents, many of whom omit confirmation. Minor indications of secularization may be found in the trend toward baptism at a later age, participation as sponsors by many non-Catholics, ceremonies involving nonessential elements directed at status considerations, and accommodations by the Church to secular concerns.

Tabus on marriage with ritual kinsmen continue in Dumaguete. Strong prohibitions exist against godparent-godchild marriage. Secondary restrictions are found against marriage of godsiblings and compadre-comadre, with marriage of the latter group the less strongly opposed. Some urban residents with high educational and status achievement dismiss these tabus as unnecessary excepting those officially set by the Church.

In summary, compadrinazgo remains a viable aspect of life in Dumaguete. Although active ties are formed with a limited number of ritual kin, and some data suggest that formal ties may constitute an increasing percentage of the total, the institution continues to serve important functions in the social system. Urban Dumagueteños are active in the institution as participants in various relationships they establish. They also serve a disproportionate number of times as sponsors for other parents. Urban selection patterns have become a model for nonurban residents whose choices have come to reflect urban occupational and prestige patterns. Compadrinazgo in Dumaguete reinforces and mirrors socioeconomic changes associated with urbanization.

Generalizations comparing the similarities and differences between rural and urban Philippine compadrinazgo are subject to numerous exceptions. Generally speaking, however, the similarities between the godparenthood complex as reported for Filipino villages and Dumaguete are greater than the differences. In striking contrast is the greater number of occasions for ritual sponsorship in Dumaguete. This may reflect, in part, the regional urban concentration of Filipino Protestants and the presence of Silliman University. Another difference is the increased frequency of multi-sponsors in this provincial capital. Finally, data from Dumaguete suggest a greater stress of the extension motive (see Graph 3).

On the whole, compadrinazgo in Dumaguete has numerous similarities to practices in rural Philippines. Ritual kinsmen have restricted spatial distribution; compadrinazgo's integrative functions are largely localized. Confirmation is the least important of the three major religious events requiring sponsorship. Incest tabus remain in force, although the prohibition of the marriage of compadres and comadres appears weakened. Kinsmen-sponsors normally are relatives in the parents' generation. Lastly, the ideal "aid and comfort" functions of compadrinazgo often are not fulfilled.

One paramount but not unlimited feature of compadrinazgo is its flexibility. It has demonstrated an ability to adapt to an amazing variety of local situations and needs, rural and urban. This flexibility and the differing value systems may assure compadrinazgo a longer and more vigorous life in industrializing, urbanizing Third World nations than was its fate in most of Europe. Specialists in urbanization in Southeast Asia have found that the large cities of this region are not duplicates of European cities, and their development must not be assumed to follow the same patterns as the latter. "They [Southeast Asian cities] will be considerably larger and structurally different; that is, they will not generally be manufacturing/industrial centers. . . . There is also apparently much less social change and mobility than occurred historically in European cities" (SEADAG 1974: 14–15).

Scattered references suggest that life in Philippine and Latin American cities is not as impersonal and instrumental as is believed. Certainly this feature is less typical of recent, including first generation, communities of migrant peasants in Philippine cities. Moreover, the impersonal nature of the city may encourage the retention or creation of personal ties as an escape from urban "freedom"; compadrinazgo is an admirable institution for such purposes. The possible structural transformation and functional modifications of compadrinazgo in non-Western urban environments remain important research problems.

Appendix

Communities Discussed in the Text

This appendix omits such major cities as Manila, Mexico City, or Buenos Aires and those communities mentioned only once or twice in the text.

Alcalá de la Sierra: Andalusian community of 2,045 people in Spain

Altaquer: Kwaiker Indian and mestizo village of 84 households in the Andean foothills of Colombia

Arembepe: Brazilian fishing village of 730 people 37 miles from San Salvador, the capital of Bahia

Aritama: A Colombian mestizo village of 1,400 people

Cabetican: Community of 4,000 Filipinos in Pampanga, Luzon

Calimera: Community of 5,803 peasants in southern Italy

Camangahan: Village of about 900 Filipinos in Panay Island

Canaman: Town of 10,655 Filipinos in southeast Luzon

Cerrada del Condor: "Shantytown" of 176 households located in the southern part of Mexico City

Chan Kom: Village of 251 people 31 miles southwest of Valladolid, Yucatan

Cherán: Town of about 5,000 people in northern Michoacán, Mexico

Coroico: Bolivian community of about 2,000 people

Cortina d'Aglio: Southern Italian village in the Molisan Appenines

Dzitas: Village of 1,200 people in Yucatan

Eleodoro Gomez: Village of about 2,000 people (including its neighborhood) 180 miles southwest of Buenos Aires, Argentine Republic

Erongaricuaro: Community of 2,000 people about 200 miles west of Mexico City

Esperanza: Village of 2,000 Filipinos in southern Leyte Island

Estancia: Town (including several adjacent villages) of some 15,000 Filipinos in northeastern Panay Island

Guinhangdan: Village of 1,200 Filipinos in eastern Leyte Island

Hualcan: Highland Peruvian community of 740 people about six miles east of Carhuaz

Huaylas: Peruvian highland district; the community of the same name had 1,156 people or 21 per cent of the district's population

Hulo: Town of 12,000 Filipinos about 15 miles from Manila

Itá: Amazon community of 500 people in northern Brazil

La Laja: Urban neighborhood of Guayana, a Venezuelan town

Los Boquerones: Village of 350 Spanish-speaking peasants west of Panama City

Malitbog: Village of about 1,000 Filipinos in central Panay Island

Manalad: Village of around 600 Filipinos in southwest Negros Island

Manta: City of 35,000 to 40,000 people located on the central coast of Ecuador in Manabí province

Martineztown: Small town in the state of New Mexico

Merida: City of 96,660 in northwestern Yucatan

Minas Velhas: County seat of about 1,500 people in central Bahia, Brazil

Mitla: Zapotecan community of 2,007 people east of the city of Oaxaca, Mexico

Moche: Peruvian coastal community of 3,178 people

Pascua: Community of 450 Yaqui on the outskirts of Tucson City

Peyrane: Village of 680 people 35 miles from Avignon, France

Potam: Yaqui village of 259 people in Sonora, Mexico

Puray: Village of about 200 Tagalogs in Rizal Province, Luzon

San Cristobal de las Casas: Town of about 30,000 people in Chiapas (southeastern Mexico)

San Cruz Chinautla: Guatemalan Pokoman Indian village of 1,672 people

San Francisco Tecospa: Village of 800 Nahuatl Indians in Mexico

San Lorenzo: Ecuadorian town of 2,221 people

San Luis Jilotepeque: Community of about 1,000 Ladinos and 2,400 Pokoman-speaking Indians 90 miles east of Guatemala City

San Miguel Milpas Atlas: Village near Antiqua, Guatemala

San Pedro: Village of 1,527 people in the Cauca valley, Colombia

Santiago Chimaltenango: Village of 908 Man-speaking Indians in northwest Guatemala

Saucío: Colombian Andes village of 356 people

Songsong: Village on Rota Island, Mariana Islands, U.S., Trust Territory of the Pacific

Suba: Ilokan village of 496 people in northwest Luzon

Tarong: Ilokan village of 294 people in northwest Luzon
Tepoztlán: Community of over 4,000 people in Morelos, Mexico
Ticul: Town of 13,000 people in Yucatan
Tlayacapan: Community of 3,000 people in Morelos, Mexico
Tobatí: Community of 1,368 people east of Asuncion, Paraguay
Tonalá: Community of 4,886 people in Mexico, about 10 miles from Guadalajara
Tusik: Mayan Indian village of 106 people in Yucatan
Tzintzuntzan: Community of 1,877 people in Michoacán, Mexico

Vasilika: Village of 216 Greek peasants in the Boeotian plain

Bibliography

Aduarte, Diego, O. P.
    1903. Historia [1596 to 1608]. In Blair and Robertson, *The Philippine Islands*, 31:23–300.

Agnir, Federico I.
    1966. Compadrazgo among the Ilocanos. Student report in Anthropology, Silliman University, Dumaguete, Philippines. Typescript.

Alzina, Francisco Ignacio.
    [1668]. Historia de las Islas e Indios de Bisayas [1668]. Reference based on preliminary translation by Paul Lietz, sponsored by the Philippine Studies Program, University of Chicago. Typescript.

Amyot, Jacques, S.J.
    1960. *The Chinese Community in Manila: A Study of Adaptation of Chinese Families to the Philippine Environment.* Philippines Studies Program, Research Series, No. 2. Chicago: University of Chicago, Department of Anthropology.

Anderson, Gallatin.
    1956. A Survey of Italian Godparenthood. *The Kroeber Anthropological Society Papers* 15:1–110.
    1957. El Comparaggio: The Italian Godparenthood Complex. *Southwestern Journal of Anthropology* 13:32–53.

Anonymous.
    1956. *Manila Bulletin.* January 1956, Manila.
    1967. *New Catholic Encyclopedia.* 15 vols. New York: McGraw-Hill.
    1971. *Rite of Baptism for Children. The Roman Ritual Revised by Decree of the Second Vatican Ecumenical Council and Published by Authority of Pope Paul VI.* Pasay City, Philippines: St. Paul Publications.
    1974. Christmas: Rituals and Remembrances. *Archipelago* 1:47–49.

Arce, Wilfredo F.
    1961. The Characteristics of Ritual Kinsmen in a Small Community. Master's thesis, Ateneo de Manila University, Quezon City, Philippines.

1973.   The Structural Bases of Compadre Characteristics in a
         Bikol Town. *Philippine Sociological Review* 21:51–71.
Beals, Ralph.
    1946.   *Cherán: A Sierra Tarascan Village.* Institute of Social An-
             thropology, Publication no. 2. Washington, D.C.: Smith-
             sonian Institution.
    1969.   The Tarascans. In *Middle American Indians,* ed. Wau-
             chope, 8:725–73.
Bernal, Rafael.
    1965.   *México en Filipinas. Estudio de Una Transculturación.*
             Mexico: Universidad Nacional Autónoma de México.
Blair, Emma E., and Robertson, James A.
    1903–   *The Philippine Islands, 1493–1898.* 55 vols. Cleve-
    1907.   land, Ohio: Arthur Clark Co.
Boissevain, Jeremy.
    1966.   Patronage in Sicily. *Man* n.s. 1:18–33.
Bourne, Edward G.
    1903.   Historical Introduction. In Blair and Robertson, *The Phi-
             lippine Islands,* 1:18–87.
Brinton, Daniel G.
    1894.   Nagualism. *Proceedings, American Philosophical Society*
             32:11–73.
Bruno, Juanito A.
    1973.   *The Social World of the Tausug. A Study in Philippine
             Culture and Education.* Manila: Centro Escolar Univer-
             sity, Research and Development Center.
Buechler, Hans C., and Buechler, J. M.
    1971.   *The Bolivian Aymara.* New York: Holt, Rinehart and Win-
             ston.
Bullough, Sebastian.
    1963.   *Roman Catholicism.* Middlesex, England: Penguin Books,
             Ltd.
Bureau of the Census and Statistics.
    1962.   *Census of the Philippines. 1960. Population, Housing.* Re-
             port by Province. Samar and Negros Oriental. Manila: Bu-
             reau of the Census and Statistics 1.
    1971.   *Total Population of the Philippines and Each Province,
             City, Municipality and Municipal District–1970.* Manila:
             Bureau of the Census and Statistics.
Campbell, J. K.
    1964.   *Honour, Family and Patronage. A Study of Institutions
             and Moral Values in a Greek Mountain Community.* Ox-
             ford: Clarendon Press.

Chirino, Pedro, S.J.
1903.   Relacion de las Islas Filipinias (1604). In Blair and Robertson, *The Philippine Islands,* 12:174–321.

Commission on Liturgy.
1971.   *Ritwal sa Bunyag (Sinugbuahon).* Cebu City, Philippines: Commission on Liturgy, Archdiocese of Cebu, Cebu Star Press.
1971.   *Ritwal sa Kasal (Sinugbuahon).* Cebu City, Philippines: Commission on Liturgy, Archdiocese of Cebu, Cebu Star Press.

Cortez, Olimpio C., Sr.
1965.   The Compadre System. *Church and Society* 5:19–22.

Crumrine, N. Ross, and Crumrine, Lynne S.
1969.   Where Mayos Meet Mestizos: A Model for the Social Structure of Culture Contact. *Human Organization* 28:50–57.

Cruz, Emeterio C.
1958.   Baptismal Customs and Beliefs. *The University of Manila Journal of East Asiatic Studies* 7:214–15. Reprinted from *The Philippine Magazine* 33 (1936):259.

Cuyás, Arturo.
1940.   *Appleton's New English-Spanish and Spanish-English Dictionary.* Revised and enlarged by Antonio Llano. New York: D. Appleton-Century Co.

Dalrymple, Alexander.
1772.   Account of Some Curiosities at Sooloo. In *An Historical Collection of the Several Voyages and Discoveries in the South Pacific Ocean,* 1:1–24. London.

Davis, William G.
1968.   Economic Limitations and Social Relationships in a Philippine Marketplace: Capital Accumulation in a Peasant Society. In *Asian Studies at Hawaii,* ed. Robert van Niel, 2:1–28. Honolulu, Hawaii: University of Hawaii Press.
1970.   Network Components in a Northern Philippine Town: Some Preliminaries. State University of California, Davis. Manuscript.
1973.   *Social Relations in a Philippine Market: Self-Interest and Subjectivity.* Berkeley, Calif.: University of California Press.

Davis, William G., and Hollnsteiner, Mary R.
1969.   Some Recent Trends in Philippine Social Anthropology. *Anthropologica* n.s. 11:59–84.

De la Fuente, Juan.
1952.   Ethnic and Communal Relations. In Tax, *Penny Capitalism,* pp. 76–96.

1967.   Ethnic Relationships. In *Middle American Indians,* ed.
        Wauchope, 6:432–448.
Deshon, Shirley K.
   1963.   Compadrazgo on a Henequen Hacienda in Yucatan: A
           Structural   Re-evaluation.   *American   Anthropologist*
           65:547–83.
Desquibel, Pedro Hurtado.
   1903.   An Act Decreeing that the Sangley Shall Not be Allowed
           to have Godchildren, on Account of the Injury which may
           Result Therefrom [1599]. In Blair and Robertson, *The Phi-
           lippine Islands,* 11:75–77.
Diaz, May N.
   1966.   *Tonalá. Conservatism, Responsibility, and Authority in a
           Mexican Town.* Berkeley and Los Angeles: University of
           California Press.
Dischoso, Rev. Fermin A.
   1965.   A Study of Life in the Slum Area of Cebu City. Master's
           thesis, University of San Carlos, Cebu City, Philippines.
Doughty, Paul L.
   1968.   *Huaylas: An Andean District in Search of Progress.* Ithaca,
           N.Y.: Cornell University Press.
Edmonson, Munro S.
   1957.   *Los Manitos: A Study of Institutional Values.* Middle
           American Research Institute, Publication No. 25. New Or-
           leans: Tulane University Press.
Eduardo, Octavio de Costa.
   1948.   *The Negro in Northern Brazil. A Study of Acculturation.*
           New York: American Ethnological Society Monograph 15.
Eggan, Fred.
   1968.   Philippine Social Structure. In *Six Perspectives on the Phi-
           lippines,* ed. George M. Guthrie, pp. 1–48. Manila: Book-
           mark.
Eggan, Fred et al.
   1956.   *The Philippines.* 4 vols. New Haven, Conn.: Human Rela-
           tions Area Files Press, HRAF–16.
Eisenstadt, S. N.
   1956.   Ritualized Personal Relations. *Man* 56 (96):90–95.
Elwood, Douglas J., and Magdamo, Patricia Ling.
   1971.   *Christ in a Philippine Context. A College Textbook in
           Theology and Religious Studies.* Quezon City, Philippines:
           New Day Publishers.
Enriquez, B. Jewel N.

1956. Marriage Practices in Tetuan District in the City of Zamboanga, Province of Zamboanga, in the Island of Mindanao, the Philippines. Student report, Silliman University, Dumaguete, Philippines. Typescript.

Erasmus, Charles J.
1950. Current Theories on Incest Prohibition in the Light of Ceremonial Kinship. *The Kroeber Anthropological Society Papers* 2:42–50.

Eslao, Nena.
1966. The Development Cycle of the Philippine Household in an Urban Setting. *Philippine Sociological Review* 14:199–208.

Fals-Borda, Orlando.
1962. *Peasant Society in the Colombian Andes: A Sociological Study of Saucío.* Gainesville: University of Florida Press.

Fél, E., and Hofer, T.
1969. *Proper Peasants: Traditional Life in a Hungarian Village.* Chicago: Aldine, Viking Fund Publications in Anthropology, No. 46.

Foster, George M.
1948. *Empire's Children: The People of Tzintzuntzan.* Institute of Social Anthropology, Publication No. 6. Mexico: Smithsonian Institution.
1951. Report on an Ethnological Reconnaissance of Spain. *American Anthropologist* 53:311–25.
1953. Cofradía and Compadrazgo in Spain and Spanish America. *Southwestern Journal of Anthropology* 9:1–28.
1960. *Culture and Conquest: America's Spanish Heritage.* New York: Viking Fund Publications in Anthropology, No. 27.
1963. The Dyadic Contract in Tzintzuntzan, II: Patron-Client Relationship. *American Anthropologist* 65:1280–95.
1967. *Tzintzuntzan: Mexican Peasants in a Changing World.* Boston: Little, Brown and Co.
1969. Godparents and Social Networks in Tzintzuntzan. *Southwestern Journal of Anthropology* 25:261–78.

Fought, John.
1969. Chorti (Mayan) Ceremonial Organization. *American Anthropologist* 71:472–76.

Fox, Robert.
1971. The Rice Wine Complex among the Tagbanuas of Palawan Island, Philippines: A Description and Social Analysis. Philippine Studies Program. Chicago: University of Chicago. Manuscript.

Freedman, Maurice.
    1957. Chinese Family and Marriage in Singapore. Colonial Re-
           search Studies No. 20. London: Her Majesty's Stationery
           Office, Colonial Office.

Friedl, Ernestine.
    1962. Vasilika. A Village in Modern Greece. New York: Holt,
           Rinehart and Winston.

Gillin, John P.
    1947. Moche: A Peruvian Coastal Community. Institute for So-
           cial Anthropology, Publication No. 3. Washington, D.C.:
           Smithsonian Institution.
    1951. The Culture of Security in San Carlos. A Study of a
           Guatemalan Community of Indians and Ladinos. Middle
           American Research Institute, Publication No. 16. New Or-
           leans: Tulane University Press.

Goldfrank, Esther S.
    1927. The Social and Ceremonial Organization of Cochiti. Wash-
           ington, D.C.: American Anthropological Association,
           Memoir 33.

Gonzalez, Mary A.
    1965. The Ilongo Kinship System and Terminology. Philippine
           Sociological Review 13:23–31.

Gowing, Peter G.
    1967. Islands under the Cross: The Story of the Church in the
           Philippines. Manila: National Council of Churches in the
           Philippines.

Grimes, Joseph E., and Hinton, Thomas B.
    1969. The Huichol and Cora. In Middle American Indians, ed.
           Wauchope, 8:792–813.

Gudeman, Stephen.
    1972. The Compadrazgo as a Reflection of the Natural and
           Spiritual Person. Proceedings of the Royal Anthropological
           Institute of Great Britain and Ireland for 1971, pp. 45–71.

Halpern, Joel M.
    1958. A Serbian Village. New York: Columbia University Press.

Hammel, Eugene A.
    1968. Alternative Social Structures and Ritual Relations in the
           Balkans. Englewood Cliffs, N.J.: Prentice-Hall.
    1969. Power In Ica. The Structural History of a Peruvian Com-
           munity. Boston, Mass.: Little, Brown and Co.

Harris, Marvin.
    1956.   *Town and Country in Brazil.* New York: Columbia University Press.
Hart, Donn V
    1954a. Barrio Caticugan: A Visayan Filipino Community. Ph.D. diss., Syracuse University.
    1954b. Preliminary Notes on the Rural Philippine Fiesta Complex (Negros Oriental Province). *Silliman Journal* 1:25–40.
    1955.   *The Philippine Plaza Complex: A Focal Point in Cultural Change.* Southeast Asia Studies, Cultural Report Series No. 3. New Haven, Conn.: Yale University Press.
    1956.   Halfway to Uncertainty: A Short Autobiography of a Cebuano Filipino. *The University of Manila Journal of East Asiatic Studies* 5:255–77.
    1959.   *The Cebuan Filipino Dwelling in Caticugan: Its Construction and Cultural Aspects.* Southeast Asia Studies, Cultural Report Series No. 7. New Haven, Conn.: Yale University Press.
    1964.   *Riddles in Filipino Folklore: An Anthropological Analysis.* Syracuse, N.Y.: Syracuse University Press.
    1965a. From Pregnancy through Birth in a Bisayan Filipino Village. In *Southeast Asia Birth Customs,* ed. Hart, Anuman, and Coughlin, pp. 1–114.
    1965b. A Personal Narrative of a Samaran Filipina. *Asian Studies* 3:55–70.
    1966.   The Filipino Villager and His Spirits. *Solidarity* 4:65–74.
    1968.   Homosexuality and Transvestism in the Philippines: The Cebuan Filipino *Bayot* and *Lakin-on. Behavior Science Notes* 3:211–48.
    1969.   *Bisayan Filipino and Malayan Humoral Pathologies: Folk Medicine and Ethnohistory in Southeast Asia.* Southeast Asia Data Paper 76. Ithaca, N.Y.: Cornell University Press.
    1975a. Christian Filipinos. In *Ethnic Groups of Insular Southeast Asia,* vol. 2, *Philippines and Formosa,* ed. Frank M. Lebar, pp. 16–22. New Haven, Conn.: Human Relations Area Files Press.
    1975b. Lanti: Sickness by Fright: A Bisayan Filipino Peasant Syndrome. *Philippine Quarterly of Culture and Society* 3:1–19.
Hart, Donn V.; Rajadhon, Phya Anuman; and Coughlin, Richard J.
    1965.   *Southeast Asian Birth Customs. Three Studies in Human Reproduction.* New Haven, Conn.: Human Relations Area Files Press.

Harvey, H. R., and Kelly, Isabel.
    1969.   The Totanaco. In *Middle American Indians,* ed. Wau-
           chope, 8:638–81.
Heath, Dwight B., and Adams, Richard N., eds.
    1965.   *Contemporary Cultures and Societies in Latin America. A
           Reader in the Social Anthropology of Middle and South
           America and the Caribbean.* New York: Random House.
Heath, Dwight B.
    1971.   Peasants, Revolution, and Drinking: Interethnic Drinking
           Patterns in Two Bolivian Communities. *Human Organiza-
           tion* 30:179–86.
Hermosisima, Thomas V., and Lopez, Pedro S., Jr.
    1966.   *Dictionary: Bisayan–English–Tagalog.* Manila: Pedro B.
           Ayuda and Co.
Himes, Ronald S.
    1967.   Cognitive Mapping in the Tagalog Area (II). In *Moderni-
           zation: Its Impact in the Philippines,* ed. George M. Guth-
           rie, Frank Lynch, and Walden F. Bello, pp. 125–68.
           Quezon City, Philippines: Ateneo de Manila University,
           IPC Papers No. 5.
Hollnsteiner, Mary B.
    1962.   The Lowland Philippine Alliance System in Municipal
           Politics. *Philippine Sociological Review* 10:167–71.
    1963.   *The Dynamics of Power in a Philippine Municipality.*
           Manila: University of the Philippines, Community Devel-
           opment Research Council Publication.
    1967.   Social Structure and Power in a Philippine Municipality.
           In *Peasant Society,* ed. Potter, Diaz, and Foster, pp. 200–
           212.
Holmes, Calixta G.
    1952.   Social Organization. In Tax, *Penny Capitalism,* pp. 97–
           118.
Hoppe, Walter A., and Weitlaner, Robert J.
    1969.   The Ichoatec. In *Middle American Indians,* ed. Wau-
           chope, 7:499–505.
Ianni, Francis A.
    1972.   *A Family Business. Kinship and Social Control in Orga-
           nized Crime.* New York: Russell Sage Foundation.
Ingham, John M.
    1970.   The Asymmetrical Implications of Godparenthood in
           Tlayacapan, Morelos, *Man* n.s. 5:281–89.
Iyoy, Margarito M.
    1950.   Marriage. Student report, Silliman University, Dumaguete,
           Philippines. Typescript.

Jacobson, Helga E.
  1969. Tradition and Change in Cebu City. A Study in a Philip-
          pine Provincial City. Ph.D. diss., Cornell University.
Jocano, F. Landa.
  1968a. *The Traditional World of Malitbog: A Study of Community
          Development and Culture Change in a Philippine Barrio.*
          Quezon City, Philippines: Community Development Re-
          search Council, University of the Philippines.
  1968b. Kinship System and Economic Development: A Case
          Study from Western Bisayas. *Southeast Asia Quarterly* 3:8
          –34.
  1968c. *Sulod Society: A Study in the Kinship System and Social
          Organization of a Mountain People of Central Panay.* In-
          stitute of Asian Studies, Monograph Series No. 2. Quezon
          City, Philippines: University of the Philippine Press.
  1969. *Growing Up in a Philippine Barrio.* New York: Holt, Rine-
          hart and Winston.
  1970. Maternal and Child Care Among the Tagalogs in Bay,
          Laguna, Philippines. *Asian Studies* 8:277–300.
  1972. Filipino Social Structure and Values. *Silliman Journal* 19:
          59–79.
Kearney, Michael.
  1972. *The Winds of Ixtepeji.* New York: Holt, Rinehart and Win-
          ston.
Kearney, Richard J.
  1925. Sponsors at Baptism According to the Code of Canon Law.
          Canon Law Studies 30:1–126.
Kenny, Michael.
  1960. Patterns of Patronage in Spain. *Anthropological Quarterly*
          33:14–23.
  1962. *A Spanish Tapestry. Town and Country in Castile.* Bloom-
          ington, Ind.: Indiana University Press.
Kiefer, Thomas M.
  1972. *The Tausug: Violence and Law in a Philippine Moslem
          Society.* New York: Holt, Rinehart and Winston.
Kluckholn, Florence R., and Strodtheck, Fred L.
  1961. *Variations in Value Orientations.* Evanston, Ill.: Row, Pet-
          erson, and Co.
Kottak, Conrad P.
  1967. Kinship and Class in Brazil. *Ethnology* 6:427–44.
Landé, Carl H.
  1965. *Leaders, Factions, and Parties. The Structure of Philippine
          Politics.* Southeast Asia Studies, Monograph Series No. 6.
          New Haven, Conn.: Yale University Press.

1973.   Kinship and Politics in Pre-Modern and Non-Western So-
        cieties. In *Southeast Asia: The Politics of National Integra-
        tion*, ed. John T. McAlister, Jr., pp. 218–33. New York:
        Random House.
Landy, David.
    1965.   *Tropical Childhood. Cultural Transmission and Learning
            in a Puerto Rican Village*. New York: Harper & Row.
Lange, Charles H.
    1959.   *Cochiti. A New Mexican Pueblo, Past and Present*. Austin,
            Tex.: University of Texas Press.
Larson, Magli S., and Bergman, Arlene.
    1969.   *Social Stratification in Peru*. Politics of Modernization Se-
            ries, No. 5. Berkeley, Calif.: Institute of International Stud-
            ies, University of California.
Laughlin, Robert M.
    1969a. The Tzotil. In *Middle American Indians*, ed. Wauchope,
            7:152–94.
    1969b. The Huastec. In ibid., 7:298–311.
Legaspi, Miguel Lopez de.
    1903.   Relation of the Voyage to the Philippine Islands [1565]. In
            Blair and Robertson, *The Philippine Islands*, 2:198–219.
Lévi-Strauss, Claude.
    1968.   The Social Use of Kinship Terms Among Brazilian Indians.
            In *Marriage, Family and Residence*, ed. Paul Bohannan
            and John Middleton, pp. 169–83. Garden City, N.Y.: The
            Natural History Press.
Lewis, Oscar.
    1960.   *Tepoztlán: Village in Mexico*. New York: Holt, Rinehart
            and Winston.
    1963.   *Life in a Mexican Village: Tepoztlán Restudied*. Urbana,
            Ill.: University of Illinois Press.
    1965.   Urbanization Without Breakdown: A Case Study. In *Con-
            temporary Culture*, ed. Heath and Adams, pp. 424–37.
    1970.   *Anthropological Essays*. New York: Random House.
Lieben, Richard W.
    1967.   *Cebuano Sorcery. Malign Magic in the Philippines*. Berke-
            ley: University of California Press.
Liu, William T.; Rubel, Arthur J.; and Yu, Elena.
    1969.   The Urban Family of Cebu: A Profile Analysis. *Journal of
            Marriage and Family* 31:393–402.
Liu, William T.; Rubel, Arthur J.; and Pate, Virginia.
    1970.   *The Cebu Family Health Project (Report on Selected Find-
            ings)*. Notre Dame, Ind.: University of Notre Dame, Cen-
            ter for the Study of Man in Contemporary Society.

Loarca, Miguel de.
    1903.   Relation of the Filipine Islands [1582–1583]. In *The Philippine Islands*, ed. Blair and Robertson, 5:34–187.
Lomnitz, Larissa.
    1971.   Reciprocity of Favors in the Urban Middle Class of Chile. In *Studies in Economic Anthropology*, ed. George Dalton, pp. 93–106. Anthropological Studies No. 7. Washington, D.C.: American Anthropological Association.
    1973.   The Survival of the Unfittest. [Mexico City, Mexico]. Manuscript.
Lynch, Frank, S.J.
    1959.   Social Class in a Bikol Town. Ph.D. diss., University of Chicago.
Lynch, Frank, S.J., and Hollnsteiner, Mary.
    1961.   Sixty Years of Philippine Ethnology: A First Glance at the Years 1901–1961. *Science Review* (Manila) 2:1–5.
Lynch, Frank, S.J., and Himes, Ronald S.
    1967.   Cognitive Mapping in the Tagalog Area. In *Modernization: Its Impact in the Philippines*, ed. Walden F. Bello and Maria C. Roldan, pp. 9–52. Quezon City, Philippines: Ateneo de Manila University, IPC Papers No. 4.
McBeath, Gerald A.
    1972.   Social and Political Assimilation of the Philippine Chinese Elite. Paper presented at the conference on "Ethnic Relations in Asian Countries," 20–21 October, State University of New York, Buffalo.
McIntyre, Mike.
    1956.   Geographical Regionalism in Samar. *Philippine Geographical Journal* 4:7–13.
Macaraig, Serafin.
    1929.   *Social Problems*. Manila: The Educational Supply Co.
Madsen, William.
    1960a.   Christo-Paganism. A Study of Mexican Religious Syncretism. In Edmonson et al., *Los Manitos*, pp. 105–79.
    1960b.   *The Virgin's Children. Life in an Aztec Village Today*. Austin, Tex.: University of Texas Press.
    1969.   The Nahua. In *Middle American Indians*, ed. Wauchope, 8:602–37.
Malay, Paula C.
    1957.   Some Tagalog Folkways. *The University of Manila Journal of East Asiatic Studies* 6:69–88.
Malay, Armando J., and Malay, Paula C.
    1955.   *Our Folkways*. Manila: Bookman.

Mallari, I. V.
    1954.   *Vanishing Dawn. Essays on the Vanishing Customs of the Christian Filipinos.* Manila: Philippine Education Co.

Mangin, William.
    1957.   Drinking Among Andean Indians. *Quarterly Journal of Studies on Alcoholism* 18:55–66.
    1965.   The Role of Regional Associations in the Adaptions of Rural Migrants in Cities in Peru. In *Contemporary Cultures,* ed. Heath and Adams, pp. 311–23.

Manners, Robert A.
    1966.   Tabara: Subcultures of a Tobacco and Mixed Crops Municipality. In *People of Puerto Rico,* ed. Steward, pp. 93–170.

Manrique, C. Leonardo.
    1969.   The Otomi. In *Middle American Indians,* ed. Wauchope, 8:682–722.

Maraspini, A. L.
    1968.   *The Study of an Italian Village.* Paris: Mouton and Co.

Mendez, Paz Policarpio, and Jocano, F. Landa.
    1974.   *The Filipino Family in Its Rural and Urban Orientation.* Mendiola, Manila: Centro Escolar University Research and Development Center.

Middleton, DeWight R.
    1975.   Choice and Strategy in an Urban *Compadrazgo. American Ethnologist* 2:461–75.

Miller, Frank C.
    1973.   *Old Villages and a New Town: Industrialization in Mexico.* Menlo Park, Calif.: Cummings Publishing Co.

Mintz, Sidney W.
    1966.   Cañamelar: The Subculture of a Rural Sugar Plantation Proletariat. In *People of Puerto Rico,* ed. Steward, pp. 314–417.

Mintz, Sidney W., and Wolf, Eric R.
    1950.   An Analysis of Ritual Co-Parenthood (Compadrazgo). *Southwestern Journal of Anthropology* 6:341–68.

Moss, Leonard W., and Thompson, Walter H.
    1959.   The South Italian Family: Literature and Observation. *Human Organization* 18:34–41.

Moss, Leonard W., and Cappannari, Stephen C.
    1960.   Pattern of Kinship, Comparaggio and Community in a South Italian Village. *Anthropological Quarterly* 33:24–32.

Nader, Laura.
    1969a. The Zapotec of Oaxaca. In *Middle American Indians*, ed. Wauchope, 7:329–59.
    1969b. The Trique of Oaxaca. In ibid., 7:400–416.

Nash, Manning.
    1958. *Machine Age Maya. The Industrialization of a Guatemalan Community.* Chicago: The University of Chicago Press.

Nelson, Cynthia.
    1971. *The Waiting Village. Social Change in Rural Mexico.* Boston: Little, Brown and Co.

Nuñez, Oscar del Prado.
    1973. *Kuyo Chico. Applied Anthropology in an Indian Community.* Chicago: University of Chicago Press.

Nurge, Ethel.
    1965. *Life in a Leyte Village.* American Ethnological Society Monograph No. 40. Seattle: University of Washington Press.

Nydegger, William F., and Nydegger, Corinne.
    1966. *Tarong: An Ilocos Barrio in the Philippines.* Six Cultures Series, vol. 6. New York: John Wiley and Sons.

Orozco y Berra, Manuel.
    1880. *Historia Antigua y de Conquista de Mexico.* 1960 ed. Mexico: Editorial Porrua.

Ortner, Donald J.
    1967. A Comparative Analysis of the Patron Saint Fiesta Complex in Middle America and the Philippines. Master's thesis, Syracuse University.

Osborn, Ann.
    1968. Compadrazgo and Patronage: A Colombian Case. *Man* n.s. 3:593–608.

Pacis, Vicente Albano.
    1971. *President Sergio Osmeña: A Fully Documented Biography.* 2 vols. Manila: Phoenix Press.

Paguio, Bernabe E.
    1965. 'Common Man's Day' Godchildren. *Philippine Free Press* 58:44.

Pal, Agaton.
    1956a. A Philippine Barrio: A Study of Social Organizations in Relation to Planned Cultural Change. *The University of Manila Journal of East Asiatic Studies* 5:391–486.

1956b. Leadership in a Rural Community. *Silliman Journal* 3:185–206.

1959. Rural Sociology in the Philippines. *Current Sociology (La Sociologie Contemporaine)* 8:16–32.

1963. Dumaguete City, Central Philippines. In *Pacific Port Towns and Cities: A Symposium,* ed. Alexander Spoehr, pp. 13–16. Honolulu, Hawaii: Bishop Museum.

Parsons, Elsie Clews.

1936. *Mitla, Town of the Souls and Other Zapoteco-Speaking Pueblos of Oaxaca, Mexico.* Chicago: University of Chicago Press.

1940. Filipino Village Reminiscence. *The Scientific Monthly* 51:435–49.

1945. *Peguche: A Study of Andean Indians.* Chicago: University of Chicago Press.

Paul, Benjamin D.

1942. Ritual Kinship: With Special Reference to Godparenthood in Middle America. Ph.D. diss., University of Chicago.

Paul, Benjamin D., and Paul, Lois.

1952. The Life Cycle. In *Heritage of Conquest,* ed. Tax, pp. 174–92.

Pearse, Andrew.

1961. Some Characteristics of Urbanization in the City of Rio de Jane iro. In *Urbanization in Latin America,* ed. Philip M. Hauser, pp. 191–205. New York: International Documents Service, Division of Columbia University Press.

Peattie, Lisa Redfield.

1968. *The View from the Barrio.* Ann Arbor: University of Michigan Press.

Phelan, John Leddy.

1955. Pre-Baptismal Instruction and the Administration of Baptism in the Philippines During the 16th Century. *The Americas* 12:3–23.

1959. *The Hispanization of the Philippines. Spanish Aims and Filipino Responses, 1565–1700.* Madison: University of Wisconsin Press.

Pierson, Donald.

1951. *Cruz das Almas: A Brazilian Village.* Institute of Social Anthropology, Publication No. 12. Washington, D.C.: Smithsonian Institute.

Pitt-Rivers, Julian A.

1958. Ritual Kinship in Spain. *Transactions of the New York Academy of Sciences.* Series 2, 20:424–31.

1961. *The People of the Sierra.* Chicago: University of Chicago Press.

1968. Pseudo-Kinship. In *International Encyclopedia of the Social Sciences,* ed. David L. Sills, 8:408–13. New York. Macmillan Co. and The Free Press.

Potter, David.

1973. Compadrazgo in the Bisayas, Philippines: Urbanization and Institutional Change. Ph.D. diss., Syracuse University.

1974. Compadrazgo in Dumaguete: The Strategy of Selection. *Silliman Journal* 21:1–28.

1975. Urban Institutional Change: Time and Space as Measures: Ritual Kinship in Dumaguete. Paper presented at the Midwest Conference on Asian Affairs, October 23–25, Ohio University, Athens. 11 pages.

Potter, Jack M.; Diaz, May N.; and Foster, George M., eds.

1967. *Peasant Society: A Reader.* Boston: Little, Brown and Co.

Press, Irwin.

1963. The Incidence of Compadrazgo among Puerto Ricans in Chicago. *Social and Economic Studies* 12:475–80.

Quijano, Ignacio T.

1937. Cebuano-Visayan Kinship Terms. *Philippine Magazine* 34:359–60.

Quisumbing, Lourdes Reynes.

1956. A Study of the Marriage Customs of the Rural Population of the Province of Cebu. Master's thesis, University of San Carlos, Cebu City, Philippines.

Ramos, Amour Mones.

1972. The Puray Remontado Family and Religion. Master's thesis, Silliman University, Dumaguete, Philippines.

Ravicz, Robert.

1966. The Washing of the Hands. A Structural Element in Indigenous Interpretation of Christian Baptism. In *Summa Anthropologica en Homenaje a Roberto J. Weitlaner,* pp. 281–90. Mexico: Instituto Nacional de Anthropologica e Historia, Secretaria de Educacion Publica.

1967. Compadrazgo. In *Middle American Indians,* ed. Wauchope, 6:238–51.

Ravicz, Robert, and Romney, A. Kimball.

1969. The Mixtec. In ibid., 7:367–99.

Redfield, Robert.

1930. *Tepoztlán: A Mexican Village.* Chicago: University of Chicago Press.

1941. *The Folk Culture of Yucatan.* Chicago: University of Chicago Press.

1965. Culture Change in Yucatan. In *Contemporary Cultures,* ed. Heath and Adams, pp. 17–29.

Redfield, Robert, and Villa Rojas, Alfonso.

1962. *Chan Kom: A Maya Village.* Chicago: University of Chicago Press.

Reed, Robert R.

1967. Hispanic Urbanism in the Philippines: A Study of the Impact of Church and State. *The University of Manila Journal of East Asiatic Studies* 11:1–222.

Reicher-Dolmatoff, Gerardo, and Reicher-Dolmatoff, Alicia.

1961. *The People of Aritama. The Cultural Personality of a Colombian Mestizo Village.* Chicago: University of Chicago Press.

Reina, Ruben E.

1966. *The Law of the Saints. A Pokoman Pueblo and Its Community Culture.* Indianapolis and New York: The Bobbs-Merrill Co.

1969. The Eastern Guatemalan Highlands: The Pokomanes and Chorti. In *Middle American Indians,* ed. Wauchope, 7:-101–32.

Reynolds, Harriett R.

1964. Continuity and Change in the Chinese Family in the Ilocos Provinces, Philippines. Ph.D. diss., Hartford Seminary Foundation.

Rheubottom, David B.

1970. Review of *Alternative Social Structures and Ritual Relations in the Balkans. American Anthropologist* 72:404–5.

Richardson, Miles.

1970. *San Pedro, Colombia: Small Town in a Developing Society.* New York: Holt, Rinehart and Winston.

Riley, Carroll L.

1969. The Southern Tepehuan and Tepecano. In *Middle American Indians,* ed. Wauchope, 8:814–29.

Roberts, Bryan R.

1973. *Organizing Strangers: Poor Families in Guatemala City.* Austin, Tex.: University of Texas Press.

Rodriguez, Eulogio B.

1941. *The Philippines and Mexico.* Documentos de la Biblioteca Nacional de Filipinas. Manila: National Library.

Romanucci-Ross, Lola.

1973. *Conflict, Violence, and Morality in a Mexican Village.* Palo Alto, Calif.: National Press Books.

Romney, K., and Romney, R.
  1966. *The Mixtecans of Juxlahuaca, Mexico.* Six Cultures Series 4. New York: John Wiley.
Rubel, Arthur J.
  1955. Ritual Relationships in Ojitlan, Mexico. *American Anthropologist* 57:1038–40.
  1966. *Across the Tracks: Mexican-Americans in a Texas City.* Published for the Hogg Foundation for Mental Health. Austin, Tex.: University of Texas Press.
Samson, Emmanuel V.
  1965. Typologies and the Filipino Temperament. *Unitas* 38:511–36.
Sanders, Irwin T.
  1962. *Rainbow in the Rock. The People of Rural Greece.* Cambridge, Mass.: Harvard University Press.
Santico, Realidad Q.
  1973. Capampangan Compadrazgo System: A Case Study. *Graduate and Faculty Studies* (Centro Escolar University, Manila) 24:20–39.
  1974. Capampangan Family and Kinship Organization: A Case Study. Ph.D. diss., Syracuse University.
Sayres, William C.
  1956. Ritual Kinship and Negative Effect. *American Sociological Review* 21:348–52.
Scheans, Daniel J.
  1962. The Suban Ilocano Kinship Configuration: An Application of Innovation Theory to the Study of Kinship. Ph.D. diss., University of Oregon.
  1963. Suban Society. *Philippine Sociological Review* 11:216–35.
  1966. *Anak Ti Digos:* Ilokano Name Changing and Ritual Kinship. *Philippine Sociological Review* 14:82–85.
Scheele, Raymond L.
  1966. The Prominent Families of Puerto Rico. In *People of Puerto Rico,* ed. Steward, pp. 418–62.
Scott, William H.
  1971. The Apo-Dios Concept in Northern Luzon. In *Acculturation in the Philippines: Essays on Changing Societies,* ed. William H. Scott and Peter G. Gowing, pp. 116–27. Quezon City, Philippines: New Day Publishers.
Seda, Elena Padilla.
  1966. Nocora: The Subculture of Workers on a Government-Owned Sugar Plantation. In *People of Puerto Rico,* ed. Steward, pp. 265–313.
Service, Elman R., and Service, Helen S.

1954. *Tobatí: Paraguayan Town.* Chicago: University of Chicago Press.

1965. General Remarks on Rural Paraguay. In *Contemporary Cultures,* ed. Heath and Adams, pp. 70–84.

Sibley, Willis E.
1958. Manalad: The Maintenance of Unity and Distinctiveness in a Philippine Village. Ph.D. diss., University of Chicago.

1965a. Persistence, Variety and Change in Visayan Social Organization: A Brief Report. *Philippine Sociological Review* 13: 139–44.

1965b. Economy, History and Compadre Choices: A Comparative Study in Two Bisayan Philippine Settlements. Unpublished paper presented at the American Anthropological Association Annual Meeting, November, Denver, Colorado, pp. 1–14 [8].

Simpich, Frederick.
1944. Mindanao, on the Road to Tokyo. *National Geographic* 86:539–74.

Southeast Asia Development Advisory Group of The Asia Society.
1974. Urban Development Panel. SEADAG Reports, 15–18 April 1974, Bali, Indonesia. New York: SEADAG.

Snyder, Patricia A.
1971. Education and the Process of Socio-Cultural Change in a Bisayan Filipino Town: A Study of Conflict in the Siaton Schools. Ph.D. diss., Syracuse University.

Spicer, Edward N.
1940. *Pascua: A Yaqui Village in Arizona.* Chicago: University of Chicago Press.

1945. *Potam: A Yaqui Village in Sonora.* American Anthropological Association Memoir No. 77. Menasha, Wisc.

Spielberg, Joseph.
1968. Small Village Relations in Guatemala: A Case Study. *Human Organization* 27:205–11.

Stein, W. W.
1961. *Hualcan: Life in the Highlands of Peru.* Ithaca, N. Y.: Cornell University Press.

Steward, Julian.
1965. Analysis of Complex Contemporary Societies: Culture Patterns in Puerto Rico. In *Contemporary Cultures,* ed. Heath and Adams, pp. 30–41.

Steward, Julian, ed.
1966. *The People of Puerto Rico. A Study in Social Anthropology.* Urbana: University of Illinois Press.

Stricken, Arnold.
    1965. Class and Kinship in Argentina. In *Contemporary Cultures*, ed. Heath and Adams, pp. 324–41.
Szanton, David L.
    1971. *Estancia in Transition. Economic Growth in a Rural Philippine Community.* Quezon City, Philippines: Ateneo de Manila University, IPC Paper No. 9.
Szanton, Maria Cristina Blanc.
    1972. *A Right to Survive. Subsistence Marketing in a Lowland Philippine Town.* University Park, Pa.: Pennsylvania State University Press.
Tax, Sol.
    1941. World View and Social Relations in Guatemala. *American Anthropologist* 43:27–42.
    1953. *Penny Capitalism. A Guatemalan Indian Economy.* Institute of Social Anthropology, Publication No. 16. Washington, D.C.: Smithsonian Institution.
Tax, Sol, ed.
    1952. *Heritage of Conquest. The Ethnology of Middle America.* Glencoe, Ill.: The Free Press.
Tax, Sol, and Hinshaw, Robert.
    1969. The Maya of the Midwestern Highlands. In *Middle American Indians*, ed. Wauchope, 7:69–100.
Tegnaeus, Harry.
    1952. *Blood Brothers. An Ethno-sociological Study of the Institutions of Blood-Brotherhood with Special Reference to Africa.* New York: Philosophical Library, Inc.
Tengco, Alfredo N.
    1962. Kinship at Christmas in the Philippines. *Asian Student,* 16 December.
Thompson, Donald E.
    1960. Maya Paganism and Christianity. A History of the Fusion of Two Religions. In Edmonson et al., *Los Manitos,* pp. 1–35.
Thompson, Richard.
    1971. Structural Statistics and Structural Mechanics: An Analysis of Compadrazgo. *Southwestern Journal of Anthropology* 27:381–403.
Tozzer, Alfredo M., ed.
    1941. *Landa's Relación de las Cosas de Yucatan.* Papers of the Peabody Museum of American Archaeology and Ethnology, vol. 18. Cambridge, Mass.: Harvard University Press.
Tuason, Romeo R.

1937. Kinship Terms Among the Aklanon. *Philippine Magazine* 34:552–571.

Tumin, Melvin M.
1952. *Caste in a Peasant Society. A Case Study of the Dynamics of Caste.* Princeton, N.J.: Princeton University Press.

Tylor, Edward B.
1861. *Anuhuaca: or Mexico and the Mexicans, Ancient and Modern.* London: Longmans, Green, Reader, and Dyer.

United Church of Christ in the Philippines.
1962. *The Book of Common Worship for Pulpit and Parish Use.* Manila, Philippines: United Church of Christ in the Philippines.

Vailoces, Aleja A.
1952. A Study of Adulthood in the Town of Payabon, Negros Oriental. In Community Studies, Student Papers prepared under the Supervision of Dr. Timoteo Oracion, Dumaguete, Philippines, pp. 99–112.

Van den Berghe, Gwendoline, and Van den Berghe, Pierre I.
1966. Compadrazgo and Class in Southeastern Mexico. *American Anthropologist* 68:1236–42.

Vanoverberg, Morice.
1936. The Isneg Life Cycle. I. Birth, Education and Daily Routine, pp. 81–189. Washington, D.C.: *Publications of the Catholic Anthropological Conference* III, no. 2.

Villa Rojas, Antonio.
1945. *The Maya of East Central Quintana Roo.* Carnegie Institution Publication 559. Washington, D.C.: Carnegie Institution of Washington.
1969. The Maya of Yucatan. In *Middle American Indians*, ed. Wauchope, 7:244–75.

Vincent, Maria Girard.
1966. Ritual Kinship in an Urban Setting: Martineztown, New Mexico. Master's thesis, University of New Mexico.

Vogt, Evon Z.
1970. *The Zinacantecos of Mexico. A Modern Maya Way of Life.* New York: Holt, Rinehart and Winston.

Wagley, Charles.
1949. *The Social and Religious Life of a Guatemalan Village.* New York: American Anthropological Association Memoir 71.
1964. *Amazon Town. A Study of Man in the Tropics.* New York: Alfred A. Knopf.
1965. Regionalism and Cultural Unity in Brazil. In *Contemporary Cultures*, ed. Heath and Adams, pp. 124–36.

1969. The Maya of Northwestern Guatemala. In *Middle American Indians*, ed. Wauchope, 7:46–68.

Wallace, Ben J.
1970. *Hill and Valley Farmers Socio-Economic Change Among a Philippine People.* Cambridge, Mass.: Schenkman Publishing Co.

Watson, James B.
1952. *Cayuá Culture Change: A Study in Acculturation and Methodology.* New York: American Anthropological Association Memoir 73.

Wauchope, Robert, ed.
1967– *Handbook of Middle American Indians.* 8 vols. Aus-
1969. tin, Tex.: University of Texas Press.

Weightman, George.
1960. The Philippine Chinese: A Study of a Marginal Trading People. Ph.D. diss., Cornell University.

Wellin, Edward.
1949. Compadrazgo in Middle America. Mimeographed. N.P.

Whitten, Jr., Norman E.
1965. *Class, Kinship and Power in an Ecuadorian Town. The Negroes of San Lorenzo.* Stanford, Calif.: Stanford University Press.

Wisdom, Charles.
1940. *A Chorti Village of Guatemala.* Chicago: University of Chicago Press.
1952. The Supernatural World and Curing. In Tax, *Penny Capitalism*, pp. 119–41.

Withycombe, E. G.
1947. *The Oxford Dictionary of English Christian Names.* New York: Oxford University Press.

Wolf, Eric R.
1966a. *Peasants.* Englewood Cliffs, N.J.: Prentice-Hall.
1966b. San Jose: Subculture of a 'Traditional' Coffee Municipality. In *People of Puerto Rico*, ed. Steward, pp. 171–264.

Wolff, John U.
1972. A Dictionary of Cebuano Visayan. Data Paper Number 87. 2 vols. Ithaca, New York: Southeast Asia Program, Department of Asian Studies, Cornell University.

Wylie, Laurence.
1961. *Village in the Vaucluse.* Cambridge, Mass.: Harvard University Press.
1966. *Chanzeaux: A Village in Anjou.* Cambridge, Mass.: Harvard University Press.

Zaide, Gregorio F.

1937. *Catholicism in the Philippines.* Manila, Philippines: Santo Tomas University Press.

1949. *Philippine Political and Cultural History,* vol. 1., *The Philippines Since Pre-Spanish Times.* Manila, Philippines: Philippine Education Co.

Zantwijk, E. A. M. van.

1967. *Servants of the Saints. The Social and Cultural Identity of a Tarascan Community in Mexico.* Assen: Van Gorcum and Co.

Index